# Quicken 6 *for* WINDOWS
# FOR BUSY PEOPLE

**Peter Weverka**

Osborne/**McGraw-Hill**

Berkeley / New York / St. Louis / San Francisco / Auckland / Bogotá
Hamburg / London / Madrid / Mexico City / Milan / Montreal / New Delhi
Panama City / Paris / São Paulo / Singapore / Sydney / Tokyo / Toronto

Osborne/**McGraw-Hill**
2600 Tenth Street
Berkeley, California 94710
U.S.A.

For information on translations or book distributors outside the U.S.A., or to
arrange bulk purchase discounts for sales promotions, premiums, or fundraisers,
please contact Osborne/**McGraw-Hill** at the above address.

**Quicken 6 for Windows for Busy People**

1234567890 DOC 99876

ISBN 0-07-882243-2


Publisher:  Brandon A. Nordin
Acquisitions Editor:  Joanne Cuthbertson
Project Editor:  Mark Karmendy
Copy Editor:  Michelle Khazai
Proofreaders:  Stefany Otis, Cynthia Douglas, Heidi Poulin
Graphic Artist:  Marla J. Shelasky
Computer Designers:  Roberta Steele, Leslee Bassin, Peter F. Hancik
Quality Control: Joe Scuderi
Series and Cover Designer:  Ted Mader Associates
Series Illustrator:  Daniel Barbeau

For information on translations or book distributors outside the U.S.A., or to
arrange bulk purchase discounts for sales promotions, premiums, or fundraisers,
please contact Osborne/**McGraw-Hill** at the above address.

For Henry, a busy lad

## About the Author

Peter Weverka is the author of *Dummies 101: Word for Windows 95* and *Word for Windows 95 for Dummies Quick Reference*. He has edited 80 computer books on topics ranging from word processors to databases to the Internet, and his humorous articles have appeared in *Harper's*.

# Contents at a glance

# Contents

# ACKNOWLEDGMENTS

**This book owes a lot to many different people. I would especially like to thank acquisitions editor Joanne Cuthbertson, who graciously gave me the opportunity to write this book and who, come to think of it, gave me my first editor job years and years ago when both of us were green and the world was young.**

I also owe a lot to copy editor Michelle Khazai. America is suffering from an acute shortage of good copy editors, and in this time of dearth and want I consider myself very lucky that a copy editor as skillful and knowledgeable as Michelle worked on my book.

I would also like to thank project editor Mark Karmendy, a level-headed individual if there ever was one, and technical editors Tom and Robin Merrin of Merrin Consulting, who poured over the manuscript to make sure that all the instructions on these pages are indeed accurate.

These people at Osborne/McGraw-Hill also gave their best to my book, and for that I am very grateful: Gordon Hurd, Cynthia Douglas, Heidi Poulin, Leslee Bassin, Jani Beckwith, Marcela Hancik, Peter Hancik, Lance Ravella, Roberta Steele, Richard Whitaker, and receptionist Kelly Young, who was very patient with some frantic phone calls I made last month.

Thanks also go to Ted Mader, who designed the excellent Busy People series for Osborne/McGraw-Hill, and Dan Barbeau, whose witty pictures you will find on the pages of this book.

A big thanks to Ari Klugman at the Intuit Corporation for all her help with my beta and online questions.

Last, and certainly not least, I want to thank my family—Sofia, Henry, and Addie—for tolerating my vampirish working hours and my strange, eerie demeanor at daybreak.

# INTRODUCTION

**All the personal finance writers agree that keeping good, accurate records is the first step toward financial security. In order to make sound financial decisions, you must be conscientious of your spending habits and know how much income you really have. How can you save for a down payment on a house if you don't know how much you are capable of saving? How can you tell if your investments are doing well if you don't track them carefully? Before you can change the way you live, from a financial standpoint at least, you have to keep accurate records.**

Quicken makes it very, very easy to do that. Balancing a checkbook and doing other mundane banking chores is simple with Quicken. Quicken users can track their investments, get information about how they spend, draw up budgets, and even pay bills and get financial information online. These days, when so many own mutual fund shares and stocks, and personal finances are more complicated than ever, having a program like Quicken is helpful indeed.

This book explains how to use Quicken to track your finances. After you have read it and started using the techniques described here, you will know what your net worth is, how much you spend in different areas, what your investments (if you have any) are worth, and how much in taxes you will owe next year. You will know how to print your own checks, generate reports and graphs that describe in clear terms what your spending habits are, plan for retirement, compare mortgages and loans, and analyze different types of investments.

# WHOM THIS BOOK IS FOR

This book is for users of Quicken 6 and Quicken 6 Deluxe, the newest versions of the Quicken computer program. It is for intelligent, busy people who want to get to the heart of Quicken and its many excellent features without having to spend a lot of time doing it.

You don't need to know much about computers to make use of this book or Quicken. What you do need to know I will explain in passing. One reason Quicken is so popular is because it doesn't ask its users to know computers well. All you have to know to run Quicken is how to turn the computer on and wiggle your fingers over the keyboard.

# WHAT'S IN THIS BOOK, ANYWAY?

Everything that is essential and helpful in Quicken, everything that might be of use to a busy person, is explained in this book. And it is explained in such a way that you understand how to make Quicken serve you. I don't describe how to use Quicken in this book—I tell you how to crack the whip and make Quicken do your bidding.

Chapter 1 explains the basics of starting the program and setting up accounts. It tells how to find your way around the screen and use Quicken's Help program. In Chapter 2, you learn how to record financial transactions, fix entry mistakes, and print a register. Chapter 3 explains everything you need to know about printing checks. Chapter 4, one of the most important chapters in the book, describes how to categorize income and expenses so you know precisely where you are spending money and what your sources of income are.

Chapter 5 simplifies the onerous task of balancing, or reconciling, a bank account. The next chapter is for people who have used Quicken for a while. Chapter 6 offers techniques for working faster and working better. After you have categorized your income and expenses, you can get a picture of your finances by generating reports and graphs. Chapter 7 explains how to do that, as well as how to get investment and other kinds of reports. In Chapter 8, you learn how to back up Quicken data, copy and delete files, and put passwords on files so others can't peek at them.

Chapter 9 explains how to budget with the program, and Chapter 10 tells how to keep track of loans, liabilities, and assets. In Chapter 11, you see how to plan for retirement, find out how much to save for a child's college education, and estimate next year's tax bill. Chapter 12 explains financial analysis techniques, including how to shop for loans and mortgages, calculate how an investment will grow, and forecast your future income and expenses.

Chapter 13 delves into the arduous problem of how to keep track of investments. It describes techniques for recording everything from stock splits to corporate securities spin-offs. In Chapter 14, you enter the exciting but scary world of cyberspace, where all money is digital and nobody pays cash for anything. It explains how to pay bills online, download account records, and get stock quotes, among other things. I hereby dedicate Chapter 14 to that brave citizen of the future, Flash Gordon.

# GETTING THE MOST OUT OF THIS BOOK

Busy person that you are, this book was designed and written to take you straight to the instructions you need. In that spirit, you will find the following elements in this book. They point to important things you should know about in the text.

## FAST FORWARDs

Each chapter begins with a handful of FAST FORWARDs. FAST FORWARDs are step-by-step, abbreviated instructions for doing things that are explained in detail later on. Each FAST FORWARD is cross-referenced to the pages in the chapter that you may turn to if you need the details. You might not need them. You might be daring enough or savvy enough to learn all you need to know from a FAST FORWARD.

## habits & strategies

Where you see habits & strategies in the margins of this book (look for the egghead chess player), prick up your ears and read attentively. Under habits & strategies you will find time-saving tips and techniques for becoming a better Quicken user. Quicken gives you lots of opportunities for tweaking and customizing and making the program work your way. I explain how to take advantage of those opportunities in the habits & strategies margin notes.

## SHORTCUTs

In Quicken, there are often two ways to do things—the fast-but-dicey way and the slow, thorough way. I explain fast-but-dicey techniques in the margin under the word SHORTCUT (look for a man with a briefcase leaping over the partially constructed fence of his unkept suburban front yard—too busy to mow the lawn, I guess).

## CAUTIONs

The Quicken computer program is for tracking money, where it goes, and where it comes from. Your money is no laughing matter, so when I describe a task that you might regret doing later or that you should think about carefully before doing, I put a word of caution in the margin. Be sure to read these CAUTIONs (look for the red-nosed pipe fitter—I hope he does his drinking after work).

*Look for cross-references and important asides in margin notes like this one.*

## definitions

Do you know what "amortized" means? How about "taskbar"? When a financial or computer term needs defining, its definition appears in the margin under the word "definition" (look for the beefy character with the overdeveloped torso and the underdeveloped thighs and brain—he has good muscle definition).

## step by step

When I describe an especially complicated or longwinded procedure, I put it in a blue "step by step" box beside a picture of a Quicken screen. These step by steps are meant to help you learn tasks quickly and thoroughly. Use them as references when you have forgotten how to do a task or when you need to brush up on a task you already know.

## tricks of the trade

Because Quicken is about tracking personal finances, some of the decisions you make when you run the program have nothing to do with computers or software. You have to make financial decisions, and to help you make those I have included "tricks of the trade" on the pages of this book. "tricks of the trade" are quotes from personal finance books and other kinds of books that are pertinent to the management of money.

By the way, I dipped into about a hundred personal finance books to get the quotes you find in this one, and almost all the advice in those books can be boiled down to this: think twice before you spend and leave your credit card at home.

## Pass GO and Collect $200

Having finished this introduction, you may now pass GO, collect $200, and learn to use Quicken to manage your personal finances. Best of luck!

MEETING
IN
PROGRESS

FAX

# The Bare Essentials

# FAST FORWARD

Quicken 6

## START QUICKEN ➤ *p. 5*
- Either double-click the Quicken 6 for Windows shortcut icon, or
- Click the Start button on the taskbar, choose Programs, choose Quicken, and choose Quicken 6 for Windows.

## GET RID OF THE QUICKEN TIPS BOX ➤ *p. 7*
1. Click Done (after you've read the tip, of course).
2. If the tip makes you curious, you can also click the More Info button before you click Done.

## CHOOSE A COMMAND FROM A MENU ➤ *p. 8*
1. Open the menu by clicking on it or by pressing ALT and the key that is underlined in the menu.
2. When the menu appears, click a command or press the underlined letter in the command name.

## REMOVE (OR VIEW) THE ICONBAR ➤ *p. 9*
1. Right-click on the gray, right side of the screen to see the shortcut menu.
2. Click Show Top Iconbar.

## SET UP A SAVINGS OR
## CHECKING ACCOUNT ➤ *pp. 11, 14-16*

1. Choose Features | Banking | Create New Account. In the dialog box, click the Checking or Savings button.
2. Click Next, and, on the EasyStep tab, enter an account name and description. Then click the Next button.
3. If you have your last bank statement, you can make sure the Yes option button is selected, click Next, enter the statement date and balance, and click Next again. However, it isn't necessary to enter the account balance information now. You can simply click the No option button, click Next, and click Next again after you've read the "That's Okay" screen.
4. The next dialog box asks about online banking. Click No if this isn't an online account. Otherwise, click Yes, enter the financial institution and the nine-digit routing number in the next tab, click Next, enter the account number and account type in the tab after that, click Next, enter your social security number, and click Next.
5. Read the Summary tab and make sure that the information you entered is indeed accurate. Then click Done.

## EXIT QUICKEN ➤ *p. 17*

- Choose File | Exit, or
- Click the Close button (the *X*) in the upper-right corner of the Quicken screen.

## USE QUICKEN'S HELP PROGRAM ➤ *pp. 17-19*

1. Press F1, click the Help button on the iconbar, or choose a command from the Help menu.
2. In a Help window, you can click Help Topics to get to the main Help Topics screen. It offers the Contents tab for searching for help by topic, the Index tab for looking up subjects in alphabetical order, and the Find tab for searching the Help program's files for advice about a topic.

This chapter gives you the lay of the land. It describes which buttons to click and which commands to choose to get around in Quicken. It explains how to start and close the program. In this chapter, I tell you the one or two things you should know right off the bat if you want to make the most out of Quicken. Here you learn how to open an account and a new file. Last of all, this chapter describes the Quicken Help commands in case you want to seek advice from Quicken itself.

# A WORD TO THE WISE

Quicken makes it very, very easy to record financial transactions. When you want to balance a savings or checking account, you don't have to punch calculator keys or scribble numbers in the margin of a checkbook, because Quicken does the math for you. You can keep track of where you spend money. To find your net worth, all you have to do is click one or two buttons. If you want to know how much you spent on groceries, federal income taxes, pet grooming, tattoos, or another spending category, you only have to give a command.

That is the good news. The bad news is that you have to enter financial data carefully for Quicken to do its job well. Not everyone is good at entering numbers with a computer keyboard, but getting the numbers right is important. To see why, take a look at the Snapshots report in Figure 1.1 (you can get a Snapshots report by choosing Reports | Snapshots). For the Expense Comparison pie chart in this report to be accurate, you must categorize your expenses carefully (categorizing is explained in Chapter 4). For the Budget report to be meaningful, you must carefully set budget goals (budgeting is explained in Chapter 9). For the Net Worth bar graph to be accurate, you must diligently record all interest income, all income from investments, and all debts.

If all you want to do is balance your checking and savings accounts, you've got it made. The program gives you lots of opportunities to double-check the accuracy of checking and savings account transac-

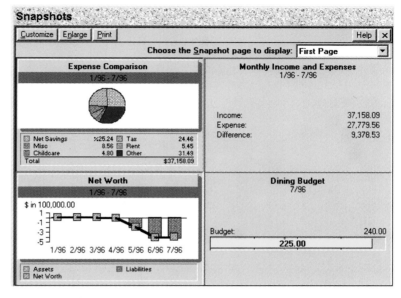

**Figure 1.1** A Snapshots report. Reports like these are only meaningful if you enter your financial data correctly.

tions. But if you are using Quicken to track investments, to budget, to compare investments, to track a loan, or to do a handful of other things, you have to be careful of how you enter data. If you do it right the first time, you will spare yourself a lot of trouble in the long run.

# STARTING QUICKEN

Starting Quicken is as easy as falling off a log. As shown in Figure 1.2, all you have to do to start the program is click the Start button on the taskbar, click Programs to see the Programs menu, and click Quicken. (Quicken Deluxe users also have to choose Quicken 6 for Windows after they click Quicken on the Programs menu.)

Another, even faster way to start Quicken is to double-click the shortcut icon on the Windows 95 screen. When you installed Quicken, the program created a shortcut icon for you. The shortcut icon is the yellow box that says "Quicken 6 for Windows" underneath it. Double-click it to start Quicken.

**definition**

**Taskbar:** *The stripe along the bottom of the Windows 95 screen. The Start button is on the left end of the taskbar.*

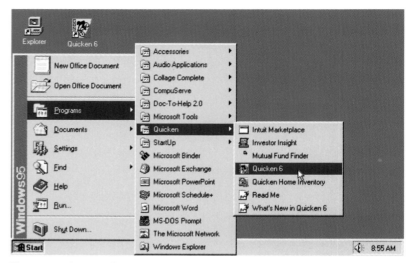

**Figure 1.2** Starting Quicken from the taskbar

# IF THIS IS THE FIRST TIME YOU'VE RUN QUICKEN

What you see after you start Quicken depends on whether you've run the program before. If you have run it before, you go straight to the Quicken screen and its imposing Quicken Tips window. "A Fast Trip Around the Screen" explains what all the clutter on the screen is.

If this is the first time you've run Quicken, you see the Quicken New User Setup dialog box. From here, you can set up your first checking account and tell Quicken how you want to categorize your income and expenses, with business or home categories (categories are the subject of Chapter 4). Click Next and you see a list of personal questions about your marital status, the number of children you have, and whether you own a house and a small business. Depending on how you answer these questions, Quicken sets up categories and tax status information for you.

After the survey, you are invited to set up a checking account and take a "QuickTour" of the Quicken wonderworld. Go ahead, if that's what you want to do. It's your party.

*Chapter 6, "Working Faster and Better," shows how to tweak the Quicken screen and make it work better for you.*

**habits & strategies**

*If it bothers you to see the Quicken Tips box each time the program starts, click the Show Tips at Startup check box to remove the check mark. Get it back again by choosing Help | Quicken Tips and putting the check mark back.*

# A FAST TRIP AROUND THE QUICKEN SCREEN

The first thing you see on the Quicken screen when the program starts is the Quicken Tips box (read the tip and click Done). The screen looks intimidating at first. Why all the buttons, pictures, doodads, and menus? With this much clutter, you could be watching MTV.

The screen is so cluttered because much of it is redundant. In other words, a lot of these buttons and whatnots activate the same commands. To create a report, for example, you can choose Reports | Home | Cash Flow, click the Reports icon on the iconbar, or click the Reports button at the bottom of the screen and choose Use More Advanced Reports from the pop-up menu. All four actions take you to the same place—the Create Report dialog box.

Don't let the Quicken screen scare you. In a few days you will know your way around the screen and know the fastest and best way to get from place to place.

Figure 1.3 shows the main ingredients of the Quicken screen. To help you get off on the right foot, the following pages describe the Quicken screen in detail.

## The Quicken Tips Box

There isn't much to know about the Quicken Tips box. Read the tip and click the Done button. If you are so inclined, you can click the Next Tip button many times and read many tips before you click Done and be done with it.

Some boxes offer a More Info button. Click it if you are curious about the Quicken tip and want to learn more. The Help program opens when you click the More Info button so you can read about the topic that so aroused your curiosity.

## QCards and What to Do About Them

Does a QCard cloud the bottom of your screen? These things are a bother. I think the best way to handle QCards is to turn them off altogether. To do that, choose Help | Show QCard. When you want to see them again, choose Show QCards again on the Help menu.

Menu bar    Iconbar

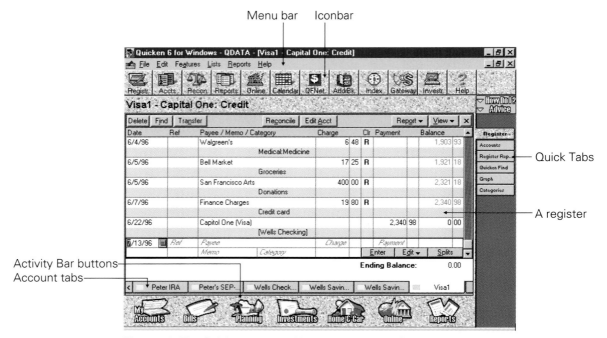

Quick Tabs

A register

Activity Bar buttons
Account tabs

**Figure 1.3** The Quicken screen with a register on top. Several windows are open; their Quick Tabs appear on the right side of the screen.

# The Menu Bar

Quicken's menu bar, found along the top of the screen, offers six menus. To open a menu and see its commands, either click on its name or press the ALT key and the letter that is underlined in its name. To open the File menu, for example, either click File on the menu bar or press ALT-F.

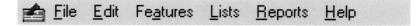

By the way, to choose a command from an open menu, either click its name on the menu or press the letter that is underlined in its name.

## The Iconbar

Below the menu bar is a long string of icons called the *iconbar.* Click an icon to give a command.

I explain what the icons do throughout this book. For now, the important thing to know is that you can make the iconbar disappear when you want more room to work in a register. To make it disappear or reappear, right-click on the gray area to the right of the screen below the Quick Tabs and choose Show Top Iconbar from the shortcut menu. Do the same to get it back again. *Right-click* means to click the mouse's right button, not its left button.

## Quick Tabs for Turning Quicken's "Pages"

On the right side of the screen are the *Quick Tabs,* one for the register, graph, report, and whatnot that you have opened or created in Quicken. Click a Quick Tab to go to another open window. In Figure 1.3, a grand total of five tabs appear. By clicking one, you could move to the Accounts List, a register report, the Find dialog box, a graph, or the Categories List.

# Registers, Registers, and More Registers

If you've ever had a job as a bookkeeper or accountant, you know that a register is a book for recording expenditures and revenue. For each account you set up, Quicken creates a register. You can see a credit card register in Figure 1.3. Registers look different, depending on the kind of account you have set up, but all registers have places for entering transaction dates and transaction amounts. Registers also show the ending balance (how much money is in the account, how much is owed, or how much the thing being tracked in the account is worth).

| Date | Num | Description / Xfer Acct / Memo | Payment | Clr | Deposit | Balance |
|------|-----|-------------------------------|---------|-----|---------|---------|
| 9/26/95 | 102 | Pacific Water Co | 20 00 | | | 20,263 23 |
| | | Utilities:Water        2 months | | | | |

# Account Tabs for Switching Between Accounts

Along the bottom of each register is a row of account tabs in alphabetical order. You will find one color-coded tab for each account you set up. Account tabs make it easy to open account registers. Rather than go to the trouble of opening an account register by going to the Accounts List first, all you have to do is click an account tab. If you have more than six accounts, arrows appear on the left and right side of the account tabs. Click an arrow to slide the tabs over and get to the one you are looking for.

# The Activity Bar Buttons

The seven Activity Bar buttons along the bottom of the screen present yet another way to give commands. Click one of these buttons and a small menu appears. I mention these buttons and menus throughout this book. For now, all you need to know is that the Online button shows a house being struck by lightning:

# SETTING UP AN ACCOUNT

When most people hear the word "account," they think of bank accounts—checking accounts, savings accounts, and the like. In Quicken, an "account" is simply a way to track the value of something. There are eight kinds of accounts: checking, savings, credit card, cash, money market, investment, asset, and liability.

Whatever the account you want to set up, the procedure is the same. These pages explain the different kinds of accounts and how to set them up.

## SETTING UP AN ACCOUNT step by step

1. Choose Features | Banking | Create New Account (or click the My Accounts button and choose Create a New Account from the menu). When Quicken asks you to choose an account type, click the button for the type of account you want, and then click Next. Fill in the two tabs in the Account Setup dialog box. When you have finished filling in a screen, click the Next button.

2. In the EasyStep tab, enter a name for the account and a description, if you want. This tab asks for your account balance, but you can enter it later.

3. If the account you're setting up can be managed online, Quicken asks if you've signed up for an online service. Click the No option button if you don't want to bank or pay bills online; otherwise, you are asked for information about the online account.

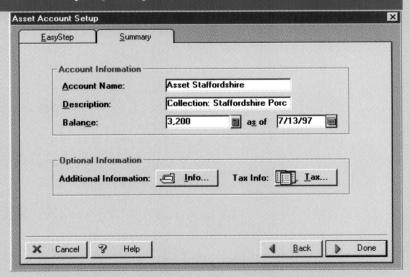

4. On the Summary tab, review the information you entered and click Done.

# The Different Kinds of Accounts

Figure 1.4 shows the dialog box for choosing which kind of account type to set up. I trust you know already what the Checking, Savings, and Credit Card buttons are for. What about the other buttons? This table explains what the eight accounts are.

| Account | What It Is For |
|---|---|
| Checking | Recording activity in a checking account. |
| Savings | Recording activity in a savings account. |
| Credit Card | Recording credit card transactions, usurious finance charges, and credit card payments. See "Recording Transactions in Credit Card Accounts" in Chapter 2 for the dirty details. |
| Cash | Recording old-fashioned cash payments and tracking petty cash accounts. See "Managing a Cash Account" in Chapter 2. |
| Money Market | Tracking the value of money market funds that you can write checks against (if you can't write checks against the money market fund, create an investment account). See Chapter 13. |
| Investment | Tracking the value of something you bought with the idea of selling it later at a profit—mutual funds, stocks, bonds, securities, IRAs, Keoghs, CDs, treasury bills, annuities, precious metals, collectibles, REITs, and unit trusts. See Chapter 13. |
| Asset | For tracking the value of things that you own—real estate, a truck, a collection of Staffordshire porcelain figurines. See "Keeping Track of Assets" in Chapter 10. |
| Liability | Tracking debt—a mortgage, car loan, or income taxes owed, for example. See Chapter 10. |

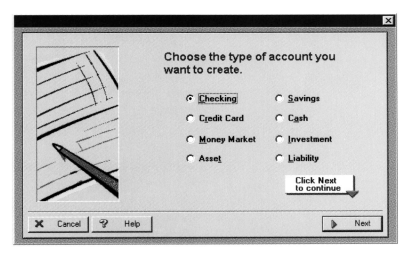

**Figure 1.4** In this dialog box, choose which kind of account to set up.

# Before You Set Up Your New Account

When you set up a new account, Quicken asks for its starting date and opening balance. It isn't necessary to give this information right away, because you can always go back and enter it later. Still, at some point or other in the life of your account you have to give some thought to its starting date and opening balance.

If you intend to use Quicken to help with taxes, you need to record transactions as of January 1. Obviously, it doesn't do any good to track itemized deductions as of July 31 or October 16, because the IRS wants to know the full story of what you did all year. An account's starting date doesn't matter if you intend to use Quicken only for balancing a checking and savings account, but it does matter for tax purposes and for some kinds of financial analysis.

Going back and recording account transactions from January 1 is a chore if today is November 11 or December 26. However, if you need to do that, get out your checkbook, bankbook, bank statements, and credit card statements, and go to it after you have set up your accounts. All I can tell you by way of encouragement is that entering transactions in Quicken is a lot easier than entering them by hand, as Chapter 2 explains.

As for the opening balance, knowing that is easy if you just opened the account. You know exactly how much money is in a new bank

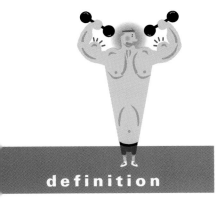

**definition**

*Balance: How much money is in a bank account. Or, in the case of asset, liability, and investment accounts, what the thing being tracked in the account is worth.*

account because no checks have been written, no deposits or withdrawals have been made, and no interest has been earned. All you have to do is tell Quicken how much your initial deposit was if you just opened the account.

But if you want to start tracking an account you've had for a while, or you need to know what your account balance was on January 1, you have some detective work to do. You have to find out how much money was in the account as of the starting date. If you kept careful records—if you balanced your checkbook each time you wrote a check, for example—knowing the balance as of a certain date is easy. But if, like me, you didn't balance your checkbook until you started using Quicken, you have to do some careful backtracking. You have to find out what your account balance was on the date you have chosen for your starting date.

## Setting Up a New Account

To set up a new account, you have to start from the dialog box shown in Figure 1.5. To get to that dialog box, click the My Accounts button and choose Create a new account from the menu, or choose Features I Banking I Create New Accounts, or click Accts on the iconbar and then click the New button in the Accounts List window.

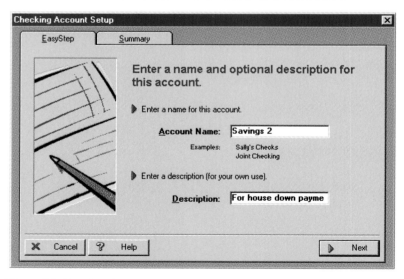

**Figure 1.5**  Entering the account name and a description. The name you enter appears on Quick Tabs and on account tabs in register windows.

Whichever account you set up, the procedure is nearly the same. In the dialog box, click one of the eight account buttons and click Next. You see the Account Setup dialog box. From there, you fill out each screen and click the Next button as you go along. To set up all eight kinds of accounts, you tell Quicken the balance (or value) of the account and give it a name. Some accounts also ask if you intend to bank online and whether the account is tax-deferred.

Click the Next button to move to the EasyStep tab shown in Figure 1.5. Next, type a name for your account. The name you type appears on Quick Tabs on the right side of the screen and on the account tabs at the bottom of registers.

In the Description text box, type a few words that describe the account you are setting up. The words you type will appear in the Accounts List, a dialog box that lists all your accounts, their balances, and your net worth. If you have, say, two checking accounts and three savings accounts, this is a good place to write a few words that help explain which account is which.

When you click Next, Quicken asks if you know the starting date and balance (or value) of the account. This question isn't as important as it seems, because you can change the starting value and starting date whenever you want after the account is set up. If you leave the Yes option button selected and click Next, an "Enter the starting point information" screen appears so you can tell Quicken how much the account was worth as of the starting date. The date and balance (or value) that you enter will be the first register entry in your new account. If you choose the No option button and click Next, Quicken consoles you with a screen that says it's okay not to know the account's value.

*In the case of an investment account, Quicken asks whether you can write checks or use a debit card against the account. Chapter 13 has instructions for setting up investment accounts.*

## tricks of the trade

*The moderate amount of discipline that smart record keeping requires is good practice for moving on in your financial life. If you don't have the discipline to file away crucial bills and chuck useless ones, for instance, how will you have the discipline for the more demanding task of saving large chunks of money for retirement?*

*Richard Eisenberg,* The *Money* Book of Personal Finance

*Click the Info button on the Summary tab to get to the Additional Account Information dialog box. This is a good place to keep phone numbers, contact names, and the like. To get back to this screen later, click Accts on the iconbar, click the account in the Accounts List, and click the Info button.*

If you are setting up a checking, savings, credit card, or money market account, the next screen asks if you intend to manage your account online. Online banking is explained in Chapter 14, where I also tell you how to come back to the Account Setup dialog box and click the Yes option here. Skip ahead to Chapter 14 if you must; otherwise, click the Next button.

The Summary tab comes next. It gives you an opportunity to double-check the information you entered and change anything, if necessary. Make changes if you wish on this tab and then click Done. You're finished—and not a moment too soon.

# CREATING A NEW FILE FOR A BUSINESS OR SECOND PARTY

All the information you keep about your finances, no matter how many accounts you open, is kept in a file called Qdata. (Actually, it's kept in seven files, each called Qdata but with a different three-letter ending. That doesn't matter, though, because the seven files are kept in one bundle to make things easier on you.) Most users of Quicken do not need to create a second file. However, you need one under these circumstances:

- You are using the program to track your business as well as your personal finances and you want to keep the two separate.
- You are tracking someone else's finances.
- Someone besides you uses Quicken on your computer to track his or her finances.

To create another Quicken file, choose File | New. A meek dialog box called "Creating a new file: Are you sure?" appears. The New Quicken File option button is already selected, so all you have to do is click OK. You see the Create Quicken File dialog box.

Type a name in the File name box. Notice the Predefined Categories check boxes. If the new file you are creating is for a business, click the Business check box to give yourself a set of business categories to work with (categories are explained in Chapter 4). Finally, click OK. Quicken opens the new file and you find yourself looking at the dialog box for creating an account.

Now that you have two (or more) files, how do you get from one to the next? To do that, choose File | Open to see the Open Quicken File dialog box, click the name of the file you want to open, and click the OK button.

# SHUTTING DOWN QUICKEN

When you want to stop using Quicken and go on to bigger and better things, either choose File | Exit or click the Close button (the *X*) in the upper-right corner of the Quicken screen.

People who use computers often are accustomed to saving their files before exiting a computer program, but you don't have to do that in Quicken. Each time you enter a transaction in a register, the data is stored on the hard disk, so you don't have to choose a Save command or click a Save button. In fact, if you look for a Save button or command in Quicken you will look in vain—there isn't one.

# GETTING HELP WHEN YOU NEED IT

Dare I say it, but this book doesn't explain every nook and cranny of Quicken. I would need two or three hundred extra pages to do that. This book covers the vital stuff and everything that a busy, intelligent, stunningly attractive person like you needs to know. It ignores the superfluous stuff. If you, however, are the type who explores nooks and crannies and is interested in the superfluous, you might need to seek help from Quicken. This part of the book explains how to do that.

When you choose the Help command, you open a separate program. I mention this not to marvel at how many computer programs you can open at once, but because having the Help program and Quicken onscreen at the same time can be very advantageous. Once you've searched the Help program and found the task you need help with, you can do the task in Quicken at the same time as you read the instructions for doing it. For example, Figure 1.6 shows a liability register for tracking mortgage payments, and, on the right side of the screen, instructions in the Help program for handling mortgages.

Quicken offers many different ways to seek help: press F1, click the Help button on the iconbar, or choose Help on the main menu and

## CAUTION

*Back up your Quicken data whenever you finish using the program. "Backing Up Financial Data" in Chapter 8 explains how to do that.*

## habits & strategies

*Treat the Help window like any program window: minimize it, maximize it, or drag it wherever you please. You can shove it to the side of the screen and read it as you do work in Quicken.*

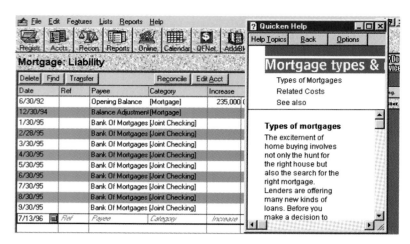

**Figure 1.6** Help is a program unto itself. You can click the Minimize and Restore buttons in the Help window to see the window or remove it, as necessary.

click an option. When you press F1, choose Help I Help on This Window, or click the Help icon; the Help program takes an educated guess about what you need help with and opens a screen with the instructions it thinks you need. In other words, if you just finished creating a graph and you press F1, the Help program offers advice for creating and editing graphs.

You can also click the Help button in dialog boxes and windows, click the How Do I? buttons that appear from time to time and give advice about specific tasks, or click the Advice buttons, which offer financial advice.

More often than not, the Help program can't read your mind and it gives you instructions you don't need. When that happens, you have to root around in the Help program to find the instructions you want. You can do that either by starting from general topics and working your way to the particulars (choose Help I Contents) or by starting right at the particulars (choose Help I Index).

When you choose the Help I Contents button in the Help window, you get a list of general topics with book icons next to them. Double-click a book, it opens, and you see more books or subtopics with question marks next to their names. Click the question mark next to the subtopic that piques your interest and you see an advice screen for doing a task. With luck and perseverance, you might find the right set of instructions. If your search takes you too far astray, you can always click the Back button in the Help program window to go back to the screens you saw earlier.

Choose Help I Index if you know by name what you need help with. The Index tab in Figure 1.7 appears.

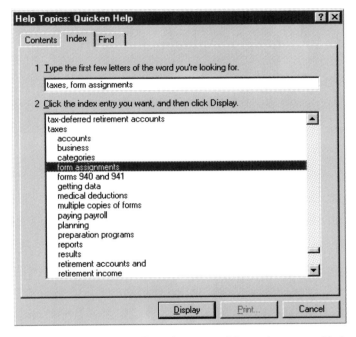

**Figure 1.7** Searching for help. Type the name of the topic you need help with in box 1. With the topic highlighted in box 2, click the Display button.

# ONWARD AND UPWARD

Now that you know the basics of using Quicken, you can forge ahead and find out how to enter transactions. That—same Bat time, same Bat channel—is the subject of the next chapter.

# Recording Your
# Financial Activity

# FAST FORWARD

## OPEN AN ACCOUNT REGISTER ➤ p. 25

1. Open the Account List window with one of these techniques: Press CTRL-A, click the Accts icon, click the My Accounts button and choose View All of My Accounts from the menu, or choose Lists I Account.
2. On the Account List window, double-click the account you want to open or select the account and then click the Open button.

## WITH A REGISTER ONSCREEN, MOVE TO ANOTHER REGISTER ➤ p. 26

1. Click one of the rectangular account tabs along the bottom of the register. Each tab has the name of an account on it.
2. If necessary, click an arrow on the ends of the row of tabs to slide the buttons over and get to the one you want.

## ENTER A TRANSACTION IN A REGISTER ➤ pp. 26-30

1. Fill in the rows. Press TAB or click in the next box to move from box to box.
2. Enter a date in the Date box.
3. Press TAB or click in the Num box and choose an option that identifies the transaction.
4. If you are writing a check or making a deposit, enter a name in the Payee box.
5. Type the amount of the transaction in the Payment or Deposit box, if necessary. Don't bother entering commas, but include a decimal point and two final numbers if you are not entering a round number.
6. Optionally, enter a description of the transaction in the Memo box.
7. Click the arrow in the Category box and choose an expense or income category for the payment or deposit.
8. Click the Enter button.

## SPLIT A TRANSACTION TO CATEGORIZE IT ACROSS MORE THAN ONE CATEGORY ➤ *pp. 30-32*

1. Fill in the register as you normally would, but click the Splits button when you get to the Category box.
2. In the Splits dialog box, click the arrow in the Category box on line 1, choose a category from the menu, and enter a dollar figure in the Amount box.
3. Do the same on line 2 and as many lines as necessary to divide the transaction across different categories.
4. When the Splits Total equals the Transaction Total, click the Finished button.

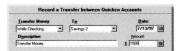

## TRANSFER MONEY FROM ONE ACCOUNT TO ANOTHER ➤ *pp. 32-33*

1. Open the register of the account from which you want to transfer money and click the Transfer button.
2. In the Transfer dialog box, enter the transfer date, if necessary. In the Amount box, enter the amount of money you are transferring. In the To box, click the arrow and choose the account the money is to be transferred to.
3. Click OK.

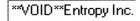

## VOID A TRANSACTION ➤ *pp. 35-36*

1. Put the cursor in the transaction you want to void.
2. Either press CTRL-V or click the Edit button on the register and choose Void Transaction. A fat **VOID** appears in the Payee box.

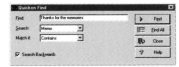

## SEARCH FOR A TRANSACTION IN A REGISTER ➤ *pp. 36-40*

1. Press CTRL-F or choose Edit I Find & Replace I Find. You see the Quicken Find dialog box.
2. Enter what you are looking for in the Find box.
3. Click the arrow in the Search box and choose an option on the menu if you know which transaction box on the register the item you are searching for is in.
4. If you are fuzzy about what you are looking for, click the arrow in the Match if box and choose an option.
5. Click the Find or Find All button.

**T**he first chapter explained how to get rolling with Quicken. In this chapter, you get down to brass tacks. This is where you learn how to enter financial transactions in a register. Here, you learn how to track where the money that comes into your accounts comes from, and where the money that goes out of your accounts goes to. I hope more money is coming in than going out, but if that isn't so, you will soon learn why.

This chapter explains how to open an account register. It tells how to record transactions and how to change, void, and delete them. It spells out how to transfer money between accounts, fix mistakes in account registers, and get around in long registers with hundreds and hundreds of transactions in them. For people who like to leave paper trails, this chapter also explains how to print an account register.

## WHAT IS A REGISTER, ANYWAY?

Chapter 1 explained how to set up an account in Quicken. For each account you set up, Quicken creates an *account register*. Figure 2.1 shows an account register for a savings account. Registers differ slightly from account type to account type, but all have a place for entering the date of the transaction and the amount of the transaction. Registers also show the account balance (how much money is in the account or, in the case of an asset, liability, or investment account, the value of the account). There is also the Clr column, which tells whether the transaction has been cleared with a bank or brokerage house.

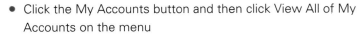

**Savings 2 - Emergency money: Bank**

| Date | Num | Payee | Category | Payment | Clr | Deposit | | Balance | |
|------|-----|-------|----------|---------|-----|---------|--|---------|--|
| 11/7/95 | | | [Wells Checking] | | R | 1,860 | 60 | 3,739 | 46 |
| 11/22/95 | | Interest Earned | Int Inc | | R | 4 | 61 | 3,744 | 07 |
| 12/2/95 | | | [Wells Checking] | | R | 1,910 | 55 | 5,654 | 62 |
| 12/22/95 | | Interest Earned | Int Inc | | R | 8 | 14 | 5,662 | 76 |
| 1/24/96 | | Interest Earned | Int Inc | | R | 10 | 22 | 5,672 | 98 |
| 2/8/96 | | | [Wells Checking] | | R | 4,000 | 00 | 9,672 | 98 |
| 2/23/96 | | Interest Earned | Int Inc | | R | 12 | 58 | 9,685 | 56 |
| 3/2/96 | | | [Wells Checking] | | R | 2,000 | 00 | 11,685 | 56 |
| 3/22/96 | | Interest Earned | Int Inc | | R | 16 | 90 | 11,702 | 46 |
| 3/30/96 | | | [Wells Checking] | | | 2,000 | 00 | 13,702 | 46 |
| 4/10/96 | TXFR | | [Wells Checking] | 6,000 00 | | | | 7,702 | 46 |
| 4/15/96 | TXFR | | [Wells Checking] | 4,000 00 | | Enter | Edit ▾ | Splits | |
| 7/13/96 | | Num | Payee | Category | Payment | | Deposit | | |

**Ending Balance:** 3,702.46

| ◄ | Savings 1 | Savings 2 | Second Ban... | SEP-IRA | Wells Check... | Cash | ► |

**Figure 2.1** An account register. Financial transactions are recorded in registers.

# OPENING AN ACCOUNT REGISTER

The first step to entering transactions is to open the register that the transaction is to be entered in. To do that, you have to get to the Account List and open the register from there. Figure 2.2 shows the Account List. Quicken offers no less than four ways to get to this sacred place:

- Click the Accts icon on the iconbar
- Click the My Accounts button and then click View All of My Accounts on the menu
- Choose Lists I Account
- Press CTRL-A

Now that the Account List is onscreen, you can open the account register of your choice. To do that, double-click the account you want to open or select the account and then click the Open button. The register appears and the cursor lands on the last row so you can start entering transactions.

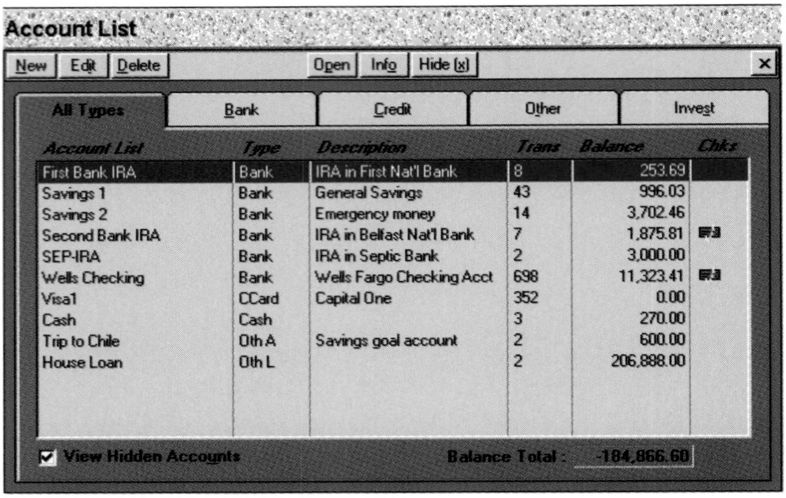

**Figure 2.2**  The Account List. Double-click an account to see its register window.

As I mentioned in Chapter 1, you can skip merrily from one account to another by clicking the account tabs along the bottom of the register.

# ENTERING TRANSACTIONS IN SAVINGS AND CHECKING ACCOUNT REGISTERS

Almost everyone has a checking and savings account, so how to fill in checking and savings account registers is explained here. (Investment registers are a bit complicated and are explained in Chapter 13. Check out Chapter 10 to learn about liability and asset registers. Handling cash and credit card registers is explained later in this chapter.) Besides filling in the different boxes in the register, the following pages explain how Quicken fills in some of the information automatically, how to split a transaction, and how to transfer money between accounts.

## ENTERING A TRANSACTION step by step

| | | Mike Mulligan | | -415.00 Home Repair | Steam shovel | |
|---|---|---|---|---|---|---|
| 7/13/96 | 1376 | Mike Mulligan | | ⬇ | *Payment* | *Deposit* |
| | | *Memo* | *Category* | | Enter | E |

1. Enter a date in the Date box either by typing it in or by clicking the baby calendar and then clicking on the month and day. Press the TAB key or click in the Num box to move there.

2. Click the arrow in the Num box and, from the menu, identify the transaction. Then press TAB or click in the Payee box.

3. Enter a name in the Payee box (for checks and deposits). If you've paid or received money from the named person or party before, the name of the party, the amount of the last transaction, and a category appear after you type the first few letters. Click in another box or press TAB if this information is correct for this transaction.

4. Enter the amount of the transaction in the Payment or Deposit box.

5. If you so desire, enter a description of the transaction in the Memo box.

6. Click the arrow in the Category box and choose an expense or income category for the payment or deposit, if necessary.

7. Click the Enter button.

# Filling in a Register

When you open a register, Quicken takes you to the first empty row at the bottom. This is where you record the transaction. Even if you are recording a transaction that occurred months ago, you can enter it on the last line because Quicken will put it in date order when you are finished recording it.

Starting on the left, the first piece of information that Quicken needs is the transaction date. Today's date appears in the Date box, but you can change that either by typing in another date or by clicking the baby calendar. When you click it, a full-fledged calendar appears. Click the arrows on either side of the month name to advance or go backward month by month, and when you've found the right month, click the day the transaction was or will be made. Or, if you are already in the right month, simply click a day. The calendar closes and there you have it—the date.

The Num box is for identifying the transaction. To move the cursor there, either click in the Num box or press the TAB key. When you've done that, click the down-arrow. Choose one of these options to describe the transaction you are about to enter:

| Num Option | What It Means |
|---|---|
| Next Check Num | The transaction is a check; kindly enter the next check number in my checkbook. (If Quicken enters the wrong number, type in the correct one.) |
| ATM | The transaction was made at an automatic teller machine. |
| Deposit | The transaction is a deposit to this account. |
| Print Check | The transaction is a check that I intend to print. |
| Send Online Payment | The transaction is an electronic payment to an online bank or CheckFree and I haven't sent it yet. |
| Transfer Funds | The transaction is a transfer of money from one account to another. |
| EFT | The transaction is an automatic transfer of funds from my account to a payee or bank. (EFT stands for *electronic funds transfer*.) |
| Edit List | Click this button to get to the Edit Num List dialog box, where you can click the New button to create a Num option of your own. |

The next box to fill in is the Payee box. If you are writing a check, enter the name of the person or business you are writing the check to. If you are entering a deposit, record the name of the person or company from whom you received the money. Don't enter anything in the Payee box if you are withdrawing money or transferring it between accounts.

If this is the first time you have written a check to or received money from this party, nothing happens. You enter the name in the Payee box and that is that. But if you have dealt with this party before, a gray box with the party's name appears above the Payee box as you type the name in. Not only does the party's name appear, but a cash amount and an expense or income category appears as well. What you are seeing is a very handy Quicken feature called *QuickFill*.

As Figure 2.3 shows, if you click the arrow on the right of the Payee box, a menu appears. This is the list of parties you have paid money to and received money from. So that you don't have to enter the same data over and over again, Quicken "memorizes" the names and transaction statistics of all parties you have paid or received money from

| 1/95 | | --Splits-- | Salary Deposit | | | | | 1,282 30 | 20,737 6 |
|---|---|---|---|---|---|---|---|---|---|
| | | Wife's Paycheck | | | | | | | |
| 3/95 | 240 | Ace Camera | | 500.00 | [Bank of B... | | | | 20,390 6 |
| | | Auto Loans by Asc... | | -440.17 | --LOAN-- | Car loan payment | | | |
| | | Bank Of Mortgages | | -1,993.15 | --LOAN-- | | | | |
| 12/95 | | Deposit | | 638.68 | [Undeposit... | Deposit from 8/21/95 | | | 20,290 6 |
| | | McMillan Photo Su... | | 328.62 | [Bank of B... | Payment to A-P Acco... | | | |
| 2/96 | 101 | Pacific Water Co | | -20.00 | Utilities:Wa... | | | | 20,290 6 |
| | | Pam Smith | | -638.68 | [Undeposit... | | | | |
| | | Runneals Furnature | | -346.95 | Household | Couch | | | |
| 3/96 | | Union Gas & Electri... | | -110.00 | Utilities:Gas... | Home electric | | | 20,270 6 |
| | | Union Gas & Electri... | | -120.00 | Utilities:Gas... | Payment for busin. ele... | | | |
| 3/96 | *Num* | | | | | *Payment* | | *Deposit* | |
| | | *Category* | *Memo* | | | | Enter | Edit ▾ | Splits |

**Ending Balance:** 20,270.6

**Figure 2.3** QuickFill at work. Click a name on the QuickFill list and the name, amount, and category are entered automatically in the register.

in the past. Click a party on the list and its name is entered automatically in the Payee box. Not only that, but the last sum you paid or received from it appears in the Payment or Deposit box, and the category you assigned it to appears in the Category box. ("Making QuickFill Work Your Way" in Chapter 6 tells how to fine-tune this excellent device.)

Press TAB or click to go to the Payment or Deposit box. Then enter the amount of the payment or deposit.

To enter an amount, it isn't necessary to enter any commas or dollar signs. All you have to do is enter the numbers themselves. As for a decimal point, enter it only if the amount includes cents as well as dollars. In other words, if your payment or deposit is $25.00, all you have to enter is **25**, but if it is $25.99, you have to enter **25.99**.

On the right side of the Payment and Deposit box is a minuscule calculator. Click it and a significantly larger calculator comes to life on your screen. You can click its buttons to add, subtract, divide, and multiply figures. When you arrive at the sum or product you want to enter as a deposit or payment, click the Enter button (it has an equal sign on it). The sum or product of your calculation is entered in the Payment or Deposit box.

When it comes to tracking where your money comes from and how you spend it, the next box is the most important of all. The Category box is where you assign an expense or income category to the transaction. Which category you choose determines where the money will show up in reports and graphs. If you are using Quicken for tax-reporting purposes, the category you choose is especially important, because it might determine how high or low your income taxes are.

The Category box is so important, I devote an entire chapter to it—Chapter 4, "Tracking Where the Money Goes and Comes From." If you have a spare hour or so, you might fold down the corner of this page, visit Chapter 4, and come back here tomorrow. Sooner or later you have to create meaningful income and expense categories that work for you, but it isn't absolutely necessary to do that now because for the time being you can use one of Quicken's ready-made categories.

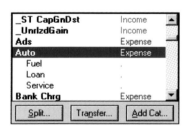

To assign a category to a transaction, click the arrow on the right side of the Category box. A list of categories appears. At the top of the list are income categories; then come expense categories; and last come transfer categories (which you can use to transfer money between accounts). Scroll through the list by pressing ↑ or ↓ on the keyboard or by clicking the up- or down-arrow on the scroll bar. When the category to which you want to assign the transaction is highlighted, either click it or press ENTER. The category you chose appears in the Category box.

Next comes the Memo box. Filling in this one is optional in the same way that filling in the memo line on a handwritten check is optional. If you think the transaction you are recording will look odd and mysterious when you review your finances months from now, you probably should type a description of some kind in the Memo box.

Now you have completed the transaction and all you have to do is tell Quicken to record it. To do that, click the Enter button. You hear a beep. The transaction has been saved to the hard disk in your computer. The cursor moves down the register and the next row is highlighted so you can enter another transaction there.

## Splitting a Deposit or Payment Across Different Categories

When you categorize a transaction as part of entering it in a register, sometimes the transaction doesn't fall neatly into one category. For example, if you were to deposit three checks, one from your place of work, one from your spouse's place of work, and one from Aunt Enid (a birthday present), the deposit wouldn't fit into a single category. It would fall into three categories: Income, Salary Spouse, and Gift Received. Likewise, if you wrote a check to the All & Sundries General Store to pay for motor oil, a submarine sandwich, stamps, and a bathing

## CAUTION

*When you split a deposit or payment, you can't assign classes to the parts of the transaction. Chapter 4 explains what classes are.*

Split...

suit, the payment wouldn't fall into a single category, but into four: Auto Supplies, Groceries, Postage, and Clothing.

To categorize a purchase like that one, you can save yourself some work and simply classify the four items under the umbrella category Misc (Miscellaneous). It depends on how carefully you want to track your spending habits. If you keep choosing the Misc category, however, you won't be able to tell how much you spent on auto supplies, groceries, and so on.

But in the case of the fictional deposit, you definitely would *split* the transaction and classify it three ways, because recording income is important for tax purposes. Splitting a transaction, in case you haven't guessed already, means to categorize the transaction in more than one way. Registers offer the Splits button for that very purpose.

To split a transaction, fill out the register in the usual way, but when you get to the Category box, click the Split button. You see the Split Transaction Window shown in Figure 2.4. Here, three checks from different categories are being deposited at once. Notice, in the lower-right corner of the dialog box, that the Splits Total and Transaction Total are equal, and that no Remainder appears. The numbers for this split deposit all add up.

To categorize the split transaction, click the arrow in the first Category box to see the Category menu and choose a category from the drop-down list. Next, go to the Amount box on line 1 and enter a number there. After you enter the amount, Quicken puts the remainder

| | Category | Memo | Amount | |
|---|---|---|---|---|
| 1. | Income:Syborex | | 1,667 00 | |
| 2. | Gift Received | Fr. Aunt Enid | 1,000 00 | |
| 3. | Salary Spouse | | 2,031 92 | |
| 4. | | | | |
| 5. | | | | |
| 6. | | | | |
| 7. | | | | |
| 8. | | | | |

Split Total: 4,698.92
Remainder: 0.00
Transaction Total: 4,698.92

Finished | Cancel | Help | Adjust ->

**Figure 2.4** Splitting a transaction across several categories. Split transactions record deposits and payments that don't fit in a single category.

on the next line in case you have only one more category to enter on line 2. Keep entering categories, amounts, and memo descriptions that explain what the transaction is, until the Splits Total equals the Transaction Total.

When the numbers in the Splits dialog box add up, click the Finished button. You go back to the register, where the word "Splits," a check mark, and an *X* appear in the Category box. Click the Enter button to record your split transaction.

To review a split transaction, click the green check mark. Quicken opens the Splits dialog box so you can have a look at the transaction and perhaps make changes.

Click the red *X* if you decide that this shouldn't be a split transaction after all. When you click the *X*, a message box asks, "Clear all split lines?" If you click the Yes button, the Category box is rendered empty so you can choose a single category and abandon the idea of splitting the transaction.

# Transferring Money Between Accounts

Sometimes not enough money is in the checking account, so you have to bolster it by transferring a few dollars from savings to checking. And sometimes, thanks to hard work or good fortune, you end up with more money in checking than you need, in which case you transfer money from checking to savings, to an IRA, or maybe to an investment account.

Transfer money between Quicken registers when you transfer money between real-life bank accounts. And transfer money between registers when you purchase stock, buy a CD, or make another kind of investment or contribute to an asset that you are tracking in a Quicken register. It seems odd to transfer money like that, but think of it this way: if you have an IRA and you write a $2,000 check for a contribution to your IRA, that $2,000 is still yours. You haven't spent it. All you have done is moved it from one account (checking) to another (an asset or investment account). Therefore, to record the $2,000 contribution in Quicken, you transfer the money from the checking account to the asset account in which you track the IRA's worth.

To transfer money between accounts, start by opening the register of the account you want to transfer money from. Next, click the Transfer button. You see the Transfer dialog box shown in Figure 2.5. Click the down-arrow in the To box and choose the account that will receive the money. Change the date, if necessary, and then enter the amount of the transfer in the Amount box. Today's date appears in the Date box, but if you transferred the real-life money between real-life accounts on a different day, enter that day in the Date box. Finally, click the OK button.

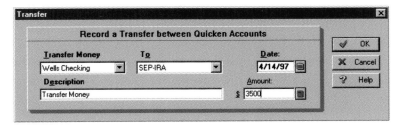

**Figure 2.5** Transferring money between accounts. You can also do this directly from a register.

You hear a beep loud enough to scare a cat. The letters TXFR (for transfer) appear in the Num box of the transaction, the words "Transfer Money" appear in the Payee box, and the name of the account you transferred the money to appears, in brackets, in the Category box. The date and the amount you entered appear, too.

| 4/14/97 | TXFR | Transfer Money | | 3,500 | 00 | | | | 6,900 | 10 |
| | | [SEP-IRA] | | | | | | | | |

## SHORTCUT

*You can also transfer money in a register by choosing Transfer Funds from the Num menu, entering the amount of the transfer in the Payment box, scrolling to the bottom of the Category menu, and choosing the destination account.*

Meanwhile, in the register that received the money transfer, the words "Transfer Money" appear in the Payee box, the amount of the transfer is entered in the Deposit box, the balance is increased, and the name of the account you transferred money from appears, in brackets, in the Category box. If you don't believe me, press CTRL-X or click the Edit button (it's next to the Enter button) and choose Go to Transfer from the menu to get to the other register.

### tricks of the trade

*Don't let your banker's hand be quicker than your eye. A checking account might deliberately carry a low monthly fee, in order to make it look cheap to price-shoppers. But the bank might recoup by charging you extra for processing checks or using the ATM machines. This is especially true of banks that tout gimmicks, like extending the manufacturer's warranty for any product that you buy by check.*

*Jane Bryant Quinn,* Making the Most of Your Money

# MOVING AROUND IN A REGISTER WINDOW

The longer you work with Quicken, the longer your account registers grow, and the harder it is to get from place to place. What if you are staring at a transaction line dated December 12 and you need to see a transaction that you made in June? This part of the chapter explains mouse and keyboard techniques for getting around in long registers.

First, the mouse techniques:

- Click the up- or down-arrow on the top or bottom of the *scroll bar*. The scroll bar is the stripe along the right side of registers (and some menus) that resembles an elevator shaft. Each time you click, the screen moves up or down by one transaction.

- Click on the scroll bar, but not on an arrow or on the scroll box. Each time you click, you see a new screenful of transactions.

- Drag the *scroll box* up or down. The scroll box is the elevator-like box in the scroll bar. As you drag, a white box appears to show you the date (and the check numbers) of the transactions you are moving to.

Next, the keyboard techniques:

| Press | To Move |
|---|---|
| ↑ or ↓ | Up or down by one transaction |
| PGUP or PGDN | Up or down an entire screenful of transactions |
| CTRL-PGUP | To the first transaction in the month |
| CTRL-PGDN | To the last transaction in the month |
| CTRL-HOME | To the first transaction in the register |
| CTRL-END | To the last transaction in the register |

# CORRECTING MISTAKES IN REGISTERS

Inevitably, everyone makes mistakes when they enter transactions in registers. Most people do not have the nimble fingers of an expert typist, magician, or shoplifter. Therefore, these pages explain how to fix entries in registers, delete and void transactions, find errors, and fix errors *en masse* with the Edit I Find & Replace I Find/Replace command.

## Changing Part of a Register Entry

Even if you've clicked the Enter button, heard the beep, and sent the financial data to the hard disk, you can go back to a transaction and change it. To do that, click where you made the mistake, press the BACKSPACE or DEL key to erase it, type the right data in, and click the Enter button.

If you make a complete botch of a transaction and want to start all over, click the Edit button (next to the Enter button) and choose Restore Transaction from the menu to erase all of the data you've entered so far.

## Voiding and Deleting Transactions

Deleting and voiding transactions are two very different things. A deleted transaction is erased from your financial records. It could just as well have never happened. A voided transaction remains in your data records (along with the word VOID and a few asterisks) so you know

## CAUTION

*Never void an online payment—it will be made anyway, since you shot it into cyberspace. Instead, choose Features I Online I Online Payments and choose Stop Payment.*

you made the transaction but voided it. If you write a check by hand and have to tear it up because you accidentally entered the wrong name in the Payee line, void the transaction instead of deleting it. That way, you have a record of what happened to the check.

To delete a transaction, put the cursor in the register row where the transaction is and choose Edit I Transaction I Delete, press CTRL-D, or click the Edit button and choose Delete Transaction from the menu. The entire transaction is deleted as though you never made it.

To void a transaction, put the cursor in the transaction, choose Edit I Transaction I Void, press CTRL-V, or click the Edit button and choose Void Transaction. A big fat **VOID** appears in the Payee box.

# Finding and Fixing Entry Errors

Suppose you made a blunder somewhere in a register but you aren't sure where you made it. You misspelled somebody's name or put an income transaction in the wrong category. Worse, suppose you made the same error many times. How can you fix your errors without wasting an afternoon?

You can use two commands: Edit I Find & Replace I Find, and Edit I Find & Replace I Find/Replace. The first one locates transactions in a register. The second finds transactions and gives you the opportunity to replace them with new entries. (Edit I Find & Replace I Find/Replace is the subject of the next part of this chapter.)

To find a single entry or all the entries of a certain kind, open the register and either click the Find button or choose Edit I Find & Replace I Find. The Quicken Find dialog box shown in Figure 2.6 appears.

**SHORTCUT**

*If you know the date of the transaction you are looking for, click the Edit button (next to the Enter button) and choose Go to A Specific Date from the menu. Then enter the date in the Go To Date dialog box and click OK.*

**Figure 2.6** Finding a transaction in a register. Click the Find button to find the last transaction; click Find All to see a list of all transactions.

Start with the Search menu, even though Find is the topmost box. The Search box is for narrowing the confines of the search and making it go faster. Quicken searches all parts of a transaction, from the Date field to the Category field, but to make the search go faster you can tell it to look in specific fields. The reason you should start with the Search menu is that the Find box changes depending on what has been chosen in the Search box. If you choose Category/Class, a menu of categories and classes appears in the Find box. If you choose Payee, the QuickFill list becomes available in the Find box.

```
All Fields
Amount
Cleared Status
Memo
Date
Category/Class
Check Number
Payee
```

Click the arrow in the Search box and choose an option from the drop-down menu. If you believe that the item you are searching for is in the Payee box, choose Payee, for example.

Now go back to the Find box and enter what you are looking for. If you are looking for a payee name or category, it should be on the drop-down menu. Type a number if you are looking for an amount.

Click the arrow in the Match if box if you don't know precisely what the name or number you are looking for is. On the Match if menu, choose Contains if you want to find all transactions that include the criterion you entered in the Find box; choose Exact to find the transactions that contain your criterion and nothing else. For example, a search for "Waldorf" with the Contains option finds "Waldorf School," "Waldorf-Astoria," and "Waldorf," but the same search with the Exact option only finds "Waldorf." Use the Starts With or Ends With option when you don't quite know what you are looking for but vaguely remember how its name begins or ends. Use the last four options on the Match if menu to search for dollar amounts.

Now that you know what to look for, tell Quicken how to conduct the search:

- **Find button:** Click the Find button to climb up the register and go to the first transaction that satisfies your search criteria. (If you want to climb down the register and search from top to bottom, click the Search Backwards check box.) If Quicken finds what you are looking for, it takes you there in the register. From there, you can either click in the register, alter the transaction and click Enter, or you can click the Find button again to see if Quicken finds another instance of the thing you so desperately seek.

- **Find All button:** Click the Find All button to open the Quicken Find window with a list of all transactions in the register that satisfy the search criteria. Figure 2.7 shows the Quicken Find window. From the list, you can zero in on a single transaction by double-clicking it. You will be taken in the register to the transaction you double-clicked. To get back to the Quicken Find window, click the Quicken Find tab on the right side of your screen.

**Quicken Find**

| Date | Acct | Num | Payee | Cat | Memo | Clr | Amount |
|------|------|-----|-------|-----|------|-----|--------|
| 2/6/96 | Wells Chec... | 1306 | Strafeway | Hair | | R | -71.64 |
| 1/21/96 | Wells Chec... | 1295 | Strafeway | Groceries | | R | -27.42 |
| 12/10/95 | Wells Chec... | 1248 | Strafeway | Hair | | R | -64.78 |
| 11/19/95 | Wells Chec... | 1219 | Strafeway | Groceries | | R | -119.07 |
| 10/8/95 | Wells Chec... | 1182 | Strafeway | Groceries | | R | -39.85 |
| 9/14/95 | Wells Chec... | 1156 | Strafeway | Groceries | | R | -58.84 |
| 8/1/95 | Wells Chec... | 1112 | Strafeway | Groceries | | R | -50.33 |
| 6/27/95 | Wells Chec... | ATM | Strafeway | Groceries | | R | -20.77 |
| 4/22/95 | Wells Chec... | 1026 | Strafeway | Groceries | | R | -57.12 |
| 4/3/95 | Wells Chec... | 991 | Strafeway | Groceries | | R | -53.89 |
| 3/29/95 | Wells Chec... | 989 | Strafeway | | | R | -48.96 |
| 3/9/95 | Wells Chec... | 966 | Strafeway | Groceries | | R | -47.24 |

☑ **Show Matches in Splits**                **Item Found in 35 Transactions**

**Figure 2.7**  The Quicken Find window. Double-click an item on the list to see it in the register.

*Quicken offers a special command for reassigning transactions to different categories. See "Fixing Mistakes in the Way Transactions Were Categorized" in Chapter 4.*

# Finding and Fixing Errors en Masse

Now that you know how to find data in a register, you can learn how to find data and replace it *en masse* with new data. To do that, you use the very powerful and sometimes mischievous Edit I Find & Replace I Find/Replace command. Finding transactions with this command is done the same way as finding transactions with the Edit I Find & Replace I Find command. The difference is, once the data is found, you can replace it with new data.

To find and replace data, open the register in question and choose Edit I Find & Replace I Find/Replace. You see the Find and Replace dialog box in Figure 2.8 (this one has been filled out already and the search has been conducted). If you look closely, you will see that the top of this dialog box is nearly identical to the Quicken Find dialog box that the previous handful of pages explained how to fill out. The only thing

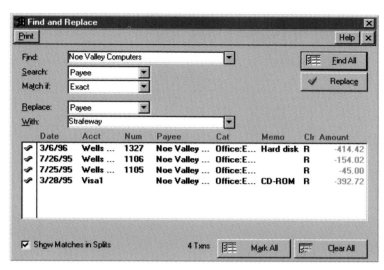

**Figure 2.8** The Find and Replace dialog box

missing is the Find button, because to conduct a find and replace operation you click the Find All button, get a list of all the transactions that meet your criteria, and then pick and choose which ones to replace with the new data.

Starting with the Search box, use the Find, Search, and Match if boxes to pinpoint the data that you want to replace. (Go back a few pages to see how to do that, if you have to.) Once you've told Quicken what you are searching for, click the Find All button. The bottom half of the dialog box shows you a list of all the transactions that could be found.

Eyeball the transactions to make sure that these are indeed the ones you want to replace. Then click the arrow in the Replace box to see the menu and choose which part of the transactions needs replacing. Which option you choose from the Replace menu determines which options, if any, become available in the With menu. If you choose Category/Class from the Replace menu, for example, you see a list of categories on the With menu. If you choose Amount, on the other hand, enter an amount yourself in the With box.

Now you are ready to tell Quicken which transactions to replace. To replace all of them, click the Mark All button at the bottom of the dialog box. To replace a few, click in the narrow column to the left of the transactions you want to replace. As you click, check marks appear. You can always click the Clear All button to remove all the check marks and start over.

The moment of truth has arrived: click the Replace button. A dialog box tells you how many replacements are about to be made and asks whether you have the guts to go through with it. Click OK. Another dialog box tells you how many replacements were made. Click OK again.

# MANAGING A CASH ACCOUNT

Chapter 1 explained how to set up an account and mentioned the different kinds of accounts you can create, including the cash account. Cash accounts are not for everybody. This kind of account might better be called a "petty cash account," because it is chiefly of use to businesses for tracking day-to-day cash spending. Rather than set up a cash account, home users can simply track cash spending from a checking account. I'll show you how.

To create a cash account if you do need one, follow the standard procedure for creating an account, and choose Cash in the Account Setup dialog box. (See "Setting Up an Account" in Chapter 1 if need be.) When your cash account is set up and you've made a few entries, its register looks something like Figure 2.9. Aren't the green stripes chic?

The money for the cash account most likely comes from a checking or savings account. When you withdraw the money from that account, transfer it to the cash account. In other words, if you withdraw $200 from a savings account for Friday night fun and frolic or a fiscal

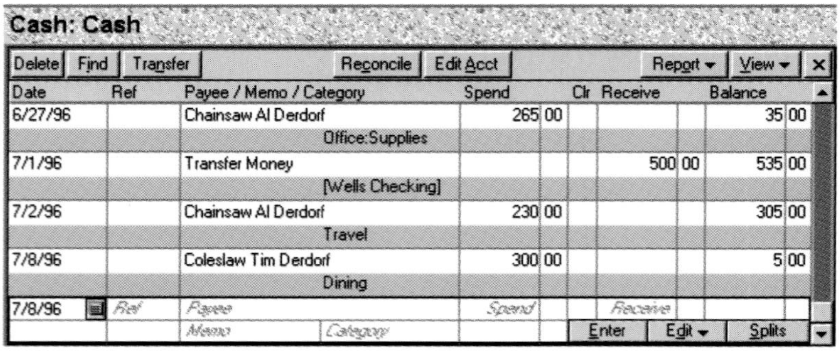

**Figure 2.9** One way to track cash spending: a cash account

year blowout bash, transfer the $200 from the savings account to the cash account. Then, as you spend the cash or your coworkers take it out of the money drawer, record those "withdrawals" in the Spend boxes. Use the Category boxes to describe what the money was spent on. You might use the Payee or Memo boxes to list the names of the people who took the cash.

So much for the cash account way to track cash spending. The other way to do it is to record cash withdrawals from savings and checking accounts. To see how this works, suppose you go to an ATM on a bustling Saturday night and take $200 cash out of a checking account. You spend $100 at dinner, and you spend the other $100 for theater tickets. In this case, you have spent $100 in two categories, Dining and Leisure. When it comes time to record these transactions in Quicken, open the checking account register, record the date and the amount of the transaction, record it as an ATM withdrawal, and click the Splits button. In the Splits dialog box, record the two spending transactions as shown here. By splitting withdrawal transactions, you can keep track of how you spend cash.

| | Category | Memo | Amount | |
|---|---|---|---|---|
| 1. | Dining | | 100 00 | |
| 2. | Leisure | Theatre tix | 100 00 | |
| 3. | | | Next  Edit ▾ | |
| 4. | | | | |
| 5. | | | | |

**Splits: Use it to itemize this transaction**

# RECORDING TRANSACTIONS IN CREDIT CARD ACCOUNTS

These days, when the mail always includes at least one invitation to get a new credit card, just about everybody has plastic. And everybody who has plastic and uses Quicken needs to set up a credit card account. Create two, three, or four, if necessary, one for each credit card you own. How to open an account is explained in "Setting Up a New Account" in Chapter 1.

The only difference between a credit card account and most other Quicken accounts is that a credit card account tracks what you owe, not what you have. Each time you charge something and record the

*To keep credit card spending under control, diligently record your charges as you make them. As you see the amount that you owe in the credit card register get bigger and bigger, you may be discouraged from spending so much.*

transaction in your credit card account, Quicken deducts the amount you charged, so the account balance almost always shows a negative number (in red, no less!). When you pay all of what you owe, the balance is brought to zero (a black zero, not a red one), as shown in Figure 2.10.

| Visa1 - Capital One: Credit | | | | | | | | |
|---|---|---|---|---|---|---|---|---|
| Delete | Find | Transfer | | Reconcile | Edit Acct | | Report ▾ | View ▾ | X |
| Date | Ref | Payee / Memo / Category | | Charge | Clr | Payment | | Balance | |
| 3/29/96 | | Chevronda | | 11 86 | R | | | 578 57 |
| | | 12/21 | Auto:Fuel | | | | | |
| 3/31/96 | | Kamei Household Wares | | 33 19 | R | | | 611 76 |
| | | | Home Repair | | | | | |
| 4/7/96 | | Finance Charges | | 23 55 | R | | | 635 31 |
| | | | | | | | | |
| 4/23/96 | | Capital Wonde | | | R | 635 31 | | 0 00 |
| | | [Wells Checking] | | | | | | |
| 7/8/96 | Ref | Payee | | Charge | | Payment | | |
| | | Memo | Category | | | Enter | Edit ▾ | Splits |

**Figure 2.10** A credit card register. Each time you charge something, record it in the register and watch the red balance—what you owe—get larger and larger.

Credit card charges are entered like other register transactions. The Payee box is for recording who the purchase was made from. The amount of the charge goes in the Charge box. The Category box is for classifying the transaction. When you make a payment to the card issuer, it is recorded in the Payment box. To make a payment, you transfer money into your credit card account from the checking account that you are using to pay the bill. I explain how to do that, and how to reconcile a credit card account, in Chapter 5.

# PRINTING AN ACCOUNT REGISTER

'Round about April 15, when your income taxes are filed and you are putting away your receipts, check stubs, and other financial papers, print a copy of your account registers for the past year and file them away, too. That way, you leave behind a wider, deeper, more distinguishable paper trail for others to follow.

To print a register, open it and press CTRL-P or choose File | Print Register. You see the Print Register dialog box. Type a descriptive name in the Title box. In the Print Transaction From and To boxes, enter a range of dates that describes which transactions to print. For example, to print all of 1996's transactions, enter **1/1/96** and **12/31/96**.

Click the Print One Transaction Per Line check box to save paper and the Print Transaction Splits check box to make split transactions appear in their entirety on the register. As for the Sort by Reference Number box, click it if you prefer transactions to be arranged in check order instead of date order. Finally, click the Print button.

Next comes the Print dialog box. Ignore the fancy gizmos on this dialog box, go straight to the OK button, and click it.

# WAGONS, HO!

So much for registers. This chapter has explained everything that you, a busy, intelligent, charming person needs to know about them. It is time to break camp and move on to Chapter 3. That chapter explains how to print checks. I suggest that you read "The Pros and Cons of Check Printing" early in Chapter 3 to see whether you need to print checks. Check printing might not be your cup of tea. If it isn't, skip to Chapter 4, which explains how to categorize your spending and income. Everybody needs to do that.

# CHAPTER 3

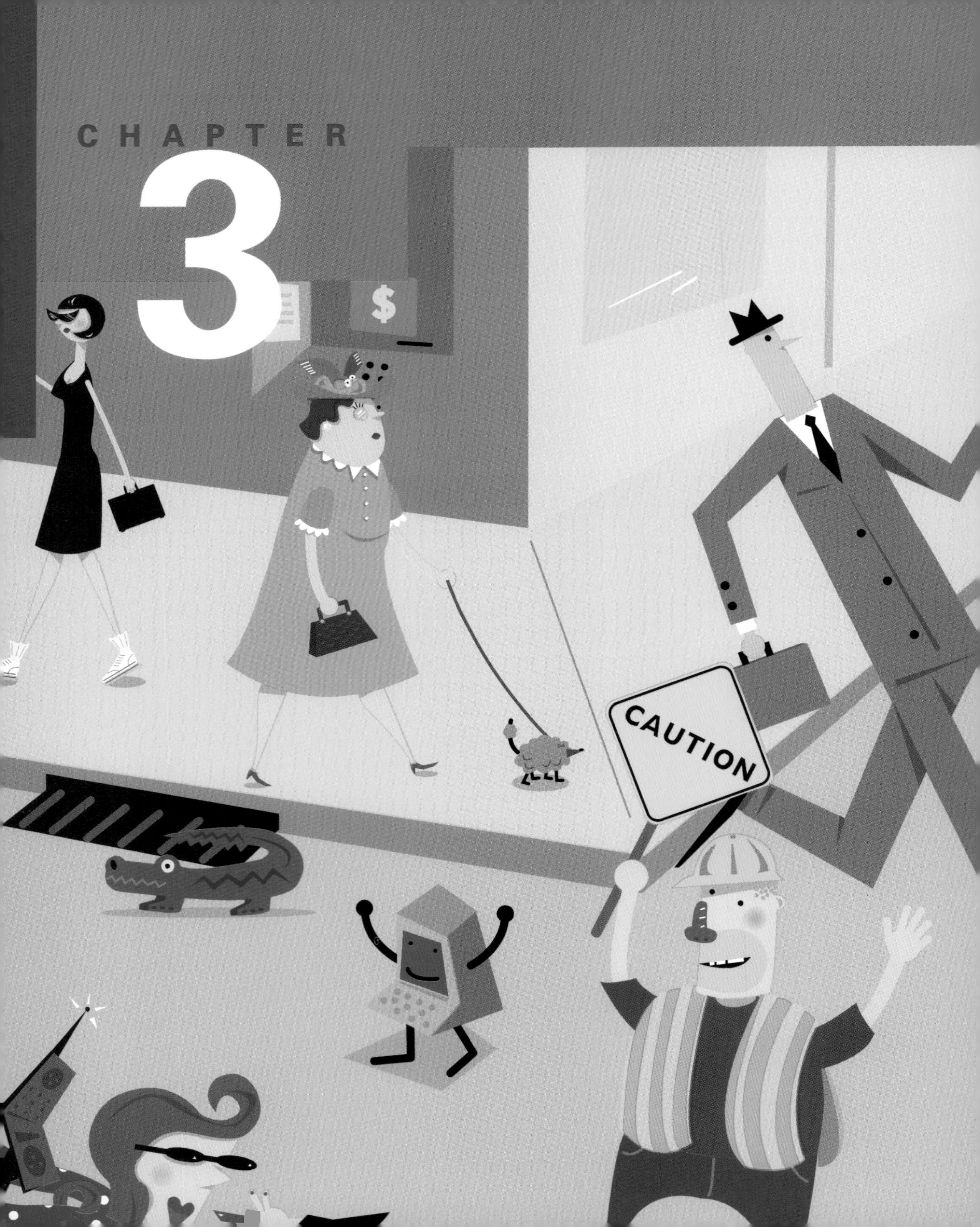

# Writing and Printing Checks

- Ordering checks

- Instructing the printer how to print checks

- Writing checks in the Write Checks window

- Moving around in the Write Checks window

- Deleting and voiding printed checks

- Choosing which checks to print

- Reprinting checks if they didn't print correctly

- Being reminded to print checks

# FAST FORWARD

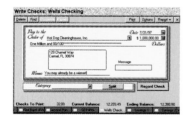

## ORDER CHECKS FROM INTUIT,
## THE MAKER OF QUICKEN ➤ *pp. 51–53*

1. Fill out the order form that came in the Quicken package and mail it to Intuit. If you have a modem, you can order checks online.
2. Choose Features | Paying Bills | Order Checks, and click the Checks button.
3. Fill in the dialog boxes and click the Order button.

## MAKE SURE YOUR CHECKS
## PRINT CORRECTLY ➤ *pp. 53–56*

1. Choose File | Printer Setup | For Printing Checks and adjust the settings in the Check Printer Setup dialog box.
2. Click the Align button, click the Full Page of Checks button, and click the Print Sample button in the Fine Alignment dialog box.
3. Depending on how your check printed, go back to the Fine Alignment dialog box and click the Vertical and Horizontal arrows to adjust by increments where text is printed on checks.

## WRITE A CHECK ➤ *pp. 56–58*

1. Open the Write Checks window pressing CTRL-W, choosing Features | Paying Bills | Write Checks, or clicking the Bills button and choosing Write a Check to Print from the menu.
2. Fill in the Write Checks window. Enter the date, payee, amount, memo, and category the same way you do in the checking register. Quicken writes out the amount for you. You can include an address in the Address box.
3. Click the Record Check button.

## REVIEW CHECKS
## BEFORE YOU PRINT THEM ➤ *pp. 60–61*

1. Click the checking register's Quick Tab in the upper-right corner of the screen and examine the checks in the register. The ones that are to be printed show the word "Print" in the Num column.
2. Edit the checks in the register. All the changes you make will also be made in the Write Checks window.

## PRINT A CHECK ➤ *pp. 61–63*

1. Click the Print button in the Write Checks window or choose File | Print Checks to see the Select Checks to Print dialog box.
2. Enter the number of the first check on the check sheet in the First Check Number box.
3. Choose All Checks to print all the checks, Checks Dated Through to print checks to a certain date, or Selected Checks and click the Choose button to open the Select Checks to Print dialog box and select checks.
4. Under Checks on First Page, choose the option that describes how many checks are on the first check sheet loaded in your printer.
5. Click OK to print your checks.

This short chapter explains how to print checks. Not everybody needs to print checks. It's expensive, for one thing. And unless you have a laser or single-sheet printer and understand how to use it, printing checks can be more trouble than it's worth. On the other hand, printed checks are neat and clean and they make a good impression on creditors and clients. They are easy to read and understand, too. I suppose you are obliged to print checks if nobody can read your handwriting.

The following pages examine the pros and cons of printing checks. They tell how check printing works, how to order checks from Quicken, how to write a check, and how to void or delete one. Last but not least, this chapter explains how to actually run a check through the printer.

# THE PROS AND CONS OF CHECK PRINTING

The literature that comes with Quicken claims that printing checks saves enormous amounts of time. Instead of filling in a check by hand and recording it in a register, you kill two birds with one stone by printing a check, because the check is automatically recorded in the register as you write it. You don't have to enter the payee name, date, and amount twice, once on the check itself and once in a register, because Quicken takes the information from you in the Write Checks window and records it automatically in the register.

Figure 3.1 shows the Write Checks window. This is where you "write" the check. Notice the Category line for categorizing the transaction and the Splits button for splitting it across several categories. Everything you can do to enter a check in a checking register can also be done in the Write Checks window. All the data you enter in this window is recorded as one transaction in the checking register.

*You can write checks by hand and print checks from the same checking account. If you opt to print checks, it doesn't mean you have to run all the checks through the printer. You can still write as many as you want by hand.*

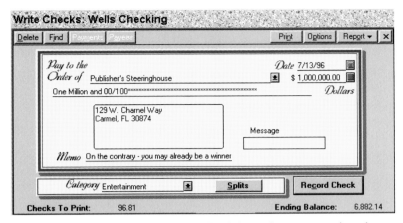

**Figure 3.1** The Write Checks window. The information you enter here is recorded in the checking register as well.

But how much time is really saved by printing checks? It takes about 10 seconds to write out a check by hand and about 10 more to enter it in a register. In that 20 seconds, you would have to fill out the Write Checks window, load checks in your printer, review the check you want to print, and give the print command if you were printing checks. How much time is saved by doing that? None, I think.

As far as time goes, the only advantage to printing checks is being able to print several at once. Running a bunch of checks through the printer does save time, especially if you intend to mail them, because the Write Checks window has a place for printing addresses in case you want to mail your checks in window envelopes.

The best reason for printing checks has nothing to do with saving time—it has to do with appearances. Depending on the type of business you are in, printed checks might increase your standing with clients and creditors. A printed check says, "I'm a very serious, prosperous individual and you should regard me as such," whereas a handwritten check with spidery lettering says, "Heaven bless you, kind sir or madam, for honoring my little check." Anyone who is in a profession where appearances are important—supermodels, for example—ought to consider printing checks.

Of course, if it improves your appearance it is bound to cost extra. As I write this, printed checks costs between 16 and 24 cents apiece, depending on the kind of check you order from Intuit. By comparison, my bank only charges around 2 cents apiece for checks.

*If you came here to learn how to record a check in a checking register, you came to the wrong place. Go see "Filling in a Register" in Chapter 2.*

# THE BIG PICTURE: CHECK PRINTING

Before you start printing checks, you should know what you're getting into. Here is the lowdown on printing checks. Everything that is outlined here is explained in detail throughout this chapter.

The first thing to do is order the checks from Intuit. As part of ordering the checks, you tell Intuit your name and address, your bank's name and address, your checking account number, where to begin numbering the checks, and everything else that concerns the checks' appearance. By the way, it isn't necessary for your bank to know that you are getting checks from Intuit. As long as the information about your bank and the checking account number are accurate, the bank will honor the checks, no matter where you got them.

After the new checks arrive, you tell Quicken how to print checks, what kind of printer you have, and what size check you ordered. Quicken can't print checks correctly until it has this information. Before you print a check for the first time, you may do a test run to see if the checks print correctly.

Next you write the checks by filling out the Write Checks window. You can write several checks at a sitting. When you are ready to print the checks, review them, tell Quicken which numbers are on the checks, and then tell Quicken which ones to print. It isn't necessary to print all of them at once. Checks are "kept" in the Write Checks window until you run them through the printer, at which time they disappear from the Write Checks window and are recorded by number in the checking register.

# ORDERING THE CHECKS FROM INTUIT

Before you order checks from Intuit, get out your checkbook. Intuit needs the following information, most of which can be found on the face of a check. You also need to answer a few questions before you order checks.

- Your name, address, and telephone number.
- Your bank's name and the city, state and zip code in which it is located.
- Your bank's *fractional number*. The fractional number looks something like this: 11-22/3456. When you deposit a check, you usually list the first four numbers of the fractional number on the deposit slip.
- The checking account number.
- The starting check number. The checks you get will be numbered starting with this number. Be sure to give Intuit a number that doesn't conflict with the numbers on checks you've already written by hand or intend to write by hand. In fact, choose a starting number that is far different from the numbers on your handwritten checks so you don't run the risk of writing two checks with the same number.
- The style of the checks—classic, prestige, or antique. Your call.
- The size of the checks—standard, voucher, or wallet. Voucher and wallet checks are for printing payroll or accounts receivable information along with the check. The standard size is for writing personal checks. Figure 3.2, taken from the Size and Style dialog box that you see when you order checks online from Intuit, shows the differences between the three check types. The following short list

## CAUTION

*Pick a starting check number that doesn't conflict with the numbers on checks you write by hand. It's okay to print checks and write them by hand from the same checking account, but you must be careful not to duplicate check numbers.*

explains the differences. I've included information about window envelopes in case you intend to send the checks you order through the mail. The prices listed here were current as of August 1996.

| Check Type | Size | No. Per Sheet | Cost Per Check | Window Envelope |
|---|---|---|---|---|
| Standard | 8.5" × 3.5" | 3 | 19¢ | Double-window/ check size |
| Voucher | 8.5" × 3.5" | 1 | 24¢ | Double-window/ check size |
| Wallet | 6" × 2.8" with 2.5" side stub | 3 | 16¢ | Double-window/ wallet size |

Once you've gathered this information, you are ready to order the checks. To do that, fill out the Intuit Supplies order form that came in the Quicken package and either send or fax it to Intuit along with a voided check.

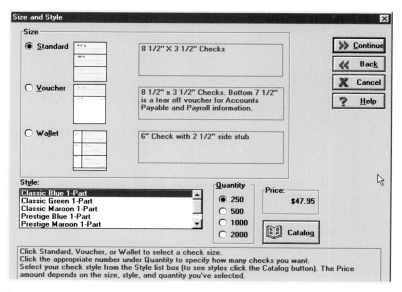

**Figure 3.2** The three types of checks. Voucher and wallet checks are for businesses; standard checks are for writing personal checks.

If you are impatient to get your hands on the checks and you own a modem, you can order checks online by choosing Features I Paying Bills I Order Checks. You see the Intuit Marketplace screen in Figure 3.3. Click the Checks button and slowly but surely fill in each dialog box as Quicken presents it. Then click the Order button when you are ready to send the order to Intuit.

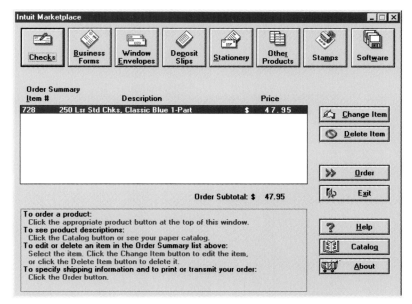

**Figure 3.3** The Intuit Marketplace dialog box. From here, you can order checks and other things—if you have a modem.

## TELLING THE PRINTER HOW TO HANDLE CHECKS

When the checks arrive, tell your printer everything you know about them. Checks are expensive. You could hurt yourself in the pocketbook if you waste them. Therefore, it behooves you to print a few checks to make sure that your printer knows what is what. After you've introduced Quicken to your printer, you never have to fool with the printer settings again.

In the Quicken package, there should be some unnumbered practice checks. Load them in your printer now. If you didn't get any practice checks, put a sheet of paper in your printer. Then choose File | Printer Setup | For Printing Checks. You see the dialog box in Figure 3.4.

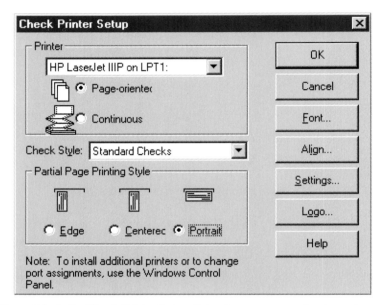

**Figure 3.4**  In the Check Printer Setup dialog box, your new checks and your printer are formally introduced to one another.

## Changing the Printer Settings

Most of the information in this dialog box should be correct already, but if it isn't, change the settings. Click the down-arrow in the Printer box and choose a new printer name from the menu. If your printer is fed paper "continuously" instead of one page at a time, click the Continuous option button. Click the arrow in the Check Style box and tell Quicken which kind of checks you ordered, Wallet, Voucher, or Standard.

The Partial Page Printing Style options are for standard and wallet-sized checks that print three to a page. You very likely won't print wallet or standard-sized checks in sets of three, which means you will be left with a "partial" page of blank checks that is one-third or two-thirds pages long. So as not to waste the leftover checks, you can feed the shortened check sheet back into your printer. To do that, however, you need to tell Quicken how paper is fed to your printer by choosing a Partial Page Printing Style option. Click the button that describes how your printer takes paper (Edge, Centered, or Portrait), even if it means burrowing through the dreary manual that came with your printer to find out.

# Doing a Test Run

From the Check Printer Setup dialog box, click the Align button to do a test printing. You see the Align Checks dialog box (people printing voucher checks bypass this dialog box and go straight to the Fine Alignment dialog box). The Align Checks dialog box is for running tests and making adjustments, if necessary, to where text lands on the checks you print. The three buttons are for making adjustments to check sheets with three checks on them, with two checks, and with only one check.

Start by clicking the Full Page of Checks button. You see the Fine Alignment dialog box in Figure 3.5. Click the Print Sample button in the Fine Alignment dialog box. Quicken prints a check made out to Jane Doe of Anytown, USA.

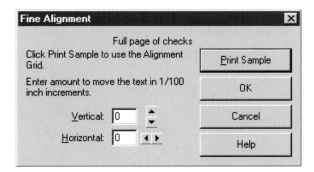

**Figure 3.5** The Fine Alignment dialog box. If necessary, click Vertical and Horizontal arrows to move the printed text on the checks a little to the east, west, north, or south.

Examine the check to see if the text landed in all the right places. (If you printed on a plain piece of paper instead of on practice checks, lay the sheet of paper over a sheet of real checks and hold both sheets to the light to see where the text fell.) I hope the printed text landed squarely where it was supposed to land, but if it didn't, start clicking the Vertical and Horizontal arrows in the Fine Alignment dialog box. With each click, you move the text ever so slightly upward, downward, left, or right. In the upper-right corner of the sample check you printed is a small grid. With each click on a Vertical or Horizontal arrow, you move the text one square on the grid. Keep clicking the Print Sample button, and keep clicking Horizontal or Vertical arrows, until the checks come out right. Then click the OK button in the Fine Alignment dialog box.

Back in the Align Checks dialog box, new Hor and Vert settings appear beside the Full Page of Checks button if you had to make adjustments. Now click the Two Checks on Page and One Check on Page buttons and perform the same diagnostic tests you just performed, but this time perform them on sheets with two checks and one check on them. When you are done testing, click OK in the Align Checks dialog box. Then click OK in the Check Printer Setup dialog box. Now stroll to the kitchen, make a cup of tea, and congratulate yourself on never having to suffer though this check alignment nonsense again.

# WRITING A CHECK

Now that you know your checks print correctly, you are ready to write and print checks. The first step is to write the checks. With that done, you can tell Quicken which ones to print.

## Filling in the Write Checks Window

First, open the register for the checking account you are going to write the check against. With the checking register onscreen, open the Write Checks window in one of these myriad ways: press CTRL-W, choose Features I Paying Bills I Write Checks, or click the Bills button and choose Write a Check to Print from the menu. You see the Write Checks window, which you saw already back in Figure 3.1.

If you've been entering checks in the register, the buttons and menus on the Write Checks window ought to look very familiar (read "Filling in a Register" in Chapter 2 to find out what the buttons and

menus do). Enter the date on the Date line, the payee on the Pay to the Order of line, and the amount next to the dollar sign. The Write Checks window also has a baby calendar and baby calculator that work the same way as the ones in registers. The Category menu works the same way. Click the Splits button to split a transaction across different categories.

QuickFill, the marvelous device for entering payee names quickly, works in the Write Checks window as well. When you type the first few letters of a familiar name, a full name appears along with an amount and category, and all you have to do then is press TAB to fill in the entire check. To move the cursor to a different part of the Write Checks window, click there or else press TAB or SHIFT-TAB.

The only differences between the Write Checks window and the checking register are the Dollars line and Address box. This being a check, you have to write the amount in words as well as numbers. However, Quicken writes the amount for you. After you enter it on the $ line and press TAB, Quicken spells out the amount of the check on the Dollars line.

## tricks of the trade

*Gold itself pays no interest and costs money to insure. It is a hedge against inflation, all right, and a handy way to buy passage to Liechtenstein, or wherever it is we're all supposed to flee to when the much ballyhooed collapse finally materializes. But if you're looking for an inflation hedge, you might do better with stocks or real estate. In the long run, they will rise with inflation, too. And in the short run, they pay dividends and rent.*

*Andrew Tobias,* The Only Investment Guide You'll Ever Need

As for the Address box, write the name and address of the party you are writing the check to in the Address box if you intend to send the check by mail. When you enter an address, Quicken remembers it. Next time you write a check to the same party, the address appears in the Address box without your having to type it there.

Scribble a few words of wisdom on the Memo line if you wish. If you're the chatty type and the Memo line isn't long enough, you can carve out more room on the check for writing pearls of wisdom. To do that, click the Options button, click the Allow Entry of Extra Message on Check option in the Checks tab, and click OK. A message box appears on your checks so you have more room to spout:

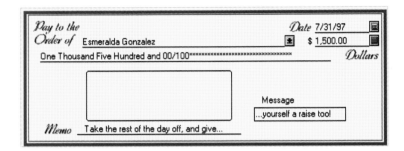

When you've filled in the Write Checks window, click the Record Check button. Write as many checks as you want. To review the ones you wrote earlier, press PGUP. To move down the list of checks you've written, press PGDN. A figure showing the sum of the checks you've written appears in the lower-left corner of the Write Checks window. A figure showing the ending balance in the checking account appears in the lower-right corner.

## What About the Check Number?

Conspicuously missing from the Write Checks window is a check number. That seems odd because all checks have check numbers, don't they? The check number, however, comes from the blank check that Intuit sent you. As part of printing a check you have written, you tell Quicken the number on the blank check. Quicken records the number on the blank check in the register when the check is printed. You will learn how to print checks shortly.

## Deleting and Voiding Printed Checks

Until you actually print a check, it has a sort of limbo status in the register. In the transaction line where the check is recorded, the word "Print" appears in the Num box. When the check is printed, however, a check number appears where "Print" used to be. Check numbers, as you will find out shortly when you learn how to print checks, come from the numbers on the blank checks that Intuit sent you. In the register shown here, some of the checks have been printed (they have numbers) and others are still waiting to be printed (notice the word "Print" in the Num column):

| 7/13/96 | 5000 | James Whitcomb Riley Hair Products | 45 | 99 | | | | 6,903 | 15 |
| | | hair brush        Gifts | | | | | | | |
| 7/14/96 | Print | Educator's Publishing | 22 | 70 | | | | 6,880 | 45 |
| | | Books | | | | | | | |
| 7/15/96 | 5001 | Big 6 | 13 | 00 | | | | 6,867 | 45 |
| | | Recreation | | | | | | | |
| 7/16/96 | Print | Dimensions in Architecture | 30 | 00 | | | | 6,837 | 45 |
| | | Books | | | | | | | |

Suppose I regret writing one of these checks. Should I delete it or void it? It depends on whether the check has been printed. A printed check must be voided, because only by voiding it can you account for the missing check number in the register, but an unprinted check can merely be deleted because it hasn't been assigned a number yet. In the register shown here, check number 5001 has been voided. By voiding check 5001, I have a record of what happened to it. I know that it isn't missing or lost somewhere. If check 5001 had not been printed, I could simply delete it, because it wouldn't have a check number in the first place.

| 7/13/96 | 5000 | James Whitcomb Riley Hair Products | 45 | 99 | | | | 6,903 | 15 |
| | | hair brush        Gifts | | | | | | | |
| 7/14/96 | Print | Educator's Publishing | 22 | 70 | | | | 6,880 | 45 |
| | | Books | | | | | | | |
| 7/15/96 | 5001 | **VOID**Big 6 | | | | R | | 6,880 | 45 |
| | | Recreation | | | | | | | |

To void a check, display it in the Write Checks window and choose Edit I Void Transaction. Be sure to write "void" across the front of the check and store it safely in the bottom of a treasure chest or filing cabinet.

To delete a check from the Write Checks window because you don't care to print it, press the PGUP or PGDN key until you can see the check, then click the Delete button in the Write Checks window. Quicken asks if it is okay to delete the transaction. Click Yes and brace yourself for a loud beep.

# PRINTING THE CHECKS

At last, you've written the checks and now you can print them. It isn't necessary to print all of them at once. This part of the chapter explains how to choose which checks to print, print on an incomplete check sheet, print the checks, and reprint them if they don't come out right.

## PRINT CHECKS step by step

1. Click the Print button in the Write Checks window.
2. In the Select Checks to Print dialog box, enter the number of the first check on the check sheet in the First Check Number text box.
3. Choose a Print option to say which of the checks you want to print.
4. Under Checks on First Page, click an option that describes how many checks are on the first page you loaded in the printer.
5. Click the OK button.

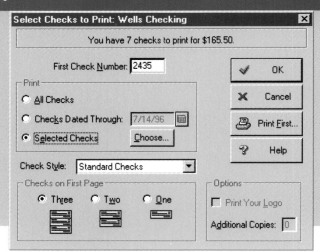

## Reviewing Checks Before You Print Them

Before you actually print the checks, take a last look at them. If a payee name, date, amount, or address is wrong, this is your last chance to correct it without wasting a check. To review checks, page through them in the Write Checks window by pressing the PGUP or PGDN key.

A faster way to review checks is to do it in the register. Click the Register Quick Tab (in the upper-right corner of the screen) to get inside the checking register, examine the checks you have written, and correct them if you have to. The word "Print" appears beside unprinted checks in the Num column:

| 7/13/96 | Print | Dimensions in Architecture | 30 | 00 | | | | 6,906 | 14 |
| | | Books | | | | | | | |
| 7/13/96 | Print | James Whitcomb Riley Hair Products | 45 | 99 | | | | 6,860 | 15 |
| | | hair brush          Gifts | | | | | | | |
| 7/13/96 | Print | Ms. Noriko O'Shaughnessy | 24 | 00 | | | | 6,836 | 15 |
| | | Babysitting | | | | | | | |

# Recording the Check Numbers

Now that you are ready to go, click the Print button in the Write Checks window or choose File | Print Checks. You see the Select Checks to Print dialog box in Figure 3.6. The top of the dialog box tells you how many checks need printing and the sum of those checks.

The first item in the dialog box is the all-important First Check Number text box. Glance at the checks as you load them in your printer and take note of the number on the first check. That is the number to

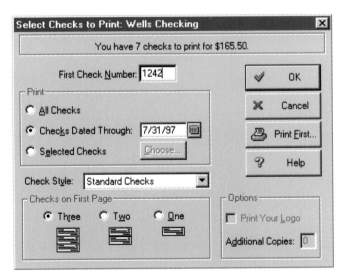

**Figure 3.6** The Select Checks to Print dialog box. This is where you tell Quicken which checks to print, how to number the checks, and how to print them.

enter in the First Check Number text box. Make sure you get this number right. If you get it wrong, your checks will be misnumbered in the register.

## Telling Quicken Which Checks to Print

To begin with, the All Checks option button in the Select Checks to Print dialog box is selected, so if you want to print all the checks, simply leave the Print options alone. However, if you want to be choosy, Quicken offers two options for deciding which checks to print:

- **Checks Dated Through:** Click this option button and enter a date to print checks up to and including those written on a particular day.

- **Selected Checks**: Click this option button and click the Choose button if you want to pick and choose which checks to print. When you click the Choose button, you see the Select Checks to Print dialog box shown here. A yellow check mark in the Print column means that the check will be printed. Click a check to remove the yellow check mark; and click again to put it back. When only the checks to be printed have a yellow check mark, click the Done button.

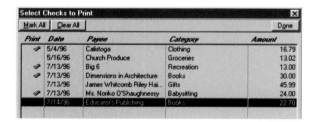

## Printing Starting with the Second or Third Check

Back in the Select Checks to Print dialog box, glance in the Check Style box to make sure Quicken knows which kind of check you are printing—Standard, Wallet, or Voucher. If you are printing voucher checks, which print one to a page, you don't have to worry about the Checks on First Page options at the bottom of the dialog box.

Standard and wallet checks, however, print three to a page. Before you print them, Quicken wants to know how many checks are on the first page of checks you loaded in the printer. If the first page is a fresh page that has never been printed on, three checks are on the first page. Otherwise, two or one remain. Investigate this urgent matter and select a Checks on First Page option to tell Quicken how many checks are on the first page of checks you will print.

## Giving the Print Command

All systems are go. Quicken knows which checks to print, how to number the checks, and how many checks are on the first page. You, my friend, may click the OK button in the Select Checks to Print dialog box.

After the checks are printed, Quicken displays the Did Check(s) Print OK? dialog box shown in Figure 3.7. I hope they printed correctly. If they did, click the OK button and be done with it. And don't forget to sign the checks. While you're at it, you might glance in the check register to make sure that the register recorded the check numbers correctly.

If the checks didn't print correctly, read on.

**habits & strategies**

*If you aren't confident that the checks will print correctly, click the Print First button to print only the first check in the batch. That way, if the checks come out wrong, you will waste only one check, not several.*

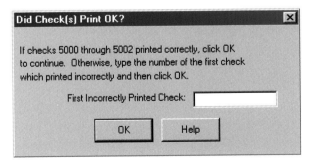

**Figure 3.7** Click OK in this dialog box if the checks printed correctly. Otherwise, enter a check number and click OK to go to the Select Checks to Print dialog box and start all over.

## If Your Checks Didn't Print Correctly

If the checks didn't come out right, examine them, find the first that didn't print correctly, and enter its number in the Did Check(s) Print OK? dialog box. When you click OK, Quicken takes you to the Select Checks to Print dialog box (see Figure 3.6), where you get another chance and can start all over. Notice that the first check number has advanced a few notches. Quicken has assumed you want to try again and is ready to print checks beginning with what it believes is the next number in the check sheet.

In the Select Checks to Print dialog box, select the checks that need printing and click OK to try again. I hope you get it right the second time around.

# BEING REMINDED TO PRINT CHECKS

If you write checks but postpone printing them for another day, Quicken reminds you to get with it and print the checks. It does this with the To Do! button, the Reminders window, and a very small check icon.

First the To Do! button. As long as you have checks to print, the To Do! button appears in the lower-right corner of the screen. Click this button and you see the Quicken Reminders window, where the checks that need printing are listed. (If the checks don't appear, click the Options button in the Reminders window, select Checks To Print in the Reminder Options dialog box, and click OK.) Click the Print Checks button in the Quicken Reminders window and you are taken to the Select Checks to Print dialog box (see Figure 3.6), where you can give instructions for printing checks.

The other way to tell if checks need printing is to glance in the Chks column in the Accounts List window. A yellow check and check mark in the Chks column mean you have written checks against the account but not printed them yet.

**habits & strategies**

*To make the Quicken Reminders window appear each time you start the program, choose Edit / Options / Reminders and click the Show Reminders on Startup and Check to Print check boxes in the Reminder Options dialog box.*

# BLAST OFF!

So much for writing checks. The whole business goes very quickly once you get the hang of it. Meanwhile, the next chapter goes to the heart and soul of Quicken. It explains how to keep track of where you spend your money and where you get it from.

# Tracking Where the Money Goes and Comes From

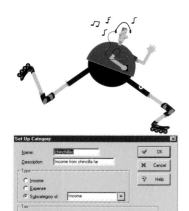

# FAST FORWARD

## CREATE A NEW CATEGORY FOR CATEGORIZING REGISTER TRANSACTIONS ➤ *pp. 74–75*

1. Choose Lists I Category & Transfer and click the New button in the Category & Transfer List.
2. In the Set Up Category dialog box, enter a name and a short description of the category.
3. Choose whether the category is an Income category, an Expense category, or a Subcategory of a known category. If you are creating a subcategory, click the down-arrow in the Subcategory box and choose the parent category.
4. Click the Tax-related check box if you want this category's data to be included in tax summary reports.
5. Click OK.

## DELETE A CATEGORY FROM THE CATEGORY & TRANSFER LIST ➤ *pp. 76–77*

1. Choose Lists I Category & Transfer.
2. Find the category you want to remove on the All Types, Income, or Expense tab and select it.
3. Click the Delete button. A message box warns you that "You are about to permanently delete a category" (read "Removing Categories and Subcategories from the List" in this chapter to see why this step is indeed a drastic one).
4. Click OK.

## RECATEGORIZE TRANSACTIONS YOU HAVE ALREADY ENTERED ➤ *pp. 77–78*

1. Choose Edit I Find & Replace I Recategorize. In the Recategorize dialog box, click the down-arrow in the Search Category box and select a category or subcategory.
2. Click the Find All button. A list of transactions with the category or subcategory you chose appears.
3. Select the transactions that should be categorized differently.
4. Choose a new category or subcategory in the Replace With box.
5. Click the Replace button.

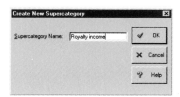

# CREATE A NEW SUPERCATEGORY ➤ *pp. 78–79*

1. Choose Lists | Category & Transfer.
2. Click the Super button in the Category & Transfer List window.
3. In the Manage Supercategories dialog box, click the New button.
4. In the Create New Supercategory dialog box, enter a name and click OK.
5. Back in the Manage Supercategories dialog box, select the supercategory you just created by clicking on it.
6. Hold down the CTRL key and click the categories for the new supercategory in the Category Name box.
7. Click the Assign button.
8. Click OK.

# CREATE A CLASS ➤ *pp. 80–81*

1. Choose Lists | Class or press CTRL-L, and then click the New button in the Class List window.
2. In the Set Up Class dialog box, enter a name and a description.
3. Click OK.

# ASSIGN A TRANSACTION IN A REGISTER TO A CLASS ➤ *p. 81*

1. Fill in the register.
2. When you get to the Category box, enter a category and then choose Lists | Class (or press CTRL-L).
3. In the Class List window, double-click a class. In the Category box, a slash and the class name appear after the category assignment.

**"Where did the money go?" is the most-asked question in American households. When you withdraw money from an ATM machine and notice the account balance dwindling, when the money in the checking account runs low, you ask yourself, "Where did I spend it all, anyway?"**

With Quicken, you can find out very quickly what your spending habits are. All you have to do is generate a report or graph to see the naked truth. And you can find out exactly where the money comes from, too. Quicken keeps close tabs on income and expenses. Whenever you record a transaction, you are given the opportunity to categorize it, and as long as you categorize transactions thoughtfully, you can learn a lot about your spending habits and sources of income. You can learn spooky things about yourself—things that even fortune tellers, clairvoyants, and psychics can't tell you.

This important chapter explains how to organize transactions into categories, classes, and supercategories, the three means by which you monitor income and spending with Quicken. It shows how to edit the list of categories and fix transactions that you categorized incorrectly. Categorizing transactions is not just important for generating reports and graphs, it is important for making tax projections and for budgeting. So read this chapter carefully.

## habits & strategies

*You can save a lot of time by getting your categories, supercategories, and classes right from the get-go. Take the time to seriously consider how expense and income transactions should be organized, even if it means talking to a tax consultant.*

# QUICKEN AND YOUR BETTER HALF

Quicken should come with a Surgeon General's warning on the side of the package: this program can be dangerous to your love life. If you are using Quicken to track a loved one's finances as well as your own, you will quickly learn things about the spending habits of your better half that you are better off not knowing. As you record checkbook and credit card transactions, you will ask your loved one, "Why did you buy this, dear?" Accusations, incriminations, and recriminations may follow.

My wife thinks it's criminal of me to spend so much money on tickets to see the Golden State Warriors, a second-rate basketball team. I acknowledge that California's public schools are grossly underfunded, but I still think she shouldn't spend quite so much on materials for her classroom. Tread softly. Be kind and generous in these matters. You have been warned.

# THE BIG PICTURE: CATEGORIES, SUPERCATEGORIES, AND CLASSES

Quicken offers three means (four if you count the tax-related identification) of tracking income and expenses: categories (and subcategories), supercategories, and classes. Very confusing, I know. Perhaps this brief list will help clarify matters:

| | |
|---|---|
| Category | A label that identifies why a transaction was made. By assigning transactions to categories, you get a better idea of how much you spend on leisure, groceries, rent, or whatever. You also get a better idea of where your earnings come from. A category can be divided into subcategories. |
| Supercategory | A group of categories that have been bundled into a single category. With supercategories, you get a better fix on your financial picture. For example, suppose you record the money you spend on a house in three categories: House Repair, Mortgage Payment, and Homeowner's Insurance. Besides knowing how much you spend in each category, you could find out how much you spend altogether on the house by creating a My Home supercategory. You could use the My Home numbers for budgeting, and the numbers would appear in budget reports, cash flow reports, and summary reports. |
| Class | A label under which transactions are organized. For example, suppose you get income from racing, training, and breeding ostriches. As the checks come in and you record them in a register, you could record them in the Racing, Training, or Breeding class. This way, you get a better picture of where you derive your ostrich income. |
| Tax-related | When you create a category, click the Tax-related check box if you want the category to be included in tax reports. Doing so makes preparing income tax reports much, much easier. You can even assign categories to tax-form line items and thereby make income tax projections with the Tax Planner. |

## Categories and Subcategories

All transactions should be assigned a category or subcategory. I regret to say it, but it's up to you to figure out which categories you need. I can't give you any advice about categories because I have not had the privilege of looking at your finances. The main thing is to create categories that give useful information about your finances. And if you want Quicken's help to prepare tax returns, make sure that the categories you create render information that is meaningful to the IRS.

## Classes

The Quicken documentation says that you should consider using classes instead of subcategories if you find yourself using a lot of subcategories with the same names. In other words, if you have subcategories named Park Place: Utilities and Marvin Gardens: Utilities for tracking the cost of utilities at those hotels, you would be better off creating two classes, one called Marvin Gardens and the other called Park Place, and recording the utility payments by class instead of subcategory. Subcategories can be confusing. It is far easier to work with categories and classes than a bunch of subcategories. On the other hand, you can't split transactions and also assign them to classes.

Classes were designed for business people who record business as well as personal transactions in the same accounts. A transaction made for the business can be recorded in the Business class, for example, and one made for personal reasons can be recorded in the Personal class or not be recorded in any class at all. That way, you can keep your business and personal transactions separate when it comes to generating reports and graphs with Quicken.

## Supercategories

Supercategories are an excellent way to cut through the details and see the big numbers. How much am I spending on my office, for supplies, computer hardware, and my telephone? By bundling the three categories into a supercategory, I can find out *pronto*.

The biggest difference between classes and supercategories is that supercategories can be used to formulate budgets as well as reports and graphs, whereas classes are of no use in budgeting.

### CAUTION

You can't assign a class to a split transaction.

Another difference between the two is that, when you assign a transaction to a class, you must do it yourself as part of entering the transaction in a register. By contrast, Quicken handles supercategories. When you assign a category to a transaction and the category is part of a supercategory, Quicken does the work for you. You don't have to concern yourself with whether the transaction has been recorded in the supercategory.

## tricks of the trade

*There is far too much preoccupation with money these days—and not enough with personal financial planning. Most people waste time thinking they would be on Easy Street if they only earned $10,000 more than they do. But $10,000, after taxes and inflation are factored in, wouldn't pay off more than one credit card balance for many people. Instead of obsessing over more money, people should be thinking of ways to do better with what they have.*

Jonathan D. Pond, The New Century Family Money Book

# MAKING YOUR OWN CATEGORY LIST

When you set up an account in Quicken, you are given the opportunity to choose between two sets of categories, business categories and home categories. Choosing a set of Quicken's categories is a good place to start, but your finances are your finances, so you need to tailor the Category List to meet your needs. This part of the chapter explains how to create categories and subcategories, delete them from the Category List, change their names, and recategorize transactions.

Categories are the basic elements for tracking income and expenses. Figure 4.1 shows an income and expense graph. It compares income and expenses in a bar graph, and, in a pie chart, shows how much was spent in the ten largest expense categories. By carefully creating and choosing categories, you can generate meaningful graphs like these.

## habits & strategies

*You can make Quicken display a message box if you try to record a transaction without categorizing it. Choose Edit / Options / Register, click the Miscellaneous tab, and click the When Recording Uncategorized Transactions check box.*

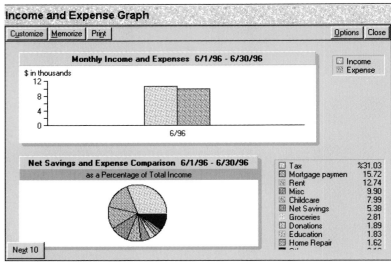

**Figure 4.1**  An income and expense graph. The names in the pie chart legend are expense categories.

*If you itemize on tax returns, see "Finding Ways to Reduce Taxes" in Chapter 11. It explains how to create categories for tracking deductible expences.*

# Adding a Category or Subcategory to the List

To create a category and add it to the list of categories that appears when you click the arrow in the Category box in a register:

1. Choose Lists I Category & Transfer. You see the Category & Transfer List shown in Figure 4.2. The All Types tab lists all categories. Other tabs list only income categories, expense categories, and, on the Transfers tab, your accounts. If you are creating an expense or income category, you might click the Expense or Income tab to get a fix on the categories that are already there.

2. Click the New button to create a category.

3. In the Set Up Category dialog box, enter a name for the category and a short description.

4. Under Type, choose whether the category is an Income or Expense category. If you are creating a subcategory, click the Subcategory of radio button, click the down-arrow, and choose which category on the list your new subcategory is to be subordinate to.

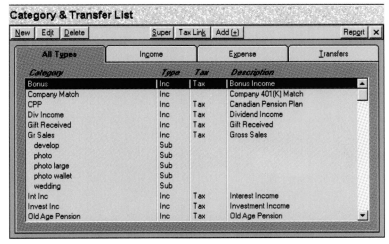

**Figure 4.2** The Category & Transfer List, where categories, supercategories, and tax links are made

5. For now, click the Tax-related check box if the category has anything remotely to do with taxes. The Tax options are discussed at the end of this chapter, under "Keeping Track of Tax-Related Expenses and Income."

6. Click OK to close the dialog box.

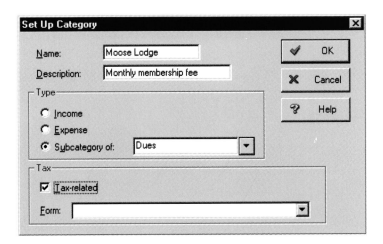

## CAUTION

*After you delete a category, transactions in the registers that were assigned the category you deleted have no category assignments. Before you delete a category, choose Edit | Find & Replace | Recategorize to reassign transactions.*

# Removing Categories and Subcategories from the List

After you have worked with Quicken for a while, you know which categories you want on the Category & Transfer List and which are merely deadwood that you have to scroll past in the Category drop-down list in registers. Go ahead and delete categories that you have not assigned to any transactions. It doesn't matter if you delete them, but deleting a category that has been recorded in a register is a serious business. In the first place, you can't get the category back after you delete it. In the second place, you end up with empty Category boxes in your registers. When you delete a category you have assigned to transactions, you end up with uncategorized transactions. Having empty Category boxes defeats the purpose of categorizing transactions in the first place.

Before you delete a category that you've assigned to transactions in registers, use the Edit | Find & Replace | Recategorize command to find all transactions that were assigned the category you are about to delete and assign those transactions to new categories. "Fixing Mistakes in the Way Transactions Were Categorized" explains how to do that.

You can't delete a category that has subcategories. Before doing that, move the subcategories to another category or else promote the subcategories and make them into full-fledged categories. The next part of this chapter explains how.

As for subcategories, when you delete a subcategory it is removed from the Category & Transfer List and transactions that were assigned to the subcategory are assigned to the parent category instead. For example, if you delete a subcategory called Railroads: B&O, all transactions that were assigned to that subcategory are given its parent category, Railroads.

Now that you know the esoterica of deleting categories and subcategories, here is how to actually do it:

1. Choose Lists | Category & Transfer.
2. On the All Types, Income, or Expense tab, find the category or subcategory you want to delete, and click it.

3. Click the Delete button.

4. A message box warns you that "You are about to permanently delete a category." Click OK and listen for the beep.

# Fixing Mistakes in the Way Transactions Were Categorized

All is not lost if you categorized transactions incorrectly, because you can use the Edit I Find & Replace I Recategorize command to fix the problem. With this command, you find all transactions that were assigned a category or subcategory, then you mark the ones that should be given another category assignment, and tell Quicken which category or subcategory assignment to give the transactions that you marked.

To recategorize transactions in a register, open the register and choose Edit I Find & Replace I Recategorize. You see the Recategorize dialog box shown in Figure 4.3 (this dialog box has been filled out). Click the down-arrow in the Search Category box and click the category or subcategory to which you've assigned the transactions whose category or subcategory you want to change. Then click the Find All button. A list of transactions appears in the dialog box.

**CAUTION**

*Unfortunately, you can't automatically recategorize split transactions. Instead, use the Find command to find the split transactions that were categorized incorrectly and recategorize them one at a time. See "Finding and Fixing Entry Errors" in Chapter 2.*

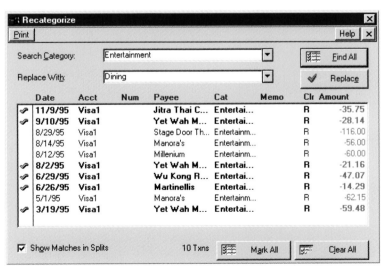

**Figure 4.3** Recategorizing transactions. Click next to the transactions that need recategorizing, then choose a new category or subcategory from the Replace With menu.

Click in the left-hand column beside the transactions that should be categorized in a different way. As you click, yellow check marks appear beside the transactions. Next, click the down-arrow in the Replace With box and choose the category or subcategory that rightfully belongs to the transactions you selected in the dialog box. Then take a deep breath and click the Replace button.

## Changing the Names of Categories and Subcategories

Changing the name of a category or subcategory is pretty darn simple. All you have to do is choose Lists | Category & Transfer. On the All Types, Income, or Expense tab, find the category or subcategory whose name you want to change, and select it. Then click the Edit button to see the Edit Category dialog box. From there, enter the new name in the Name box and click OK. Transactions in the register that were assigned the old name are given the new one automatically.

# SETTING UP AND MANAGING SUPERCATEGORIES

As you know if you read the beginning of this chapter, a super-category is a group of categories that have been bound together for the purpose of budgeting and getting a clearer look at your finances. After you have created a supercategory, you tell Quicken which categories to include in it. How to do both is explained on these pages.

## Creating a Supercategory

To create a supercategory, choose Lists | Category & Transfer. In the Category & Transfer List window, click the Super button. You see the Manage Supercategories dialog box shown in Figure 4.4.

The names of the categories and subcategories in your Category & Transfer List are shown in the Category Name column on the left side of the dialog box. In the Supercategory column are the supercategory assignments that Quicken makes on its own. There are four default supercategory assignments: Discretionary Income, Non-Discretionary Income, Other Income, and Salary Income. You can see the names of these supercategories in the Supercategory Name box. Each category can belong to only one supercategory.

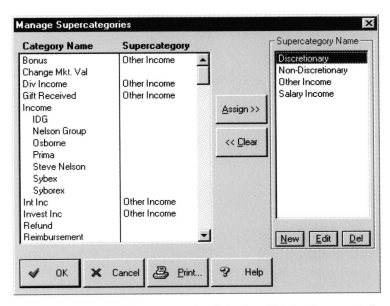

**Figure 4.4** The Manage Supercategories dialog box. This is where you tell Quicken which categories to include in the supercategory.

To create your own supercategory, click the New button (it is below the Supercategory Name box). When the Create New Supercategory dialog box appears, enter a name and click OK.

Back in the Manage Supercategories dialog box, the name you entered appears with the other supercategory names. Now you have to tell Quicken which categories to include in your new supercategory. Read on.

# Putting Categories in a Supercategory

With the Manage Supercategories dialog box open (see Figure 4.4) and the new name in the Supercategory Name box, you are ready to assign categories to your new supercategory. First, in the Supercategory Name box, click the name of the supercategory you want to assign categories to. With that done, select the categories in the Category Name box by holding down the CTRL key and clicking on them. As long as you hold the CTRL key down, you can click as many categories as you want. When you've selected all the categories, click the Assign button.

## CAUTION

*A category can only be part of one supercategory, not two or three.*

Now when you categorize a transaction in a register, the income or expense you record will be recorded in a supercategory as well as a category.

To remove a category from a supercategory, highlight its name in the Category Name column and click the Clear button.

# Deleting and Renaming Supercategories

If you need to delete a supercategory, choose Lists | Category & Transfer and click the Super button in the Category & Transfer List window to get to the Manage Supercategories dialog box (see Figure 4.4). From there, click the supercategory you want to delete in the Supercategory Name box, and then click the Del button. All assignments from the supercategory you deleted disappear from the Supercategory column on the left side of the dialog box.

To rename a supercategory, get to the Manage Supercategories dialog box and click its name in the Supercategory Name box. Then click the Edit button (it's below the Supercategory Name box). Enter a new name in the Edit Supercategory dialog box and click OK.

# WORKING WITH CLASSES

Classes are helpful for examining your finances in different ways. This part of the chapter explains how to create a class, assign a transaction to a class in a register, and delete and rename classes. As I explained at the start of this chapter, classes give you a window on one aspect of your finances.

The report in Figure 4.5 shows a class comparison of July income from two different years, 1995 and 1996. The three classes are ostrich breeding, ostrich racing, and ostrich training. By dividing ostrich income into three classes, the Australian who generated this report can tell at a glance where the income is coming from.

# Creating a Class

To create a class, choose Lists | Class or press CTRL-L to see the Class List window. From there, click the New button. In the Set Up Class dialog box, enter a name and a few words that describe your new class

## CAUTION

If you intend to use classes, you must be diligent about it. Quicken displays a message box if you forget to categorize a transaction, but it is as silent as the grave if you forget to assign a class to one.

| Wells Checking | | | | 8/23/96 |
|---|---|---|---|---|
| | **Comparison Report** | | | |
| | 7/1/95 Through 7/31/96 | | | |
| Class Description | 7/1/96-<br>7/31/96 | 7/1/95-<br>7/31/95 | **Amount<br>Difference** | |
| Ost breed | 1,115.00 | 1,890.00 | 775.00 | |
| Ost race | 0.00 | 2,290.00 | 2,290.00 | |
| Ost train | 1,342.00 | 1,456.00 | 114.00 | |
| OVERALL TOTAL | 2,457.00 | 5,636.00 | 3,179.00 | |

**Figure 4.5** The data in this report was gathered from three classes. Classes add another dimension to financial tracking.

eloquently. (The Copy Number box is for businesses that receive more than one copy of tax forms—see the Help program if that pertains to you.) Click OK when you are done filling in the Set Up Class dialog box.

The class name and description appear in the Class List window. Click the Close button (the *X*) to remove the window. Now you can assign transactions to this class.

# Assigning a Class to a Register Transaction

Assigning a class to a transaction is done as part of assigning a category. To assign a class:

1. Fill in the register as you usually do.
2. When you get to the Category box, make a category assignment.
3. With the cursor still in the Category box, choose Lists | Class or press CTRL-L. You see the Class List window.
4. Double-click on the class that you want to assign to this transaction. When you do, the Class List window disappears and you see the register again, where a slash and the class name appear after the category in the Category box:

| Great Blight Derby | | | | 2,546 | 00 | 15,997 | 59 |
|---|---|---|---|---|---|---|---|
| Income/Ost race | | | | | | | |

## Deleting and Renaming Classes

To delete a class, choose Lists I Class, select the class you want to delete in the Class List window, and click the Delete button. A dialog box appears and tells you that the class will be permanently deleted. Click OK. Transactions in your registers that were assigned to the class you deleted are no longer assigned that class. They aren't assigned to any class. You could say that those transactions no longer have class.

Renaming a class is pretty simple. Just open the Class List window by choosing Lists I Class, click the class whose name needs changing, and click the Edit button. In the Edit Class dialog box, enter a new name and click OK. Transactions in your registers that were classified under the old name are classified automatically under the new one.

# KEEPING TRACK OF TAX-RELATED EXPENSES AND INCOME

Quicken offers both a simple and complex way to use the category feature to help with income tax reporting. The simple way is to tell Quicken which categories relate to income taxes. By doing that, you can get detailed summary reports that list your sources of income and all expenses that pertain to income tax reporting. Figure 4.6 shows part

| TEST-Non Tax-Deferred Accts | | | | | | | 7/14/96 |
|---|---|---|---|---|---|---|---|
| **Tax Summary Report** | | | | | | | |
| 1/1/95 Through 12/31/95 | | | | | | | |
| Date | Acct | Num | Description | Memo | Category | Clr | Amount |
| | Rent | | | | | | |
| 1/6/95 | Well... | 900 | Albert Landlord | | Rent | R | - 475.00 |
| 2/14/95 | Well... | 932 | Albert Landlord | | Rent | R | - 475.00 |
| 4/3/95 | Well... | 992 | Albert Landlord | | Rent | R | - 950.00 |
| 5/3/95 | Well... | 1042 | Albert Landlord | | Rent | R | - 475.00 |
| 6/20/95 | Well... | 1071 | Albert Landlord | | Rent | R | - 950.00 |
| 7/23/95 | Well... | 1099 | Albert Landlord | | Rent | R | - 475.00 |
| 9/8/95 | Well... | 1154 | Albert Landlord | | Rent | R | - 475.00 |
| 10/16/95 | Well... | 1200 | Albert Landlord | | Rent | R | - 1,350.00 |
| 12/22/95 | Well... | 1265 | Albert Landlord | | Rent | R | - 675.00 |
| 12/30/95 | Well... | 1273 | Albert Landlord | | Rent | R | - 675.00 |
| | | | | | **TOTAL Rent** | | - 6,975.00 |

**Figure 4.6** A Tax Summary Report. This report lays out the numbers for all categories that pertain to income tax reporting.

of a Tax Summary Report. A report like this comes in very handy right around April 15.

Everybody can take advantage of the simple way, but the complex way requires a bit of moxie and an understanding of the tax forms. With the complex way, you tag each category to a line on an income tax form. Then, you plug the data from categories into lines on whichever form (1040, Schedule A, B, etc.) you use to report income taxes. With that done, you can export the information to the Tax Planner and get accurate estimates of how much tax you will owe come next April. "Estimating How Much in Taxes You Will Owe" in Chapter 11 explains this way.

To tell Quicken that a category is related to taxes and should be part of the Tax Summary Report and reports like it, start by choosing Lists I Category & Transfer. The All Types, Income, and Expense tabs in the Category & Transfer List window all have a column called Tax. If the word "Tax" appears next to a category or subcategory, the category or subcategory's totals will appear on tax reports.

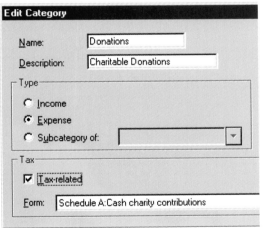

Scroll down the Category list and make sure that categories that pertain to taxes show the word "Tax" in the Tax column. If a category or subcategory needs to be tax-related but isn't, click it and then click the Edit button. You see the Edit Category dialog box. Under Tax, click the Tax-related check box. If you know which line on the tax forms the category or subcategory is reported on, click the Form down arrow and choose the line from the drop-down list. Then click OK.

If a category in the window says it is tax-related but it really shouldn't be, click it and click the Edit button. In this case, the Tax-related check box has a check mark in it. Click the box to remove the check mark, and then click OK to close the Edit Category dialog box.

## ¡VAMANOS!

So ends our little adventure with categorizing, classifying, and codifying transactions. The next chapter explains how to complete an extremely onerous chore in a matter of minutes. It explains how to reconcile a checking account, savings account, or credit card account.

# Reconciling a Bank or Credit Card Account

# FAST FORWARD

**WHAT DOES "RECONCILE" MEAN?** ➤ *pp. 88–89*

It means to compare the transactions that the bank shows as cleared on its statement with the same transactions in your register. As part of reconciling, you make sure that the amounts, payee names, and so on in your records match those of the bank, and you clear the transactions in your register.

**RECONCILE A CHECKING OR SAVINGS ACCOUNT** ➤ *pp. 91–93*

1. Open the register of the account you want to reconcile and either click the Recon button on the iconbar or click the Reconcile button in the register window.
2. In the Reconcile Bank Statement dialog box, take note of the number in the Opening Balance box—it shows the amount of money in the account as of the last time you reconciled it. Change the number, if necessary, and enter the closing balance that is shown on your bank statement in the Ending Balance box.
3. Enter a service charge, if one appears on the statement, in the Service Charge box, enter the date of the charge (probably the statement date), and categorize this charge. Do the same if you earned interest on the account by filling in the Interest Earned information from your statement.
4. Click the OK button to get to the Reconcile Bank Statement window.
5. While studying your bank statement and looking in the window, click in the Clr column next to each transaction in the window that also appears on the bank statement.
6. When the Cleared Balance and Statement Ending Balance in the lower-right corner of the dialog box are the same and the Difference is 0.00, click the Finished button.
7. Click Yes or No on the Congratulations screen to say whether you want to create a Reconciliation report.

**New**

**Edit**

**Delete**

**Statement...**

## DO THE FOLLOWING IF AN ACCOUNT WON'T RECONCILE ➤ *pp. 94–95*

- Click the New button to enter a transaction from the bank statement that you forgot to record in the register.
- Click the Edit button to go back to the register and fix a transaction. Quicken takes you to the transaction that is highlighted in the Reconcile Bank Statement window.
- Click the Delete button to delete the highlighted transaction in the Reconcile Bank Statement window. Delete a transaction if you entered it twice by accident.
- Click the Statement button to go back to the Reconcile Bank Statement dialog box and adjust the information there if you entered it incorrectly.

## RECONCILE A CREDIT CARD ACCOUNT ➤ *pp. 96–98*

1. Open the credit card register and either click the Recon button on the iconbar or click the Reconcile button in the register window.
2. In the Credit Card Statement Information dialog box, enter the total for the purchases and cash advances on your statement in the Charges, Cash Advances box.
3. Enter the total of the payments you made to the credit card company and any credits the company owes you in the Payments, Credits box.
4. In the Ending Balance box, enter the total new balance that the statement says you owe.
5. If you were late in paying last month, enter, date, and categorize the finance charges you must pay for being late in part 2 of the dialog box. Then click OK.
6. On the Charges side of the Pay Credit Card Bill window, click off the transactions that also show on your monthly statement. As you click, the Cleared Balance and Statement Ending Balance should come into agreement. When the difference between the two numbers is 0.00 (or as close to 0.00 as you can afford to get), click the Finished button.
7. Fill in the Make Credit Card Payment dialog box and click Yes if you want to pay all or part of the credit card bill now.

**O**ne of the best things about Quicken is being able to reconcile an account in a matter of minutes. What used to take an hour or so to accomplish—comparing your records to the bank's monthly statement, punching keys on a calculator—can be done in the time it takes to boil an egg at sea level.

This short chapter explains how to reconcile checking accounts, savings accounts, and credit card accounts. I'll show you a tried-and-true technique for making this tedious chore go as fast as possible. This chapter also shows you what to do when an account doesn't balance.

# WHAT DOES "RECONCILE" MEAN?

In financial terms, "reconcile" means to compare one set of records against another for the sake of accuracy. When you reconcile a bank account, you compare the bank's records against your records. In other words, you compare what it says on the bank statement with what you recorded in the Quicken register. If the numbers are different, you have to reconcile them somehow. Almost always, that means changing a transaction in the Quicken register to make it match what is on the bank statement. Banks *are* good at record-keeping even though they aren't good at making lines move faster.

As part of reconciling a bank account with Quicken, you record the bank fees and interest payments that appear on the bank statement. For example, if the bank charged for new checks and the charge appears on your statement, you record it as a payment in the checking account register. If your savings account earned interest, the bank statement tells you so, and you record the interest as a deposit. Likewise, the bank statement might show ATM withdrawals or checks that you forgot to record. When you reconcile, you find out how forgetful you are, and you get the opportunity to record the wayward transactions that you forgot to enter in the Quicken registers.

In my experience, it is very easy to reconcile a savings account. Savings deposits, withdrawals, and transfers are recorded by the bank almost as soon as they are made, so they show up on monthly statements. Checks, on the other hand, sometimes get lost in coat pockets and desk drawers for months and months before they are cashed. When you reconcile a checking account, you sometimes have to sift through transactions from months past to find and clear them in the register.

# THE BIG PICTURE: RECONCILING AN ACCOUNT

Reconciling is sort of confusing at first, so before you learn the details, here are the mechanics of reconciling.

To start with, you click the Recon button and fill in the Reconcile Bank Statement dialog box, which is shown in Figure 5.1. This is where, in the Ending Balance box in part 1, you report to Quicken what the bank statement says your closing balance is. You also enter bank service charges or interest payments that show on your statement. The Opening Balance box is the amount of money in the account as of the last time you reconciled it (or the date you opened it). A number already appears there.

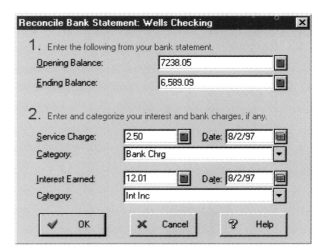

**Figure 5.1** The Reconcile Bank Statement dialog box. This is where you tell Quicken what the ending balance on your bank statement is.

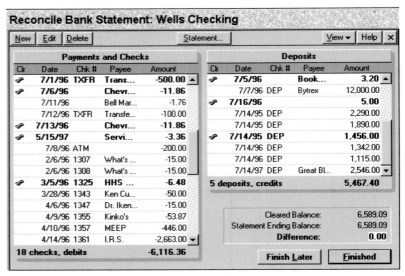

**Figure 5.2** The Reconcile Bank Statement window. Click the Clr column of transactions that show on your bank statement.

When you click OK, you see the Reconcile Bank Statement window shown in Figure 5.2. It lists all uncleared transactions in the register. On the left side of the window are transaction records of payments and transfers of money out of your account, and on the right side are transaction records of deposits and transfers of money into your account.

Comparing the transactions on your bank statement with the transactions in the Reconcile Bank Statement window, you click the Clr (Clear) column next to transactions that show on the statement. As you click, check marks appear and the numbers in the lower-right corner change:

- **Cleared Balance:** As you click the Clr column next to transactions in the window, you clear transactions and change this balance. When you click transactions on the right-hand Deposit side of the window, you add to the cleared balance; when you click on the left-hand Payments and Checks side, you subtract from the cleared balance.

- **Statement Ending Balance:** This is the ending balance you got from your bank statement. You entered it in the Reconcile Bank Statement dialog box. It doesn't change. When you have cleared all the transactions in the Quicken register that appear on the bank statement, the statement ending balance and the cleared balance are the same.
- **Difference:** Lists the difference between the cleared balance and the statement ending balance. As you click off transactions in the Reconcile Bank Statement window, this number shrinks. When it reaches zero, you have reconciled the account.

When the cleared and bank ending balance are the same and you click the Finished button, Quicken places an *R* in the Clr box of transactions that have cleared the bank. That *R* means that the transaction has cleared the bank and been reconciled. Notice the *R*s in this register:

| Date | Ref | Payee | Category | Charge | | Clr | Payment | | Balance | |
|------|-----|-------|----------|--------|--|-----|---------|--|---------|--|
| 3/1/96 | | Schnell Market | Groceries | 21 | 33 | R | | | 1,370 | 05 |
| 3/5/96 | | BP Oil | Auto:Fuel | 11 | 73 | R | | | 1,381 | 78 |
| 3/5/96 | | Walgreen's | Office:Supplies | 29 | 98 | R | | | 1,411 | 76 |
| 3/8/96 | | Schnell Market | Groceries | 31 | 25 | R | | | 1,443 | 01 |
| 3/9/96 | | | [Wells Checking] | | | R | 1,370 | 05 | 72 | 96 |

# RECONCILING A CHECKING OR SAVINGS ACCOUNT

The first thing to do when you want to reconcile an account is open the account's register. To do that, click a rectangular account button along the bottom of a register or click the Accts button on the iconbar and double-click the account name in the Account List.

Now you are ready to click the Recon button on the iconbar and get going. Oops, I forgot to mention one important thing...

## Getting the Paperwork Ready

Before you reconcile an account, put the paperwork in order. Spread the bank statement across your desk and note what the bank says your ending balance is. Arrange your deposit and withdrawal slips (you've been saving them, haven't you?) in date order. In the case of a checking account, put the checks in numerical order.

Very shortly, you will undertake a three-way comparison to determine precisely which transactions cleared in the past month. You will compare the deposit slips, withdrawal slips, and checks on your desk with the transactions that are listed in your bank statement with the transactions in the Quicken account register.

## Telling Quicken What the Bank Told You

With the account register onscreen and the paperwork in order, either click the Recon button on the iconbar or click the Reconcile button in the register window. You see the Reconcile Bank Statement dialog box (see Figure 5.1). A number already appears in the Opening Balance box. This is the amount of money in the account as of the last time you reconciled it or, if you recently opened the account, the opening balance. If the number is incorrect, enter a new number.

In the Ending Balance box, enter the closing balance that is shown on your bank statement.

In part 2 of the dialog box, enter a service charge if one appears on the statement. These days, banks charge extra for all kinds of things so they can overpay their executive presidents. If you are being gouged for using an ATM, for new checks, or for anything of that kind, enter the amount that the statement shows you were gouged in the Service Charge box. Also enter the gouge date listed on your statement in the Date box, and categorize the transaction by clicking the down-arrow in the Category box and choosing a category from the list. The Category is Bank Chrg if you are using Quicken's ready-made categories.

In the Interest Earned box, enter the amount of interest the account generated, if any. Also enter the date that the interest payment was received, or if no such date is listed, enter the bank statement date. Don't forget to categorize the interest payment. Probably the category is Int Inc (Interest Income).

*When I reconcile, I use only the bank statement and Reconcile window for the first try. Sometimes I get lucky and don't have to examine the paperwork. If the numbers don't add up, then I get out the checks, deposit slips, ATM slips, and so on.*

# Reconciling Your Records with the Bank's

Now that Quicken knows what the bank knows, you can begin the dirty work of actually reconciling your Quicken transactions with the account transactions that the bank has recorded. Click the OK button to get to the Reconcile Bank Statement window (see Figure 5.2). This window shows all transactions, including money transfers, that have not yet cleared the bank. If you entered a service charge, it appears with a yellow check mark beside it on the left-hand Payments and Checks side of the window; if you entered an interest payment, it appears with a yellow check mark in the right-hand Deposits side of the window.

Looking at the bank statement, looking at the computer screen, and looking at the paperwork you assembled on your desk if necessary, click in the Clr column next to each transaction in the window that also appears on the bank statement. When you click, a yellow check mark appears in the Clr column. Meanwhile, the Cleared Balance in the lower-right corner gets larger or smaller, depending on whether you clicked a Deposit transaction on the right side of the screen or a Payments and Checks transaction on the left side. To remove a check mark if you need to, click the transaction again.

Start from the first transaction on your bank statement and work your way down, clicking transactions in the window as you do so. If all goes well, the Difference number in the lower-right corner that expresses the difference between the Statement Ending Balance and the Cleared Balance gets smaller and smaller. You want the Difference number to reach zero. When it reaches zero, the ending balance as reported by the bank and the cleared balance of this month's transactions are one and the same, and the account is reconciled.

When the Cleared Balance and Statement Ending Balance are the same and the Difference is zero, click the Finished button. As shown in Figure 5.3, you see a happy-looking Congratulations screen that asks if you want to create a reconciliation report. Only do that if you are keeping the books for someone else. It isn't necessary otherwise, and all you have to do is click the No button.

By the way, if this reconciliation business drags on too long and you have important things to do, you can always procrastinate by

**Figure 5.3** Congratulations, it's morning in America and your account is reconciled.

clicking the Finish Later button. Quicken will save your work in the Reconcile Bank Statement window until you return there by clicking Recon again or by clicking the Recon Quick Tab on the right side of the screen. And if you really get fed up with reconciling, click the Cancel button and start all over.

## What to Do If an Account Doesn't Balance

When an account doesn't balance and you can't reconcile your records with the bank's, a bunch of different things could be wrong. To help you make corrections, Quicken offers these four buttons in the Reconcile Bank Statement window:

You may have entered an amount incorrectly in the register. Compare the bank statement, paperwork, and register transactions carefully to find the error. And look for transposed numbers and num-

bers entered backwards. For example, $21.23 and $22.13 look very much alike at a glance, but there is a difference of 90 cents between the numbers.

When you find an amount error or any other error that needs correcting, select it on the Reconcile Bank Statement window and click the Edit button. Quicken takes you straight to the transaction in the register so you can fix it. When the fix is in, click the Enter button on the register and then the Recon button on the iconbar to get back to the Reconcile Bank Statement window.

Another common reason why accounts don't reconcile is forgetfulness on your part. If an ATM withdrawal, check, or other transaction appears on the bank statement but not in the register, you probably forgot to record it. To record it now, click the New button on the Reconcile Bank Statement window. The register opens so you can enter the transaction. After you enter it, click Enter and click the Recon Quick Tab or the Return to Reconcile button (it's below Enter, Edit, and Splits) to get back to the Reconcile Bank Statement window.

Look for transactions that were entered twice, perhaps a few days apart. To fix this error, select one of the transactions, click the Delete button, and click Yes when Quicken asks if you really want to go through with it.

Perhaps your account doesn't balance because you entered the ending balance, a service charge, or an interest payment incorrectly to begin with in the Reconcile Bank Statement dialog box. Check it out by clicking the Statement button. You go back to the Reconcile Bank Statement dialog box, where you can make adjustments. When you've made them, click OK.

Finally, if worse comes to worst, you can always force a reconciliation by clicking the Finished button even though there is still a difference between the cleared and bank ending balances. Only do this as a last, drastic measure if you cannot find the error. Quicken displays the Adjust Balance dialog box when you click Finished. Enter today's date in the Adjustment Date box, take note of how much Quicken will add to or subtract from your account, and click the Adjust button.

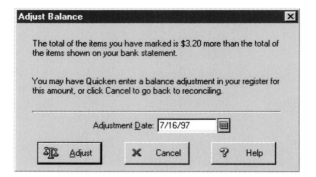

# RECONCILING A CREDIT CARD ACCOUNT

Reconciling a credit card account is nearly the same as reconciling a savings or checking account. The only difference is in the dialog box where you enter the ending balance. When you reconcile a credit card account, you also have to enter the total of the charges and cash advances, as well as any payments or credits that the card issuer awarded you. Of course, you also have to deal with recording the excessive finance charges that card issuers are so famous for.

## Entering the Statement Information

To reconcile a credit card account, lay the monthly statement flat on your desk, open the credit card register, and either click the Recon button on the iconbar or click the Reconcile button in the register window. You see the Credit Card Statement Information dialog box shown in Figure 5.4. All the information you enter here should be listed in black and white on your credit card statement. You have to put numbers in the top three boxes, even if you only enter a zero.

In the Charges, Cash Advances box, enter the total for the purchases and cash advances on your statement. If this is the first time you have reconciled this account and you owe from previous monthly statements, add the previous balance to the total as well.

In the Payments, Credits box, enter the total of the payments you made to the credit card issuer as well as credits that the issuer bestows upon you, if any.

*As you fill in part 1 of the Card Statement Information dialog box, you can click the calculator icon and use the calculator to add charges to cash advances (for the first box) or payments to credits (for the second).*

**Credit Card Statement Information: Visa1**

1. Enter the following from your statement.

Charges, Cash Advances: `987.79`
(other than finance charges)

Payments, Credits: `0`

Ending Balance: `1899.60`

2. Enter and categorize your interest charges, if any.

Finance Charges: `35.87`   Date: `6/7/96`

Category: `Credit card`

OK   Cancel   Help

**Figure 5.4** Get the information for this dialog box from your monthly credit card statement.

In the Ending Balance box, enter the total new balance. This number is the easiest to find on the credit card statement. It is the total amount that you owe and is probably located in the lower-right corner of the statement, on the "bottom line." It includes the finance charges, if any. You will enter those charges next.

In the Finance Charges box, enter the total finance charges from your statement. I hope they are not too high. Enter the date on the credit card statement in the Date box. In the Category box, click the down-arrow and choose an expense category (most likely Finance Charges or Usury).

## tricks of the trade

*Credit has been called another form of slavery because it binds the user to a life of work without reward. With credit you enjoy goods and services now while paying for it later. In reality, a $2,500 credit card balance at an interest rate of 18 percent (common in America) takes 25 years to pay off if the user makes the minimum payment each month. Think about that. And what is worse, the card user often does not even know or remember what he or she bought with the credit card.*

Ivory Muhammed C.C.C., The Credit Builder: A Black Perspective

Click OK when you're finished filling in the Credit Card Statement Information dialog box.

# Reconciling Your Records with the Card Issuer's

Now the reconciling begins. When you click OK, you see the Pay Credit Card Bill window, which is shown in Figure 5.5. Starting at the top of the credit card statement, compare the transactions on the statement with the ones in the window. (Or, if you're like me and you don't record credit card transactions as you make them, click the Statement button to go to the credit card register, enter all the transactions on the statement, and then come back to the Pay Credit Card Bill window.) When a transaction appears on both the window and the statement, click it in the window. Yellow check marks appear in the Clr column beside the transactions as you clear them.

As you click transactions, the Cleared Balance (the total of the transactions you are clicking off) and the Statement Ending Balance (the ending balance from your credit card statement that you entered in the Ending Balance box back in the Credit Card Statement Information

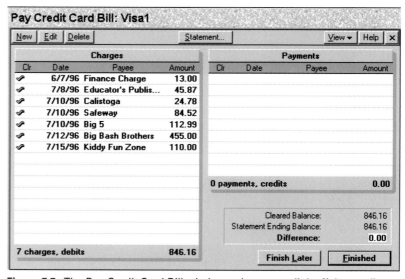

**Figure 5.5** The Pay Credit Card Bill window, where you click off the credit card transactions that appear on your statement.

dialog box) should slowly draw closer together. When the difference between the two is zero, you have reconciled your account and cleared all the transactions on the statement.

At that point, click the Finished button. Your credit card account is reconciled and you see the Make Credit Card Payment dialog box, which asks if you want to pay the bill now.

By the way, if this reconciliation rigmarole gets to be too much for you, you can always postpone it by clicking the Finish Later button. Your work in the Pay Credit Card Bill window will be saved until you return there by clicking Recon again.

## Paying the Credit Card Bill

If, once you have reconciled a credit card account and clicked the Finished button, you decide to pay all or part of the bill, you can do that from the Make Credit Card Payment dialog box. It is shown here:

In the Bank Account box, click the down-arrow and select the account from which you will pay the bill. Under Payment Method, choose the means by which you will produce the check. Then click Yes.

Quicken opens either the register of the account you chose or the Write Checks window. The total amount you owe appears in the Payment box or Pay to the Order of line. If you want to pay only part of the bill, change the amount. Notice that the payment is categorized as a transfer of money between accounts. That seems odd at first, since it's not as though you are transferring money from a savings to a checking account, for example. But you are transferring money. In this case you are doing it to cover a bill.

## If Your Credit Account Doesn't Reconcile...

Your credit card account may not reconcile for the same reasons that a checking or savings account won't reconcile. Therefore, I strongly suggest turning several pages back to "What to Do If an Account Doesn't Balance." The same buttons, the same techniques that are described back there can be brought to bear on the problem of making a credit card account balance. Turn back a few pages. I'll wait for you here, I promise.

## HIGHER, FARTHER, FASTER

Now that you've reconciled yourself to reconciling checking, savings, and credit card accounts, you are ready to go on to the next chapter. It explains how to make Quicken work a bit more smoothly and a bit more quickly.

# Working Faster and Better

# FAST FORWARD

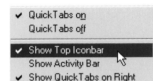

## PACK MORE TRANSACTIONS
## ONTO A REGISTER WINDOW ➤ *p. 106*

1. Click the View button in the register window.
2. From the drop-down menu, choose One-Line Display.
3. Do the same to get the two-line view of the register back.

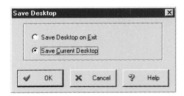

## REMOVE THE ICONBAR
## FROM THE SCREEN ➤ *p. 107*

1. Right-click on the right side of the screen below the Quick Tabs and choose Show Top Iconbar from the shortcut menu. *Right-click* means to click with the right mouse button, not the left.
2. To get the iconbar back, right-click again and choose Show Top Iconbar.

## DECIDE FOR YOURSELF
## WHAT APPEARS ONSCREEN
## EACH TIME YOU START QUICKEN ➤ *pp. 107-108*

1. Open the register, windows, graph, reports, and so on that you want to be available each time you start the program.
2. Choose Edit | Options | Desktop.
3. In the Save Desktop dialog box, click the Save Current Desktop option and click OK.

## MAKE USE OF QUICKEN'S CALCULATOR ➤ *p. 108*

1. Choose Edit | Use Calculator. This calculator works like a hand-held calculator.
2. When you're done using it, either click its Close button or click Paste to enter the number in the calculator window in a register or dialog box.

## USE QUICKFILL TO ENTER PAYEE, AMOUNT, AND CATEGORY DATA QUICKLY ➤ pp. 108-110

1. Move the cursor to the Payee box in the register and enter a few letters of the payee's name. A box appears with the payee's full name, the last amount you paid or deposited, and a category.
2. Press the TAB key, and the payee name, amount you last paid the payee, and category are entered in the register. You can also enter this data by clicking the arrow in the Payee box and choosing a transaction from the QuickFill list of memorized transactions.
3. Click in the Payment or Deposit box and change the amount of the transaction, if necessary.
4. Click the Enter button.

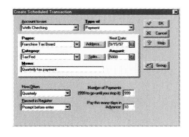

## SCHEDULE A FUTURE TRANSACTION SO THAT IT IS RECORDED AUTOMATICALLY ➤ pp. 113-115

1. Choose Lists | Scheduled Transaction (or press CTRL-J).
2. In the Scheduled Transaction List window, click the New button to see the Create Scheduled Transaction dialog box.
3. At the top of the dialog box, tell Quicken which account to make the payment from and what type of payment you want to make.
4. In the yellow part of the dialog box, tell Quicken who the payee is, how to categorize the payment, the amount of the payment, and when the next payment is due.
5. In the bottom of the dialog box, say how often to make payments or deposits, how many to schedule, whether they should be recorded automatically, and how many days in advance you want to be warned of the scheduled transaction.
6. Click OK.

## PAY A SCHEDULED TRANSACTION ➤ pp. 115-117

1. Select the transaction in the Scheduled Transactions Due dialog box (this dialog box appears when you start Quicken if you have scheduled payments or deposits to make).
2. Click the Record button.

**J**ulius Caesar said, "What is done well is done quickly." And if Caesar read this book, this might be the first chapter he'd turn to. It offers two dozen or so shortcuts for getting in and out of Quicken in a hurry. After you've read this chapter, Quicken will work for you, instead of the other way around.

This chapter explains how to push parts of the screen aside so you can see exactly what you want to see. It tells how to adjust the already fast QuickFill feature to make it work even faster. In this chapter, you discover how to schedule transactions in advance so you don't forget to make them and how to use the Financial Calendar to organize your chaotic life.

# GETTING MORE ROOM TO WORK ONSCREEN

The Quicken screen is claustrophobic. When you have to enter a lot of transactions at once, the buttons, menus, and whatnots get in the way. What can you do about that? This part of the chapter tells you what.

## Seeing a One-Line View of a Register

After you've been around Quicken for a while and you know how to fill in a register, you might try working with a single-line display instead of a double-line display. Figure 6.1 shows what a single-line display looks like. In a single-line display, each transaction occupies one line in the register instead of two. Meanwhile, the Enter, Edit, and Splits buttons move to the lower-right corner of the register window.

To get a one-line display, click the View button in the register window. From the drop-down menu, choose One-Line Display. When you want to see two lines again, do the same, only this time click to remove the check mark from the One-Line Display option on the menu.

*"QCards and What to Do About Them" in Chapter 1 explains how to keep Guide Cards from cluttering your screen.*

| Delete | Find | Transfer | | | Reconcile | Edit Acct | | | Report ▾ | View ▾ | × |
|---|---|---|---|---|---|---|---|---|---|---|---|
| Date | Ref | Payee | | Category | Charge | | Clr | Payment | | Balance | ▲ |
| 3/29/96 | | Chevronda | | Auto:Fuel | 11 | 86 | R | | | 578 | 57 |
| 3/31/96 | | Kamei Household \ | Home Repair | | 33 | 19 | R | | | 611 | 76 |
| 4/7/96 | | Finance Charges | | | 23 | 55 | R | | | 635 | 31 |
| 4/23/96 | | Capital Wonde | | [Wells Checking] | | | R | | 635 31 | 0 | 00 |
| 6/7/96 | | Finance Charges | | Credit card | 13 | 00 | R | | | 13 | 00 |
| 7/8/96 | | Educator's Publishi | Education | | 45 | 87 | R | | | 58 | 87 |
| 7/10/96 | | Big 5 | | Recreation | 112 | 99 | R | | | 171 | 86 |
| 7/10/96 | | Safeway | | Groceries | 84 | 52 | R | | | 256 | 38 |
| 7/10/96 | | Calistoga | | Groceries | 24 | 78 | R | | | 281 | 16 |
| 7/12/96 | | Big Bash Brothers | Entertainment | | 455 | 00 | R | | | 736 | 16 |
| 7/15/96 | | Kiddy Fun Zone | | Leisure | 110 | 00 | R | | | 846 | 16 |
| 7/16/96 | | | | [Wells Checking] | | | | Enter | Edit ▾ | Splits | |
| 7/17/96 | Ref | Payee | | Category | Charge | | | Payment | | | ▼ |
| | | | | | | | | **Ending Balance:** | | 0.00 | |

**Figure 6.1** To get a single-line view of a register, click the One-Line Display option on the View drop-down menu.

# Removing (and Viewing) the Iconbar

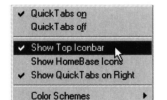

The iconbar is mighty convenient, because all the important commands are there and lined up like ducks in a shooting gallery. Nevertheless, the iconbar does take up a lot of space onscreen. To remove it, right-click on the right side of the screen below the Quick Tabs. On the shortcut menu that appears, click Show Top Iconbar.

To get the iconbar back, all you have to do is right-click again and choose Show Top Iconbar again. By the way, *right-click* means to click the right mouse button instead of the left mouse button.

# CHOOSING WHAT YOU SEE WHEN YOU START QUICKEN

When you start Quicken, it opens the windows and register that were open the last time you closed the program. In other words, if you close the program while the Accounts List window is onscreen, you see the Accounts List window the next time you start Quicken. And if you close the program while a report, a checking account, and a graph Quick Tab appear on the right side of the window, the same three Quick Tabs appear again when you start the program.

You can, however, make a certain register appear whenever you start the program. Likewise, you can make the same reports, graphs, or whatever appear in Quick Tabs each time you start the program.

To decide for yourself what you see when the program starts, put the things you want to see onscreen. If you do most of your work in a checking register and you want to see it when you start Quicken, put the checking register onscreen. Open other windows too and make sure their names appear on Quick Tabs. Then choose Edit | Options | Desktop. In the Save Desktop dialog box, click the Save Current Desktop option and click OK.

If you want to go back to seeing what was onscreen the last time you exited the program, choose Edit | Options | Desktop again, but choose the Save Desktop on Exit button instead.

# USING QUICKEN'S POP-UP CALCULATOR

As you know if you've been horsing around with Quicken for a while, the program offers baby calculators in registers, the Write Checks window, the Reconcile Bank Statement dialog box, and other places where you might need a calculator. When you need to cipher something, you click the baby calculator, it grows to adult proportions, you do the math, and that's all there is to it.

Besides baby calculators, Quicken offers an adult-sized calculator that you can use no matter where you are. To use Quicken's calculator, choose Edit | Use Calculator. I trust you know what all the keys do. Notice the Paste button at the bottom. By clicking that button, you can paste the sum or product of the equation you did at the place where the cursor is. When you're done with the calculator, click its Close button (the *X*) in the upper-right corner.

# MAKING QUICKFILL WORK YOUR WAY

QuickFill is a mighty handy invention. Instead of having to enter the full name of payees in registers or in the Write Checks window, you only have to type the first three or four letters, and Quicken does the rest. It fills in the name of the payee as well as the last amount you paid or received. It even categorizes the transaction for you. On the Write Checks window, QuickFill remembers the address of the payee and puts his or her name in the address box.

QuickFill, as good as it is, can be made even better. And that is the subject of this part of the chapter.

## USING QUICKFILL step by step

1. In a register, move the cursor to the Payee box and type the first few letters of the payee's name. A box appears above the register line with the payee's full name, the last amount you paid or deposited, and a category.

2. Press the TAB key to move out of the Payee box and record an amount and category as well as the payee name in the register. You can also click the arrow in the Payee box and choose a transaction from the Memorized Transaction List.

3. Click in the Payment or Deposit box and change the amount, if necessary.

4. Click the Enter button to record the transaction.

## The Ins and Outs of QuickFill

Whenever you record a transaction, Quicken "remembers" it and puts it on the Memorized Transaction List (to see the list, press CTRL-T or choose Lists | Memorized Transaction). Quicken remembers the payee name, the amount of the transaction, and the category you put it under so you don't have to enter this information all over again whenever you record a transaction to the same party.

*If Quicken isn't memorizing transactions automatically, choose Edit | Options | Register, click the QuickFill tab in the Register Options dialog box, click the Auto Memorize New Transactions check box, and click OK.*

Next time you record a transaction that involves the same payee, Quicken throws out the same information you entered last time around with the idea that you want to enter the same or similar information again. In the register shown here, the user has moved to the Payee box and has typed the letters **sc**. Quicken, well aware that this person wrote a check to "Schnell Market" for $28.76 and categorized the transaction under Groceries, displays a box and offers to enter the same information again:

| | | Schnell Market | -28.76 Groceries | | | | |
|---|---|---|---|---|---|---|---|
| 7/17/96 | 1378 | Schnell Market | ± | *Payment* | | *Deposit* | |
| | | *Memo* | *Category* | | | Enter | Edit ▾ | Splits |

If the user presses the TAB key now, all the QuickFill information is recorded in the register again, like so:

| 7/17/96 | 1378 | Schnell Market | 28.76 ▣ | c | *Deposit* | | |
|---|---|---|---|---|---|---|---|
| | | *Memo* | Groceries | | | Enter | Edit ▾ | Splits |

Another way to enter a memorized transaction is to click the arrow in the Payee box and choose the transaction, Schnell Market in this case, from the Memorized Transaction List:

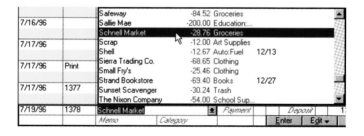

Probably, the loyal customer of Schnell Market did not spend $28.76 this time around, so he or she has to enter a new amount in the Payment box. Nevertheless, not having to enter the payee name or categorize the transaction has spared the user from having to do that all over again.

# Pruning the Memorized Transaction List

The longer you use Quicken, the longer the Memorized Transaction List becomes. If you're the mouse type who likes choosing payees from the list to enter them in registers, your list soon gets too long. At some point, you have to get out your pruning shears and cut the Memorized Transaction List down to size.

To delete transactions from the Memorized Transaction List, choose Lists | Memorized Transaction (or press CTRL-T). You see the Memorized Transaction List shown in Figure 6.2. To remove a transaction from the list, click it, click the Delete button, and click OK when Quicken asks if you want to go through with it. When you delete a memorized transaction, nothing happens to it in the register. The transaction in the register stays the same, but it stops appearing in the Memorized Transaction List.

Another way to keep the list of QuickFill transactions from growing too long is to tell Quicken to discard transactions on the Memorized Transaction List after a certain number of months have elapsed. To do that, choose Edit | Options | Quicken Program and click the General tab in the General Options dialog box. Then click the Remove Memorized Transactions Not Used in Last Months check box and enter the number

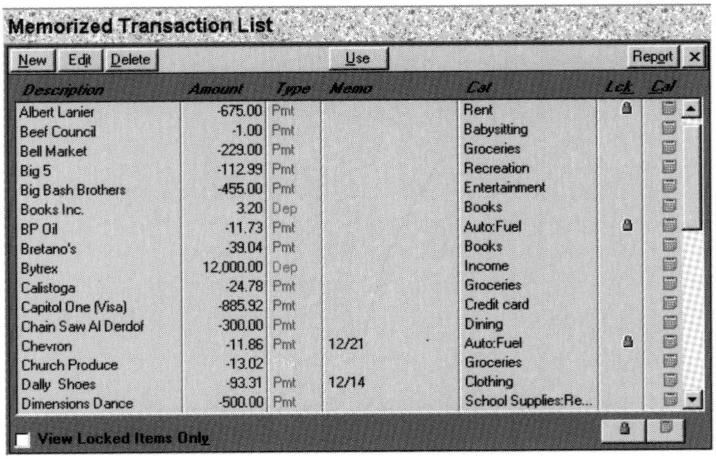

**Figure 6.2** The Memorized Transaction List window. Click a transaction and click Delete to remove it from the list.

of months that memorized transactions should stand before they are forgotten. If you enter 3 months, for example, all memorized transactions that have not been chosen from the list in the past three months are removed from the list. Click OK when you're done.

## QuickFill and "Locked" Transactions

QuickFill "memorizes" all transactions. It remembers payee names, how much you paid out last time around, and how you categorized the transaction last time around. Suppose, however, that you want QuickFill to stay put and not memorize the most recent transaction. Suppose you want the same amount and the same category to appear on the QuickFill list regardless of what your most recent transaction was.

To "lock" a transaction this way, open the Memorized Transaction List by choosing Lists | Memorized Transaction (or pressing CTRL-T), click on the transaction you want to lock in the Memorized Transaction List window, and click the Lock icon in the lower-right corner of the screen. Transactions on the list that have been locked all show a picture of a padlock in the Lck column. To "unlock" a transaction on the list, click its lock icon to remove it.

# SCHEDULING TRANSACTIONS SO THAT YOU DON'T FORGET TO MAKE THEM

Most people make transactions of the same kind over and over. Mortgage payments, car payments, the rent, and quarterly tax payments, for example, are usually the same amount. They are made at regular intervals—weekly, monthly, bi-monthly, or quarterly. Certain kinds of deposits are made on a regular basis, too. Most salaried employees receive the same pay whether they take long lunches or work on weekends.

To help you record and remember to make transactions that are the same or nearly the same, you can schedule them. After you schedule a transaction, you can ask Quicken to remind you to make it. And that, ladies and gentlemen, is the subject of these pages.

# The Big Picture: Scheduling Transactions

To schedule a transaction, you start by telling Quicken what the transaction is. Among other things, you say how often it is to be made, whether it is to be recorded in a register automatically, how many payments or deposits to schedule in a row, and how many days in advance you want to be warned of the scheduled transaction.

When it comes time to actually pay up or deposit the money, Quicken tells you so with the Scheduled Transactions Due dialog box. It appears as soon as you start the program. From this dialog box, you can record the transaction, change it, skip it altogether, or postpone it. Scheduled transactions also appear in the Quicken Reminders window, which also comes onscreen when you start the program. And for the especially forgetful, you can also be reminded about scheduled transactions in the Billminder window. It appears when you turn on your computer.

## Scheduling a Transaction

To schedule a transaction such as a mortgage payment, rent payment, or deposit that is made at regular intervals, choose Lists | Scheduled Transaction (or press CTRL-J). That takes you to the Scheduled Transaction List window. From there, click the New button. You see the intimidating Create Scheduled Transaction dialog box shown in Figure 6.3.

Actually, this dialog box isn't as intimidating as it seems. Many of these text boxes, buttons, and drop-down lists also appear on registers. I'm not going to explain what the Payee, Category, and Memo boxes are, or what the Splits button does, because I'm sure you know already if you are sophisticated enough to schedule transactions. What about the other boxes, drop-down lists, and buttons? Here is what they are for:

- **Account to use:** Choose the account that the transaction is to be paid from or paid to.

- **Type of:** The first two choices, Payment and Deposit, are self-explanatory. If you choose Print Check, the scheduled transaction makes the Checks to Print button in the Quicken Reminders window light up, so you know that a

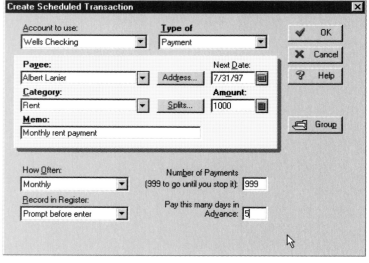

**Figure 6.3** The Create Scheduled Transaction dialog box, where you describe the scheduled transaction in great detail.

check—in this case the scheduled transaction—is ready to print. Choose Online Pmt, the last option, if you are enrolled in the online banking service and want to make the scheduled transaction electronically.

- **Next Date:** Enter the date when the first of the series of scheduled transactions is to be made.

- **How Often:** The frequency at which the transaction is to take place. Intervals range from Only Once at the top of the scroll list to Yearly at the bottom.

- **Number of Payments:** In the case of a paycheck, leave the number of payments at 999. You will be paid at least that many times, I hope. The 999 setting simply means that the deposit or payment is an ongoing one. If you know the number of payments, enter it. To schedule 359 mortgage payments, for example, enter **359**.

- **Record in Register:** Choose Automatically enter to record transactions like direct-deposit paychecks automatically in the register. With this option, the transaction goes in the register and you don't review it first. Choose Prompt before enter if you want the chance to review the transaction first in the Scheduled Transactions Due dialog box.

- **Pay this many days in Advance:** The number of days beforehand that you want to be warned to make a scheduled transaction. The warning appears in the Scheduled Transactions Due dialog box when you start Quicken. Meantime, Quicken enters the scheduled transaction as a postdated entry in the register. The entry is postdated the number of days you enter in the Advance box.

- **Group:** Believe it or not, you can schedule groups of scheduled transactions by clicking this button. See Quicken's Help program if you are banking online and this slice of esoterica interests you.

Click OK when you are done filling in the Create Scheduled Transaction dialog box.

## Paying and Recording Scheduled Transactions

Now that you've gone to all that trouble to schedule a transaction, you will be glad to know that paying and recording it is far easier than scheduling it.

When a scheduled transaction is ready to be completed, you see the Scheduled Transactions Due dialog box when you start Quicken. From this dialog box, which is shown in Figure 6.4, you can record the transaction, change it, skip it, or postpone it by selecting the transaction in the dialog box and clicking one of these four buttons:

- **Record:** Enters the transaction in the register.

- **Edit:** Opens the Edit Transaction dialog box so you can change the transaction somehow. Edit is the button to click if you want to adjust the amount, for example. By the way, after you change the amount or any other part of the scheduled transaction, your original transaction stays intact. If you want to change a scheduled transaction permanently, choose Lists | Scheduled Transaction and click the Edit button in the Scheduled Transaction List window.

### CAUTION

*If you click the Record button, don't forget to write the check or make the deposit right away. Many a Quicken user has clicked this button but quickly forgotten to actually do the paperwork.*

## habits & strategies

*To make the Quicken Reminders window appear onscreen, choose Edit | Options | Reminders and, in the Reminder Options dialog box, click the Show Reminders on Startup and Scheduled Transactions check boxes.*

- **Delete:** Tells Quicken not to make the transaction this week, month, quarter, or whatever you chose as the interval. If you click the Delete button, the scheduled transaction is not removed from the Scheduled Transaction List window (to see that window, choose Lists | Scheduled Transaction). It is still scheduled for the next time interval and will appear in the Scheduled Transactions Due dialog box next time around. To delete a scheduled transaction altogether, click the Delete button in the Scheduled Transaction List window.

- **Done:** Postpones the transaction. Clicking this button tells Quicken not to record the transaction just yet, but to offer another opportunity to record it the next time you start Quicken.

To be doubly sure that you handle scheduled transactions in a timely manner, they also appear in the Quicken Reminders window. This window is shown in Figure 6.5. It comes onscreen when you start Quicken if you have checks to print, scheduled transactions to make, online payments to send, or online banking to do. To handle a scheduled

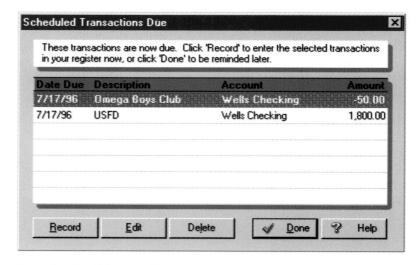

**Figure 6.4** The Scheduled Transactions Due dialog box. From here, you can record, change, skip, or postpone the transaction.

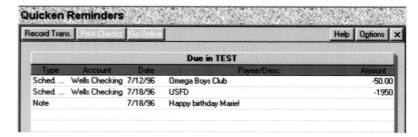

**Figure 6.5** The Quicken Reminders window. Click a scheduled transaction here and click Record Trans. to get to the Scheduled Transactions Due dialog box.

transaction, click it in the Reminders window and then click the Record Trans. button. You land back at the Scheduled Transactions Due dialog box shown in Figure 6.4, where you get another crack at the Record, Edit, Skip Payment, or Done button.

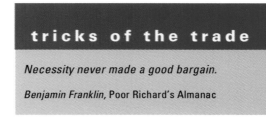

**tricks of the trade**

*Necessity never made a good bargain.*

*Benjamin Franklin,* Poor Richard's Almanac

# Making a Scheduled Transaction Early

Suppose you are taking a month-long trip to Chile, the most beautiful country in the world. Before you go, you want to pay off scheduled transactions in the next month so that you don't come home to a mountain of unpaid bills.

To make a scheduled transaction early, choose Lists | Scheduled Transaction (or press CTRL-J). You see the Scheduled Transaction List window. From there, click the transaction you want to pay early, and then click the Pay button. You see the Record Scheduled Transaction dialog box shown in Figure 6.6. Choose an option from the Num drop-down list and click the Record button.

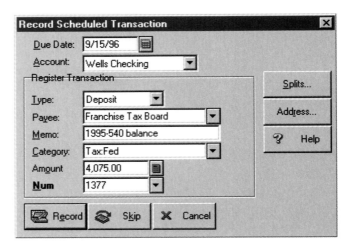

**Figure 6.6** The Record Scheduled Transaction dialog box. Change the date and click Record to pay early; click Skip to skip a scheduled payment.

# Skipping a Scheduled Transaction

To bypass a scheduled transaction and tell Quicken that you won't make it this week, month, quarter, or whatever, choose Lists | Scheduled Transaction (or press CTRL-J). In the Scheduled Transaction List window, click the transaction, and then click the Pay button. You see the Record Scheduled Transaction window shown in Figure 6.6. Click the Skip button.

# Changing a Scheduled Transaction

To change a scheduled transaction, you have to go to the home of scheduled transactions—the Scheduled Transaction List window. It is shown in Figure 6.7. In this window, find the transaction you want to change, click it, and click the Edit button. You see the Edit Scheduled Transaction dialog box, a carbon copy of the Create Scheduled Transaction dialog box (see Figure 6.3 and the accompanying explanations of that dialog box). Fill in the boxes to taste, as they say in cookbooks, and click the OK button when you are done.

To delete a transaction, click it in the Scheduled Transaction List and then click the Delete button. Click OK when Quicken asks if you really want to go through with it.

**Scheduled Transaction List**

| New | Edit | Delete | | Pay | | | | ✕ |
| --- | --- | --- | --- | --- | --- | --- | --- | --- |

| Description | Amount | Pmts | Frequency | Next Date |
| --- | --- | --- | --- | --- |
| Albert Lanier | -675.00 | | Monthly | 9/20/96 (Friday) |
| Franchise Tax Board | 4,075.00 | | Quarterly | 9/15/96 (Sunday) |
| Omega Boys Club | -50.00 | | Monthly | 10/17/96 (Thursday) |
| USFD | 1,800.00 | | Monthly | 7/17/96 (Wednesday) |

Sort by: [ Description ▼ ]

**Figure 6.7** The Scheduled Transaction List window. Click an option in the Sort by box in the lower-left corner to change how the transactions are listed.

# STAYING ORGANIZED WITH THE FINANCIAL CALENDAR

The Financial Calendar is a handy little device. You can use it to write reminder notes, to examine past transactions and scheduled transactions, and even to see a glorious tricolor depiction of your account balances, past, present and future.

## A Trip Around the Financial Calendar Window

Figure 6.8 shows the Financial Calendar window. To get there, click the Calendar icon on the iconbar or choose Features | Paying Bills | Financial Calendar. The window shows all recorded and scheduled transactions, as well as a graph of account balances along the bottom. On the right is a menu of memorized transactions.

To view different months, click the Prev Month or Next Month button. The calendar shows all transactions to begin with, but you can unclutter the calendar by choosing commands on the View menu:

- Click the Show Recorded Transactions in Calendar command to remove or display recorded transactions.

- Click Show Scheduled Transactions in Calendar to remove or see the transactions you have scheduled.

The account graph along the bottom of the screen shows the sum of daily account balances. The yellow bars represent balances before today, the green bar represents balances as of today, and the blue (or red) bars represent projected balances for coming days and months:

# Jotting Down Reminders on the Calendar

I think being able to jot down reminder notes is the best part about the Financial Calendar. Once you put a note on the calendar, it shows

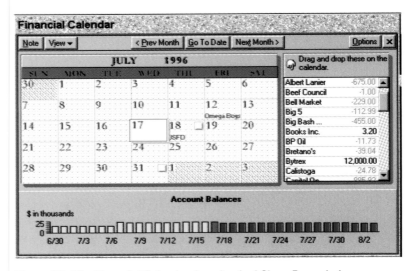

**Figure 6.8** The Financial Calendar. I unchecked Show Recorded Transactions in Calendar on the View menu, so only memorized transactions appear on this calendar.

up in the Quicken Reminders window, the window you see when you start Quicken. It is hard to ignore a note in a prominent place like that.

To put a note on the calendar, click on the day on which you want the note to appear in the Quicken Reminders window, and then click the Note button in the upper-left corner of the Financial Calendar window. You see the Note dialog box.

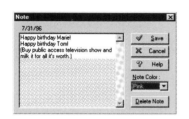

Write a note and click the Save button. Back on the calendar, Quicken has put a box on the day that you chose for your note. To read a note on the Financial Calendar, click its box.

Next time you start Quicken, your note appears in the Quicken Reminders window (if it doesn't appear there, click the Options button in the Reminders window and then click the Show Calendar Notes check box). Notes also appear in the Billminder when you start your computer. And, to top it off, the To Do! button in the lower-right corner of the screen appears when there are notes to read.

| Due in TEST | | | | |
|---|---|---|---|---|
| Type | Account | Date | Payee/Desc. | Amount |
| Note | | 7/31/96 | Happy birthday Marie! | |

# OLLIE OLLIE OXEN FREE!

For some years now, I have been trying to find out the origin of the expression that children use when the game of hide-and-seek is over: Ollie Ollie Oxen Free! If you know where this expression came from, send an e-mail message to me at 74364.50@compuserve.com. Meanwhile, like the children at the end of the hide-and-seek game, you are free either to stop reading this book or to go on to the next chapter, which is about generating charts and reports with Quicken.

CHAPTER

7

# Reports and Graphs for Gauging Your Finances

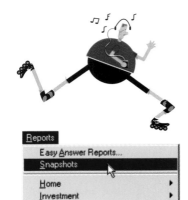

# FAST FORWARD

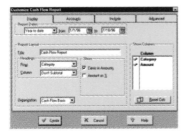

### GET A "SNAPSHOT" OVERVIEW
### OF YOUR FINANCIAL SITUATION ➤ *pp. 126-127*

1. Choose Reports | Snapshots. You see the Snapshots window with an expense comparison chart, a net worth graph, a table showing year-to-date income and expenses, and a bar graph that determines whether you met your budget.
2. Double-click a chart to get a good look at it.

### GENERATE ONE OF QUICKEN'S
### REPORTS ➤ *pp. 127-128*

1. Click the Reports button on the iconbar.
2. Find the report you want to generate in the Create Report dialog box. You might have to click tabs and use the scroll bars to find the one you want. Click a report's name (not its icon) to get a sample glimpse of what it looks like when it has been generated.
3. Change the report dates, if necessary.
4. To generate the report, click the icon beside its name or click the Create button.

### PRINT A REPORT ➤ *pp. 130-131*

1. Create the report.
2. Click the Print button in the report window or press CTRL-P.
3. Select options in the Print dialog box, if necessary, and click OK.

### GENERATE A CUSTOM-MADE REPORT ➤ *pp. 131-132*

1. Create the report that most resembles the one you want to create.
2. In the report window, click the Customize button.
3. Choose options in the Customize Report dialog box. The Display tab handles the title and layout of the report; the Accounts tab lets you choose which accounts to include; the Include tab lets you choose categories, classes, or supercategories; and the Advanced tab lets you choose which transactions to include and exclude.
4. Click the Create button.

## CREATE ONE OF
## QUICKEN'S FIVE GRAPHS ➤ *pp. 136-138*

1. Choose Reports | Graphs, and then click one of the five graph types—Income and Expenses, Budget Variance, Net Worth, or Investment Performance, or Investment Asset Allocation.
2. In the Graph Dates part of the Create Graph dialog box, tell Quicken which time period to use for generating the graph.
3. Either click the icon of the graph you want to create, or click its name and then click the Create button.

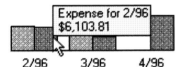

## SEE WHAT A PIE SLICE OR BAR ON A GRAPH
## REPRESENTS IN MONETARY TERMS ➤ *pp. 138-139*

1. Move the mouse over the part of the graph you are interested in. The pointer changes into a magnifying glass and a box appears with the numeral that that part of the graph represents.
2. Double-click to see another graph that gives more detail about the thing you clicked on.

**A** picture is worth a thousand words, so they say, and one financial graph is worth a fair number of words, too. With Quicken, you can get pie charts, bar charts, and other kinds of charts that show right away where you stand financially. You can also get detailed reports, 25 kinds in all, about everything from investment performance to missing checks.

This chapter explains how to get the lowdown on your finances by generating reports and graphs. It describes how to use one of Quicken's prefab reports and how to fashion reports of your own. It tells how to generate and tinker with graphs. It explains how to print graphs and reports, too.

And it's a rather important chapter—reports and graphs can be very useful. After I discovered the Tax Summary report, I stopped staying up late on April 14. I had a foggy notion at best of how I spent money until the day I generated my first Income and Expense graph. It was a revelation. The fog cleared. I heard angels sing. I became a new man.

## GETTING A "SNAPSHOT" OF YOUR FINANCES

Perhaps, instead of fooling around with Quicken's reports and graphs, what you want to know is right in front of your nose on the Snapshots window. To see a "snapshot" of your finances similar to the one in Figure 7.1, choose Reports | Snapshots. The Snapshots window is divided into four parts that describe your financial picture in the year so far: an expense comparison pie chart, a table showing your monthly income and expenses, a net worth bar graph, and a budget graph.

If one of the four parts of the window piques your interest and you want to investigate it more closely, click it and then click the Enlarge button. You see a more detailed picture of the graph or table you clicked on.

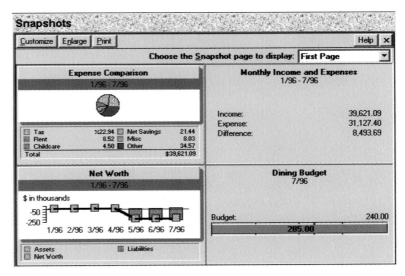

**Figure 7.1** The Snapshots window. Choose Reports | Snapshots to get a quick look at your financial situation.

# EASY ANSWER REPORTS AND GRAPHS

The surest way to find out anything is to ask, and that is the premise behind the Reports | Easy Answer Reports command. Choose that command to see a simple report or graph that answers a common question about finances. When you choose Reports | Easy Answer Reports, you see the Easy Answer Reports & Graphs dialog box shown in Figure 7.2.

If one of these questions is the one you have been aching to have answered, click it. One, two, or three boxes appear in the Details section, depending on the question you clicked. Usually, all you do is choose a time period, but Quicken needs category names and account names to answer some of the questions. When you have made entries in the Details boxes, click the Show Report or Show Graph button to see a report or graph that answers your question (unfortunately, for some questions you cannot get a graph).

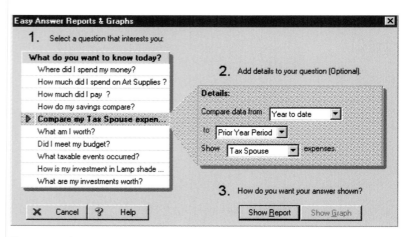

**Figure 7.2** Click the question you want an answer to on the left, fill in the box or boxes on the right, and then click either Show Report or Show Graph to see a report or graph that answers your question.

# READY-MADE REPORTS FROM QUICKEN

Chances are, you can find a ready-made report that tells you exactly what you need to know about your finances. Quicken offers 25 different reports. And if one of them isn't quite right, you can always tweak it. This part of the chapter describes Quicken's ready-made reports and explains how to generate them. "Fashioning a Report of Your Own," a few pages hence, explains how to get a tailor-made report of your own.

## CREATE A REPORT OR GRAPH FROM A REGISTER step by step

1. Click the Report button in the register window.

2. From the drop-down menu, choose Register Report to get a by-date listing of all transactions in the register, or choose Expense Summary Graph to get a pie chart of the ten highest expenditures by category in the register.

3. Click a transaction to get a detailed report about the payee in the transaction or the category you assigned to it.

4. From the Report drop-down menu, choose Amount spent on to see a by-date category report of all transactions you assigned to the category, or choose Payments made

Amount spent on Travel
Payments made to Chainsaw Al Derdorf

Expense Summary Graph...

to in order to see a by-date payee report of all payments you made to the party listed in the Payee box.

# The Different Kinds of Reports

Here is an exercise to show you all the reports that Quicken offers: click on the Reports menu and slowly slide the mouse pointer past Home, to Investment, Business, and Other. As you slide the mouse down, submenus appear. Each submenu lists a handful of reports you can generate:

| Cash Flow... | | |
|---|---|---|
| Monthly Budget... | | |
| Itemized Categories... | | |
| Tax Summary... | | |

| Net Worth... |
|---|
| Tax Schedule... |
| Missing Checks... |
| Comparison... |

| Portfolio Value... |
|---|
| Investment Performance... |
| Capital Gains... |

| Investment Income... |
|---|
| Investment Transactions... |

| P&L Statement... |
|---|
| P&L Comparison... |
| Cash Flow... |

| A/P by Vendor... |
|---|
| A/R by Customer... |
| Job/Project... |

| Payroll... |
|---|
| Balance Sheet... |
| Missing Checks... |
| Comparison... |

| Transaction... |
|---|
| Summary... |
| Comparison... |
| Budget... |
| Account Balances... |

| Memorized Reports... |
|---|

Now click the Reports button on the iconbar. You see the Create Report dialog box with its five tabs, four of which are familiar to you from the Reports menu—Home, Investment, Business, and Other. The point is, you can go directly to the Create Report dialog box and create any kind of report you want merely by clicking the Reports button on the iconbar or by choosing Report and one of the Report commands. Whichever route you take, you end up at the Create Report dialog box shown in Figure 7.3.

The Create Report dialog box lists every kind of report you can generate, as well as the reports you fashion yourself, which are placed on the Memorized tab. To find a report that meets your needs, click the different tabs, click on a scroll bar if necessary, click on a report name (but not on its icon), and glance at the midget sample report on the left side of the dialog box. Besides looking at the sample, you can also find out what a report is by generating it. It takes about two seconds to generate a report. Better read on...

# Generating Reports and QuickZoom Reports

When you've found your report in the Create Report dialog box, choose report dates to tell Quicken which time period to cover in the

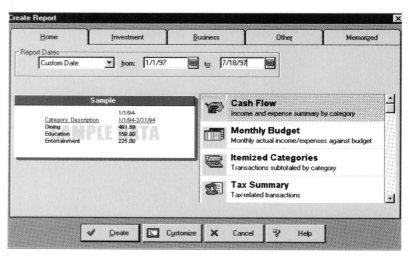

**Figure 7.3** The Create Report dialog box. Click the scroll bar to move down the list of reports, then click on a report name (not its icon) and glance at the sample to see what the report is.

report. Then either click the report's icon or click the report's name and click the Create button. Soon you see your report in all its pristine glory. You will probably have to click the scroll bar to move down the "pages" and read the whole thing.

If something on a report arouses your curiosity, move the mouse pointer over it. With any luck, the mouse pointer changes into a magnifying glass with a *Z* in it. Double-click at that point and you see what Quicken calls a *QuickZoom report.* QuickZoom reports are "reports within reports" that clarify the thing you clicked on, whatever it happened to be.

# Printing a Report

To print a report after you generate it, click the Print button in the report window (or press CTRL-P). You see the Print dialog box shown in Figure 7.4. In case you were wondering, the Portrait option button under Orientation is for printing on paper that is long on the sides and narrower on the top, like the pages of this book, whereas the Landscape option prints on paper that is wider on top than it is on the sides, like a landscape painting.

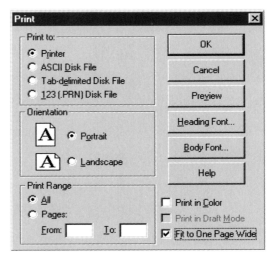

**Figure 7.4** The Print dialog box, where you tell Quicken how to print the report

The three check boxes in the lower-right corner are for telling Quicken that you have a color printer, that you want to print quickly by doing so in draft mode, and that you want Quicken to squeeze a wide report so it fits across the page. Click the Preview button to see what your report looks like, and if it looks good, click Print in the Print Preview dialog box.

# FASHIONING A REPORT OF YOUR OWN

Rugged individualists and mavericks of all stripes will be glad to know that you don't have to rely solely on ready-made reports, because you can fashion reports of your own. To create a report tailored especially for your finances, you start by generating a ready-made report, and then you click the Customize button in the report window to mold the report into something entirely new.

Besides creating new reports, you can change the way they look. And when you're finished doing that, you can tell Quicken to "memorize" your new report so you can call on it again without having to go through all that shaping and molding a second time.

**habits & strategies**

*When it comes to fashioning a report of your own, you should start with a report on the Other tab of the Create Report dialog box. The five reports on that tab are the basic report types on which all of Quicken's ready-made reports are built.*

# "Massaging" a Quicken Report

After you have generated a ready-made report, you can start fooling with it by clicking the Customize button in the report window (for that matter, you can start fooling around from the get-go by clicking the Customize button at the bottom of the Create Reports dialog box). When you click the Customize button, you see a Customize Report dialog box similar to the one in Figure 7.5. Four tabs can be found in this dialog box: Display, Accounts, Include, and Advanced.

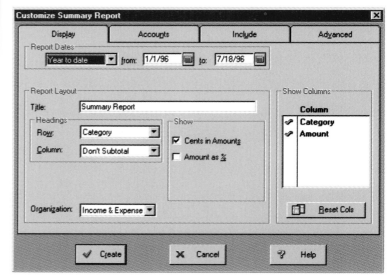

**Figure 7.5** The Display tab of the Customize Report dialog box. These are the options for customizing a summary report.

Depending on the kind of report you are trying to modify, the options in the Customize Report dialog box differ a little bit. Don't be afraid to click the Help button in the dialog box to get descriptions of the options you have to choose from. You are on your own when it comes to modifying a report, since I don't know what you want to do or which report you are trying to modify, but to help you, here is a brief rundown of what is on the four tabs:

| Tab | What It Does |
|-----|--------------|
| Display | Changes the title and layout of the report |
| Accounts | Tells Quicken from which accounts to draw data for the report |
| Include | Tells Quicken which categories, classes, or supercategories to report on |
| Advanced | Weeds out transactions that you do not want included in the report |

When you are done filling in the four tabs of the Customize Report dialog box, click the Create button to generate your newfangled report. If it doesn't come out right, click the Customize button again to get back to the Customize Report dialog box and start all over.

# Changing the Look of a Report

Besides changing the layout and content of a report, you can change its appearance. By dragging the column markers, you can change the width of columns. And you can also choose a new typeface for the headings and the body text of a report.

To change the width of a column in a report, move the mouse pointer over the gray, diamond-shaped marker that separates the name of one column heading from the next. If you do this correctly, the mouse pointer changes into a cross with arrowheads on two sides. Click, hold down the mouse button, and drag the cross to widen or narrow the column.

Changing the typeface that is used in the headings and body text of a report is done from the Print dialog box (see Figure 7.4). Click the Print button in a report window (or press CTRL-P) to get to that dialog box. It offers two buttons called Heading Font and Body Font. Click the Heading Font button to open the Report/List Header Font dialog box shown in Figure 7.6 and choose a new font, font style, and font size for the headers in your report.

Headers are the names that appear at the top of columns. Click the Body Font button to open a similar dialog box for choosing a typeface for the main text of the report. Don't forget to look in the

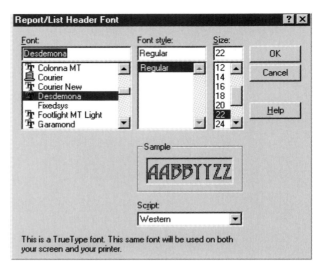

**Figure 7.6** Choose a font, font style, and font size for the column headers in your report from this dialog box.

Sample box to see what your choices will look like when the report is printed. When you have made your choices, click the OK button.

## tricks of the trade

*Where time is money, it's hard to protect time for those who—such as low-wage workers, children, aged parents, or community organizations—can't pay for it. And it's hard to protect time for ourselves, for relaxation, hobbies, sleep. The pressures toward long working hours have become too powerful. But common sense tells us that working hours can be too long. Excessive hours are unhealthy and antisocial, and ultimately erode the quality of life.*

*Juliet B. Schor,* The Overworked American

# Memorizing Your New Report So You Can Call on It Again

After you go to the trouble of creating a report of your own, you might as well tell Quicken to "memorize" it. That way, you can generate the report again without having to go to all the trouble of modifying one of Quicken's reports. When you memorize a report, you give it a name, and Quicken puts its name on the Memorized tab of the Create Report dialog box (see Figure 7.3).

To memorize a report that you have created yourself, generate the report and then click the Memorize button in the report window. You see the Memorize Report dialog box shown in Figure 7.7. In the Title box, type a descriptive name for the report. The name you enter will appear on the Memorized tab of the Create Report dialog box, as will the description if you enter one in the Description box at the bottom of the screen. Click an icon at the bottom of the dialog box if you want an icon to appear beside the report name (yes, that is a rubber ducky you're seeing among the icons).

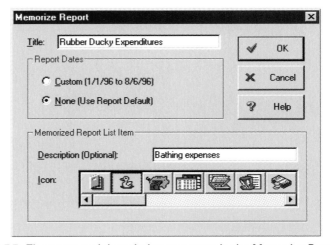

**Figure 7.7** The name and description you enter in the Memorize Report dialog box will appear on the Memorized tab of the Create Report dialog box so you can generate your report again.

The Report Dates options determine which days the report covers:

- **Custom:** Generates a report that covers the dates shown to the right of the option button. For example, if those dates are 1/1/97 to 6/3/97, the memorized report always covers that time period.

- **None:** Generates a report that covers the default dates for reports. (To find out what those are and to change them if you want, click the Options button in a report window to get to the Report Options dialog box. Then, under Default Report Date Range, choose a time period and click OK.)

Click OK when you've made your choices. Next time you visit the Memorized tab of the Create Report dialog box, you will see your memorized report. To generate it, select it and click the Create button.

# GRAPHING YOUR FINANCES

The quickest way to see how you stand financially is to generate a graph. Graphs tell it like it is. The slices of the pie and the bars on the graph tell you instantly what your finances look like.

It's pretty easy to create a graph with Quicken. And, like reports, you can tinker with graphs to make them display the financial data you are curious about. This part of the chapter shows you how to create a graph, "zoom in" to look at it more closely, create graphs of your own, and change the appearance of graphs.

## The Four Types of Graphs

To create one of Quicken's four ready-to-wear graphs, choose Reports | Graphs and click one of the five graph commands on the menu. No matter which command you choose, you end up at the Create Graph dialog box shown in Figure 7.8. This dialog box serves up five types of graphs, four of which are shown in Figure 7.9. Click the option button next to the graph you want to create:

- **Income and Expenses graph:** A bar graph comparing monthly income and expenses, and a pie chart showing each expense as a percentage of total expenses.

- **Budget Variances graph:** Two bar graphs, one that compares your budget income goals to your actual income, and another that compares your actual spending by category to your budget's spending goals.

- **Net Worth graph:** A bar graph that shows, month by month, how your assets and liabilities stack up to produce your net worth.

- **Investment Performance graph:** Two bar charts, one that shows the month-by-month value of your portfolio and another that shows your average return for the year. The Investment Asset Allocation graph is a pie chart that compares income by asset class.

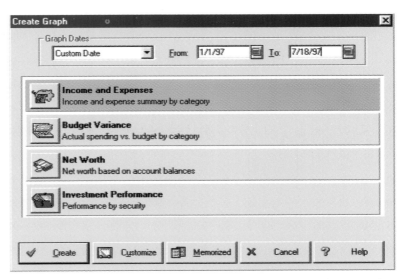

**Figure 7.8** The Create Graph dialog box. This is where you tell Quicken what kind of graph to make.

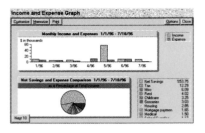
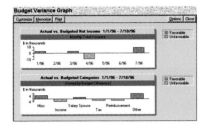
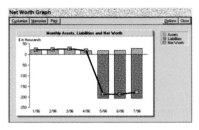
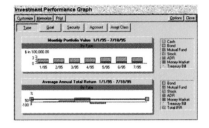

**Figure 7.9** Clockwise from upper-left: an Income and Expense graph, Budget Variance graph, Net Worth graph, and an Investment Performance graph.

# Getting a Closer Look at Graph Data

Graphs are plotted from the data in registers. As such, each bar, pie slice, line, and box represents a number of some kind. To find out what those numbers are, move the mouse pointer over the part of the graph you are interested in. The pointer changes into a magnifying glass and you see a dollar figure.

If you double-click while you see the magnifying glass and dollar figure, Quicken shows you a "QuickZoom graph" with detailed information about the thing you clicked. For this illustration, I double-clicked the "Office" slice of an expense comparison graph. The QuickZoom graph I got shows me how much I spent each month in the Office category:

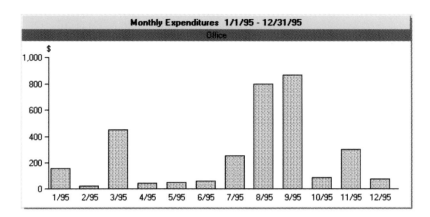

QuickZoom graphs are a convenient way to look more closely at the data on a graph. When you are finished scrutinizing a QuickZoom graph, click the Close button to get back to the original graph.

# Creating Your Own Graph

When Quicken makes a graph, it includes data from all the accounts. All categories and all classes go into the making of a graph. As for the time period covered, Quicken graphs cover the year to date. You can, however, change these settings. You can exclude certain accounts, certain categories, and certain classes. And you can tell Quicken to plot data from past years or from this quarter or from last month. You don't have to stay with the year-to-date time period if you don't want to.

Changing the way graphs are plotted is called "customizing," and it is done by clicking the Customize button in the graph window. When you click this button, you see the Customize Graph dialog box shown in Figure 7.10.

Click the Accounts, Categories, or Classes tab to keep data from accounts, categories, or classes from being plotted in the graph. When you click one of those buttons, you get a list of accounts, categories, or

**SHORTCUT**

*To include only a few items in the Select to Include dialog box, start by clicking the Clear All button. That removes all the check marks.*

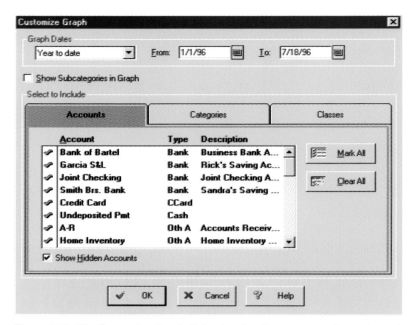

**Figure 7.10** The Customize Graph dialog box is where you tweak graphs and tell Quicken precisely what data you want them to display.

classes. Click items to exclude them. As you click, the yellow check marks beside items are removed. Only items with check marks beside their names are plotted in the graph. Choose a new date for plotting the graph, if you want to, and then click the OK button.

Back in the Customize Graph dialog box, Quicken generates your newfangled graph.

# Memorizing a Graph So You Can Use It Later

Graphs, like reports, can be memorized and called to use another day. If you have gone to the trouble to create an elaborate, intricate graph, you owe it to yourself to save it for another day. To do that, click the Memorize button. In the Memorize Graph dialog box, enter a description for your graph and click OK.

To create the graph again, choose Reports | Graphs | Memorized Graphs, click the name of the graph in the Memorized Graphs window, click the Use button, and click OK in the Recall Memorized Graph dialog box. By the way, the Edit button in the Memorized Graphs window is for changing the names of memorized graphs and the Delete button is for removing them from the Memorized Graphs window.

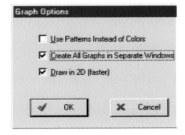

# Changing the Look of a Graph

Appearances count for a lot, so Quicken gives you a handful of ways to change how graphs look. The most dramatic way to change the look of a graph is to click the Options button in a graph window and choose among the options in the Graph Options dialog box. Click Use Patterns Instead of Colors to see crosshatch patterns in graphs instead of colors. If your printer is a black-and-white job, you absolutely *must* choose this option. A graph with patterns instead of colors is shown in Figure 7.11.

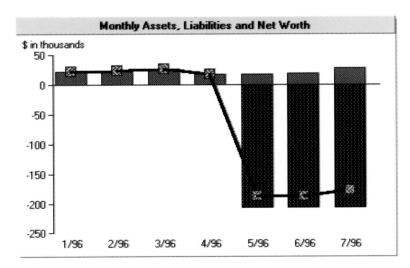

**Figure 7.11** For *film noir* fans: click the Options button in a graph window and choose Use Patterns Instead of Colors to see patterns instead of colors on graphs.

The Create All Graphs in Separate Windows check box tells Quicken to print graphs like Income and Expense, which are really two graphs, on separate pages. It is a printing option, truth be told. The Draw in 2D (faster) check box robs one dimension from Quicken's graphs and renders all graphs in two dimensions instead of three. If you have a good eye, you might have noticed that the graphs shown in this chapter are two-, not three-dimensional. Three-dimensional graphs look good on computer screens, but not on paper, which is why I chose two-dimensional graphs for this book.

Another way to change the appearance of a graph is to do it from the Report Printer Setup dialog box. To get there, choose File | Printer Setup | For Reports/Graphs Printer Setup. Click the Heading Font button to open a dialog box where you can choose a new typeface for headings and titles. Click the Body Font button to get to a dialog box where you can choose a new typeface for the text and labels in graphics.

## Printing a Graph

Printing a graph is pretty darn simple. All you have to do is glance at your graph to make sure it is just-so and click the Print button. Don't forget to turn the printer on first.

## TALLYHO!

So much for the exciting chapter about generating reports and graphs. I started this chapter by saying that a picture is worth a thousand words, but I wonder if that is still true. With TV, MTV, the Internet, and so many magazines and newspapers, I think we may be suffering from picture inflation. A picture can't be worth a thousand words anymore. It might be worth ten, maybe fifteen words at the most. The next chapter, to change subjects as abruptly as they do on MTV, is about the onerous chores you have to do to keep Quicken in good working order.

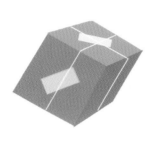

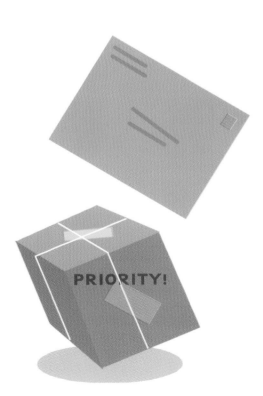

PRIORITY!

# Getting the Housekeeping Done

# FAST FORWARD

**BACK UP A QUICKEN FILE** ➤ *pp. 149-150*

1. Put a floppy disk in the drive to which you will make the backup copy.
2. Choose File | Backup (or press CTRL-B) to see the Select Backup Drive dialog box.
3. If necessary, click the down-arrow in the Backup Drive drop-down list and choose a new drive letter.
4. Click OK.

**REPLACE THE ON-DISK COPY OF
A QUICKEN FILE WITH ITS BACKUP** ➤ *pp. 150-151*

1. Put the floppy with the backup copy on it in the A drive of your computer.
2. Choose File | Restore. You see the Restore Quicken File dialog box.
3. Click the Up One Level button twice until you see the 3½ Floppy (A:) icon.
4. Double-click the 3½ Floppy (A:) icon. You see the .qdb backup file or files in the dialog box.
5. Click the backup file that is to take the place of the file that is on the hard disk now.
6. Click OK. A message says, "If you proceed with restoring, you will overwrite an existing file."
7. Click the OK button.

**CREATE AN ARCHIVE FILE FOR STORING THE
PREVIOUS YEAR'S TRANSACTIONS** ➤ *pp. 152-153*

1. Choose File | File Operations | Year-End Copy.
2. Since Archive is already selected, click OK in the Year-End Copy dialog box.
3. In the Archive File dialog box, enter a name for the archive file in the Archive Old Data to File box.
4. Enter a date in the Archive Transactions Prior to and Including box. Transactions recorded previous to the date you enter, and transactions recorded on the date you enter, will be stored in the archive file.
5. Click OK.
6. Click OK in the File Copied Successfully dialog box.

## RENAME A QUICKEN FILE ➤ *p. 154*

1. Choose File | File Operations | Rename.
2. Find and click on the file you want to rename in the Rename Quicken File dialog box.
3. Enter a name for the file in the New Name for Quicken File box.
4. Click OK.

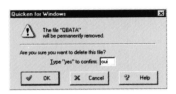

## DELETE A QUICKEN FILE ➤ *p. 156*

1. Choose File | File Operations | Delete.
2. Click the file you want to delete, and then click OK.
3. In the message box that appears, type **yes** to confirm that you want to delete the file.
4. Click OK.

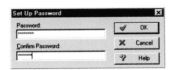

## CREATE A PASSWORD FOR A QUICKEN FILE ➤ *pp. 157-158*

1. Choose File | Passwords | File.
2. Type the password twice in the Set Up Password dialog box, once in the Password and once in the Confirm Password box.
3. Click OK.

This short and to-the-point chapter explains the necessary housekeeping chores you have to do in Quicken. It tells how to back up Quicken data for safekeeping and how to create a year-end or archive file of the previous year's financial transactions. It also explains how to rename, copy, and delete Quicken data files. Last but not least, this chapter has something for the espionage fan—it explains how to create passwords so others can't look at your precious financial data.

# PROTECTING DATA AGAINST A COMPUTER FAILURE

Computers are marvelous machines until they break down. A broken computer is worse than useless. The data stored on its hard disk is trapped inside and will never be of use to anyone. Unless someone had the foresight to back up the data, no one will ever be able to see or use it again.

In computer lingo, *backing up* means to make a second copy of a computer file and keep it in a safe place where nothing can harm it. Usually, files are backed up to floppy disks or tape drives. The second, backed-up copy is a sort of insurance policy in case something bad happens to the original copy, the hard disk gets warped, the computer is stolen, the house catches on fire, or another morbid catastrophe strikes. As long as the data has been backed up, you can get it back and use it, no matter what happens to your computer.

The financial data you worked so hard to assemble with Quicken is very important. Therefore, you ought to back it up. Backing up a Quicken data file and restoring data from a backed-up file are the subjects of this part of the chapter.

**habits &
strategies**

*Quicken makes it very easy to
back up a data file. Do it each
time you finish running the
program. That way, you always
have an up-to-date copy of your
financial records.*

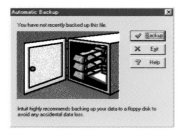

# Backing Up Financial Data

Nothing could be easier than backing up a Quicken data file. To
do so, put a floppy disk in the floppy drive, glance at the computer screen
to make sure that the Quicken file you want to back up is onscreen, and
then choose File | Backup (or press CTRL-B). You see the Select Backup
Drive dialog box shown in Figure 8.1.

Make sure the backup drive letter shown in this dialog box is the
right one. Very likely, Quicken made the right choice, drive A (the floppy
disk drive), but if you want to back up the data to another drive, click
the down-arrow and choose a new letter from the Backup Drive
drop-down list.

Click OK when you are done. You hear a grinding noise as the data
is copied to the floppy disk, and when the grind is over a dialog box tells
you that the file backed up successfully. Click OK, put the floppy disk
or tape aside in a safe place, and rest assured that your financial data is
safe and sound.

By the way, backing up data is so important, Quicken reminds you
to back up if you forget to do it. If you lackadaisically use the program
for awhile without backing up your data, you see the Automatic Backup
dialog box. This dialog box is your cue to get with it and back up your
financial records. Click the Backup button and you see the Select
Backup Drive dialog box (see Figure 8.1). From there, you can back up

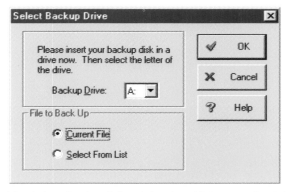

**Figure 8.1** The Select Backup Drive dialog box. Make sure the right letter
appears in the Backup Drive box and then click OK to make a backup copy of
your Quicken data.

the Quicken data file. (To make sure you see the Automatic Backup dialog box, choose Edit | Options | Quicken Program, click the General tab in the General Options dialog box, make sure the Prompt to Backup Files on Shutdown check box is selected, and click OK.)

# Restoring Data from Backed Up Files

If something evil this way comes and you lose your Quicken financial data, you can always restore it from the backup copy you made. Or, if you bungle a find-and-replace operation, for example, and make a hash of your data files, all is not lost because you can get a clean copy of your financial records from the backup copy.

Using the backup copy of a file in place of the parent copy is called "restoring." When you restore a Quicken data file, you erase the data on the hard disk and replace it with the backup file on a floppy disk. If you take my advice and back up Quicken files each time you finish running the program, you will always have a sound backup file to use in case of an emergency.

To restore a Quicken data file, put the floppy disk with the backup copy on it in a disk drive. Next, choose File | Restore. You see the Restore Quicken File dialog box shown in Figure 8.2. Select the backup file that is to take the place of the original. Unless you gave the original

**habits & strategies**

*Quicken keeps backup copies of files in a folder called Backup. If you forgot to back up your files, you might try getting backup copies from this folder, but they're made sporadically—I wouldn't count on them to be up-to-date and accurate.*

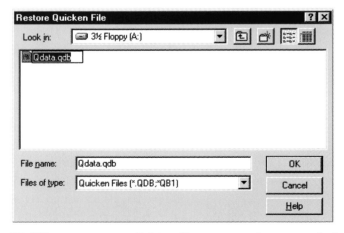

**Figure 8.2**  When you restore a Quicken file, you erase the copy on the hard disk and replace it with the backup copy. Click the backup file in this dialog box and then click OK.

file a new name or created a new Quicken file, the backup file is called Qdata.qdb. When you click the OK button, a message warns, "If you proceed with restoring, you will overwrite an existing file. Continue anyway?" Click the OK button in the message box.

Now all you have to do is enter the financial transactions that you entered between the time you last backed up the file and the time you "restored" it. I hope there aren't many transactions to enter.

---

**tricks of the trade**

*Put not your trust in money, but put your money in trust.*

*Oliver Wendell Holmes,* The Autocrat at the Breakfast Table

---

# CLOSING OUT THE YEAR

In traditional accounting methods, the books are "closed" at the end of the year and a new set of books is "opened." To accommodate traditionalists, Quicken offers a command for starting a new file at the end of the year. You can also create an "archive file," a second file where all the transactions from a single year are kept.

## The Big Picture: Archive Files and Year-End Files

An *archive file* is simply a copy of all financial records from a single year. When you create an archive copy of a file, the original file you have been working with all along stays intact and you end up with two files, one with data from the previous year and one with all your Quicken data.

When you create a *year-end file*, on the other hand, the original file does not stay intact—instead, it is broken in two, and all transactions from the previous year are removed from it and stored in the year-end file. Meanwhile, the original file is "shrunk" because—except for investment records—only transactions from the present year remain in the original file. Quicken keeps investment records from past years in the original file so you can track investment histories.

**CAUTION**

*Don't create a year-end or archive file on January 1. Wait until you have filed your income taxes, made the necessary end-of-the-year reports, and cleared all transactions from the past year.*

Create an archive file so you have a record of each year's transactions. As for year-end files, there are only two valid reasons for creating them. Sometimes the Quicken data file grows too large and it can't fit on a floppy disk. When that happens, backing up the file is impossible, so you have to create a year-end copy to remove past years' transactions and make the original file small enough to fit on a floppy disk. The other good reason has to do with standard accounting practices. Standard accountants always start a new file each year. They also—the men at least—wear tasseled loafers. But you don't have to wear tasseled loafers or start a new file each year if you don't want to.

Year-end files have real disadvantages. You can't see year-to-year comparison reports after you create a year-end file. A year-end file severs one year from the next and makes it impossible to compare one year's data to another year's.

## Putting Data from the Past Year in an Archive File

To create an archive file, choose File | File Operations | Year-End Copy. You see the Year-End Copy dialog box. The Archive option button is already selected, so click the OK button. You see the Archive File dialog box shown in Figure 8.3. This is where you tell Quicken what to call the archive file and which transactions to put in it.

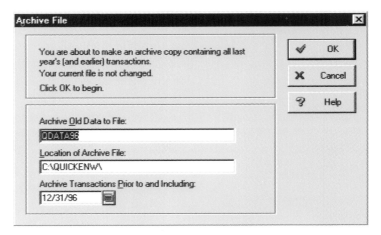

**Figure 8.3**  To create an archive file, enter a name and an inclusive date, and click OK.

In the Archive Old Data to File box, Quicken suggests calling the archive file by its present name followed by the last two digits of the previous year's name, but you can choose a name of your own by typing it in the box.

In the Archive Transactions Prior to and Including box, Quicken has entered the last day of the previous year. The archive file will hold all financial transactions made in the past year or years unless you change this date. Change the date if you wish by entering a new one or clicking on the baby calendar and choosing a new date. Click OK when you are done filling in the Archive File dialog box.

After Quicken creates the archive file, you see the File Copied Successfully dialog box. The Current file option is selected. That's the one you want to work with, so click OK in this dialog box.

To view an archive file (or any Quicken file for that matter), choose the File | Open command, select the archive file in the Open Quicken File dialog box, and click OK.

## Creating a Year-End File for Your Financial Records

To create a year-end file for your financial records and remove the past year's records from the Quicken data file, choose File | File Operations | Year-End Copy. In the Year-End Copy dialog box, click the Start New Year option button, and then click OK. You see the Start New Year dialog box shown in Figure 8.4.

In the first box, Copy All Transactions to File, enter a name for the year-end file. The second box, the one with the long name, is for telling Quicken what the cut-off date is. All transactions (except investment transactions) before the cut-off date will be removed from the file you work with and put in the year-end file. Very likely, you want to remove transactions made before January 1, the date Quicken has entered in the dialog box, but you can enter a different cut-off date if you wish.

Quicken keeps the year-end file in the Quickenw folder along with all the other data files, but if you want to put the file elsewhere, enter a new path name in the Move Current File to box. Finally, click OK.

You see the File Copied Successfully dialog box. The Use file for new year option is already selected, so click OK to see the original file *sans* the transactions you just removed from it.

**CAUTION**

*Be sure to back up the Quicken file before you create a year-end file. That way, if you regret shrinking the original file, you can restore it from the backup copy.*

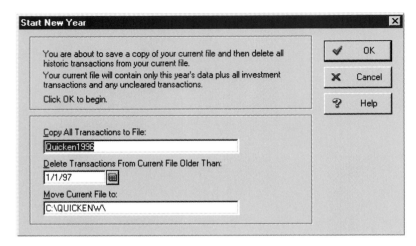

**Figure 8.4** Creating a year-end file. Enter a name for the file in the topmost box and then click OK.

To see transactions in a year-end file, do what you would do to open any Quicken file: choose the File | Open command, select the file in the Open Quicken File dialog box, and click OK. You can look at the file, but don't alter it in any way.

# RENAMING A QUICKEN FILE

To rename a Quicken file, all you have to do is choose File | File Operations | Rename. You see the Rename Quicken File dialog box shown in Figure 8.5. Click the file you want to rename and then enter a new name in the New Name for Quicken File box. When you have named and christened the file, click the OK button.

# COPYING A QUICKEN FILE

To make a copy of all or part of a Quicken file, open the file and choose File | File Operations | Copy. You see the Copy File dialog box shown in Figure 8.6. Enter a descriptive name in the Name box. Quicken suggests putting the copy alongside the other files in the Quickenw folder, but you can put it elsewhere by entering a path name in the Location box.

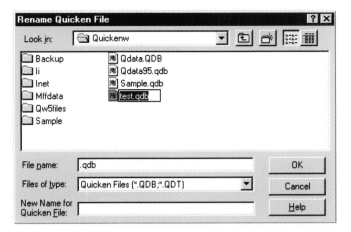

**Figure 8.5** To rename a Quicken file, click the file in this dialog box, enter a new name in the New Name for Quicken File box, and click OK.

The Copy Options part of the dialog box is for telling Quicken which transactions to copy. To begin with, Quicken wants to copy all the transactions, and it says as much in the From and To Copy Transactions boxes, but you can change these dates. Do so if you want to copy a part of the file.

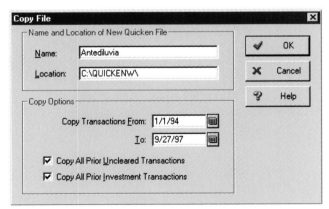

**Figure 8.6** The Copy File dialog box, where you name the copied file and tell Quicken which transactions to include in it.

As for the Copy All Prior Uncleared Transactions check box, click it if you are copying part of the file and you want to copy uncleared transactions that fall before the date range you entered in the Copy Transactions From and To boxes. Unless you copy the uncleared transactions, you can't reconcile your accounts in the copied file.

If you keep investment accounts, a check box called Copy All Prior Investment Transactions also appears in the dialog box. Make sure it is clicked if you want the copied file to show a complete history of your investment transactions.

Not a moment to soon, click OK when you are done filling in the Copy File dialog box. Then, in the File Copied Successfully dialog box, click OK to keep working in the original file, or click the New copy option button and click OK to open the copy you just made.

# DELETING A FILE

To delete a Quicken data file, make a backup copy first. With that done, choose File | File Operations | Delete. You see the Delete Quicken File dialog box. Click the to-be-deleted file and then click the OK button. An ominous message box appears and warns you that the file will be permanently deleted. The message box gives you a last chance to keep the file:

Type **yes** in the confirm box and click OK, or click Cancel if you get cold feet and decide not to go through with it.

## CAUTION

*Before you delete a Quicken file, make a backup copy. Someday you might need the file you deleted. Moreover, unlike other files, Quicken data files don't land in the Windows 95 Recycle Bin after they are deleted.*

*An ideal password is hard to
decipher but also easy to
remember. Here's a trick for
choosing a password: decide
what your favorite foreign city is
and spell it backwards. If I
needed a password for my
Quicken file, it would be "sirap."*

# PROTECTING YOUR FINANCIAL RECORDS WITH PASSWORDS

To keep others from snooping, you can assign passwords to Quicken files. After a password has been assigned to a file, no one can open it without the password. Besides protecting a file, you can also keep transactions that were recorded previous to a particular day from being changed. For example, you might protect the previous year's transactions with a password.

A password can be any combination of characters. Quicken doesn't distinguish between upper- and lowercase letters in passwords. As long as "Peter" is the correct password, it doesn't matter if you enter peter, Peter, or PETER in Quicken's password dialog boxes.

It almost goes without saying, but you must never, never, never forget a password. A Quicken file whose password has been forgotten is as good as useless, because no one can get into it. Write down passwords in a secret place where no one would expect to find them.

## Assigning a Password to a File

To clamp a password on a file and keep others from opening it, choose File | Passwords | File. Then, in the Set Up Password dialog box, type your password twice, first in the Password box and then in the Confirm Password box. Instead of letters, you see asterisks. That is so anyone looking over your shoulder doesn't see the password (although a cunning spy could watch your fingers on the keyboard and get the password that way!).

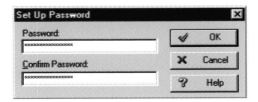

Click OK when you are done entering and confirming the password. As long as you entered it the same way twice, the password is in place. Next time you or a cat burglar start Quicken or open this data file, you see the Quicken Password dialog box:

Enter the password and click OK. Devious souls who try to get into your data file without knowing the password are told that they have the incorrect password and are sent packing.

# Assigning a Password to Register Transactions

Assigning a password to transactions in a register is similar to assigning a password to a file. The only difference is, you tell Quicken to protect transactions that were recorded before a certain day.

To assign a password to register transactions, open the register whose transactions you are so keen on preserving. With that done, choose File | Passwords | Transaction. You see the Password to Modify Existing Transactions dialog box:

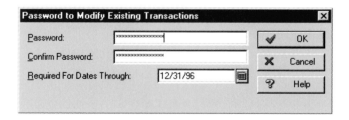

Enter the password twice, once in the Password box and once in the Confirm Password box. In the Required For Dates Through box, enter the date on or before which a password will be required in order to alter a transaction. In the illustration shown here, for example, users will need the password to change any transaction that occurred on or before December 31, 1996.

Click OK when you are done entering passwords and a date. If you or anyone else goes into the register, changes a transaction that occurred on or before the date, and clicks the Enter button, the Quicken Password dialog box appears. As long as you enter the password correctly in this dialog box, you hear the beep when you click OK, and the transaction change is recorded. Enter the password incorrectly and Quicken stomps on your toe.

# Changing and Doing Away with Passwords

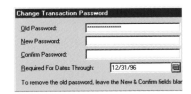

To change or get rid of a password to either a file or transactions in a register, choose File | Passwords and click either File or Transaction on the submenu. If you choose Transaction, you see the Change Transaction Password dialog box. The dialog box for changing or dropping file passwords looks the same except it doesn't have a Required For Dates Through box.

What you do next depends on whether you want to remove or change the password:

- **Remove:** Enter the password in the Old Password box and click the OK button.

- **Change:** Enter the present password in the Old Password box and the new password in both the New Password and Confirm Password boxes, then marvel at all those asterisks and click OK.

In the case of transaction passwords, you can also change the date through which a password is required for altering transactions. Do that by entering a new date in the Required For Dates Through box.

# SO LONG, CHARLIE!

So ends the chapter about housekeeping chores in Quicken. Nobody likes housekeeping chores, so to make up for this chapter I've included a lot of fireworks and histrionics in the next one. It is about saving money and budgeting with Quicken.

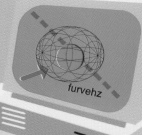

# Budgeting and Saving Money with Quicken

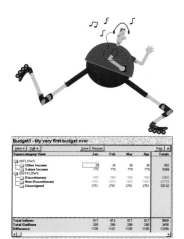

# FAST FORWARD

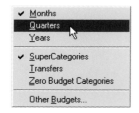

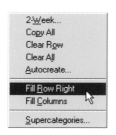

## OPEN THE BUDGET WINDOW AND START PREPARING A BUDGET ➤ *pp. 165-166*

1. Choose Features | Planning | Budget. You see the Budget window. The "inflows" at the top of the screen are income categories; the "outflows" at the bottom are expense categories.
2. To prepare a budget, enter what you expect your income to be in the inflow rows and columns and what you would like to spend in each expense category in the outflow rows and columns.

## BUDGET BY YEAR, QUARTER, OR MONTH ➤ *p. 167*

1. Click the View button in the Budget window and choose Months, Quarters, or Years from the drop-down menu.
2. Click SuperCategories as well if you want to budget by supercategory instead of by category.

## ENTER NUMBERS IN THE BUDGET WINDOW ONE AT A TIME ➤ *p. 168*

1. Click in the Budget window and enter the numbers in the rows and columns.
2. Click the Edit button in the Budget window and choose Fill Row Right to copy the amount at the location of the cursor across all the rows to the right.
3. Choose Clear Row to remove budget numbers from the row so you can start anew.

## ENTER BUDGET NUMBERS AUTOMATICALLY FROM YOUR QUICKEN REGISTERS ➤ *pp. 169-170*

1. Click the Edit button in the Budget window.
2. Choose Autocreate from the drop-down menu to see the Automatically Create Budget dialog box.

3. In the From and To boxes, enter the date range for Quicken to draw data from.
4. Choose $1, $10, or $100 in the Round Values to Nearest box.
5. Click the Use Monthly Detail option button to use real amounts from the time period you chose, or click Use Average for Period to average out your spending and income so that the same figures appear across all columns in the Budget window.
6. Click OK.

## GENERATE A BUDGET REPORT OR BUDGET GRAPH ➤ *pp. 172-173*

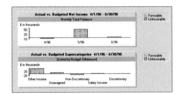

1. Choose Reports | Easy Answer Reports.
2. Click the "Did I meet my budget?" question in the Easy Answer Reports & Graphs dialog box.
3. In the Details part of the dialog box, choose a time period from the list.
4. Click the Show Report button or Show Graph button.

## SET UP A SAVINGS GOAL ACCOUNT ➤ *p. 176*

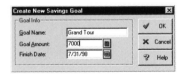

1. Choose Features | Planning | Savings Goals and click the New button in the Savings Goals window to get to the Create New Savings Goal dialog box.
2. Enter a name for the goal in the Goal Name box.
3. Enter the amount you want to save in the Goal Amount box.
4. In the Finish Date box, enter the date by which you want to have saved the money.
5. Click OK.

## "TRANSFER" MONEY TO A SAVINGS GOAL ACCOUNT ➤ *p. 176*

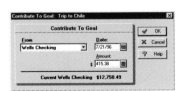

1. Choose Features | Planning | Savings Goals.
2. In the Savings Goals window, select the savings goal account, and then click the Contribute button.
3. In the Contribute to Goal dialog box, click the From down-arrow and choose the account from which you want to make the pseudo-contribution.
4. Enter the amount of the contribution in the Amount box and click OK.

**S**hort of winning the lottery, there are only three legal ways to get more money (without borrowing) when you need it. You can tighten your belt, you can squirrel it away, or you can make more. Quicken can't help you make more money, but it can help you manage the money you do have. This chapter explains how, with Quicken's help, to draw up and live within a budget, and to work toward a savings goal.

# BUDGETING WITH QUICKEN

When bills arrive in the mail with ominous red warnings on them, or when you want to start saving for a house or a South American vacation, it is time to put yourself on a budget. Going on a budget, like going on a diet, is not easy. It requires self-discipline. However, Quicken offers ways to plan realistic budgets. Just as important, the program shows you in no uncertain terms whether you have met your budget and precisely where you need to spend less or can allow yourself to spend more.

## The Big Picture: Budgeting

Budgeting with Quicken is a two-step business. First you prepare the budget by telling Quicken what you expect your income to be and how much you prefer to spend in each category or supercategory. After a few months pass, Quicken accumulates enough data to see whether you have met your budget, and you create a budget report or budget graph. The report or graph compares what you thought you would earn and spend with what you really earned and spent so you can see right away whether you stuck to your budget.

Figure 9.1 shows a budget graph. On the top, you can see that this person took in much more income than the budget allotted, since the blue "favorable" bar is quite high on the chart. However, as the pink "unfavorable" bar chart on the bottom shows, this person paid more in taxes than he or she budgeted for (couldn't help it, I guess).

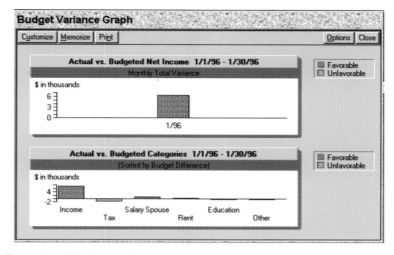

**Figure 9.1** A budget variance graph. The bar chart at the top shows whether budget goals were met; the one on the bottom compares budget projections to real spending and income.

*Before you draw up a budget, choose Reports | EasyAnswer Reports and generate a "Where did I spend my money?" report. Create an Income and Expense graph, too. They will help you formulate your budget.*

# Deciding How to Draw Up the Budget

Quicken gives you lots of choices when it comes to drawing up a budget. You can budget by month, by quarter, or by year. You can crunch the budget numbers by supercategory or by category. You can create budgets for a single category or for every category and subcategory in the Category & Transfer window. This part of the chapter lays out the choices you make when you draw up a budget.

To get going, open the Budget window shown in Figure 9.2 by choosing Features | Planning | Budget or by clicking the Planning button and choosing Budget My Spending from the menu. You will enter the numbers in the columns and rows of this window. In the figure, numbers have already been entered.

At first the Budget window looks confusing, but stare at it for awhile and you notice that the "inflows" at the top of the window are income categories. Besides entering amounts in expense categories, you estimate what your income will be in income categories. Click the down-arrow on the scroll bar along the right side of the window and you

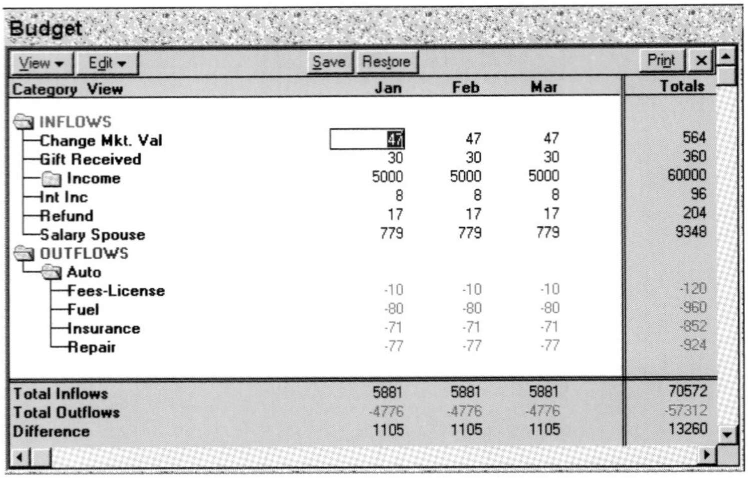

**Figure 9.2** The Budget window. Click the scroll bars to move from month to month or down the screen from income categories (inflows) to expense categories (outflows).

soon come to "outflows." "Outflow" is a fancy name for "expense category."

Besides budgeting for categories and subcategories, you can make budgeting easier by budgeting for supercategories. Figure 9.3 shows the Supercategory View of the Budget window. Here, inflows (income) and outflows (expenses) are divided into two and three supercategories, respectively.

Notice that the Budget window in Figure 9.3 is set up for budgeting on a quarterly instead of a monthly basis. This budget would be easy to prepare because you would only enter four quarterly amounts instead of twelve monthly amounts, and you would only enter a few supercategory amounts instead of dozens of category and subcategory amounts. It would be easy to prepare, but it wouldn't provide as much detail as the monthly, category-and-subcategory budget shown in Figure 9.2.

After you have entered the numbers, the Totals column on the right side of the Budget window shows how much you think you will earn in each inflow category (the numbers are positive) and how much you think you will spend in each outflow category (the numbers are

| Supercategory View | Q1 | Q2 | Q3 | Q4 | Totals |
|---|---|---|---|---|---|
| **INFLOWS** | | | | | |
| Other Income | 114 | 114 | 114 | 114 | 456 |
| Salary Income | 2337 | 2337 | 2337 | 2337 | 9348 |
| **OUTFLOWS** | | | | | |
| Discretionary | -1740 | -1740 | -1740 | -1740 | -6960 |
| Non-Discretionary | -5679 | -5679 | -5679 | -5679 | -22716 |
| Unassigned | 8283 | 8283 | 8283 | 8283 | 33132 |

**Figure 9.3** Budgeting by supercategory on a quarterly basis. Quicken gives you many options for deciding how detailed a budget you want.

negative). Meanwhile, the three rows at the bottom of the window summarize the total income and expenses in each column.

# Laying Out the Columns and Rows

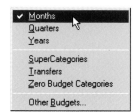

As the longwinded last few pages of this book pointed out, you have a lot of choices to make when it comes to preparing a budget. And the first decision you have to make is whether to budget monthly, quarterly, or yearly. A month-by-month budget makes you think long and hard about your spending habits and income, but it takes a long time to prepare. A yearly budget doesn't take long to prepare, but it doesn't force you to peer at yourself as closely, either.

To tell Quicken how to budget, click the View button in the Budget window and choose Months, Quarters, or Years. The number of columns in the Budget window changes accordingly.

The other strategic decision you have to make is whether to budget by category or supercategory. To make this choice, click the View button in the Budget window and click to put a check mark next to SuperCategories if you want to budget by supercategory. Remove

## tricks of the trade

*Leave room in your budget for slipups. The worst thing you can do is to set unrealistic spending goals, similar to trying to stick to a 500-calorie-per-day diet. If you are like many people I know, you may give up completely and end up spending more than you were before you started!*

*Ginger Applegarth,* The Money Diet

**habits & strategies**

*If you make a hash out of your budget, you can always click the Restore button in the Budget window to go back to the budget you had when you first opened the window or you last clicked the Save button.*

the check mark if you want to budget by category. You can save a lot of time by budgeting with supercategories. How to create them is explained in "Setting Up and Managing Supercategories" in Chapter 4.

# Entering the Numbers

Now that you have told Quicken how to lay out the budget, it's time to enter the numbers. This is the hard part. This is where you give serious consideration to how much money you take in and how much you spend. My advice is not to be ambitious. Set realistic goals for yourself (and for your family, too, if you are preparing a budget for your family). The idea is to curb your spending, not set yourself up for failure.

Enter budget numbers in the Budget window. If you don't want to include a category or supercategory in the budget, leave it alone. Quicken doesn't count supercategories and categories with zeros in them in budgets. If you don't get it right the first time, no problem. You can always go back and fool with your budget later on.

Folder icons appear beside supercategories, if you're using them to budget, and beside some categories that you're using. As you enter the numbers, click a closed folder to see the categories or subcategories inside it. Click an open folder to tuck the categories or subcategories back into their parent supercategory or category.

Quicken offers two ways to enter the budget numbers, the "from scratch" method and the automatic method. Stay tuned.

## Entering the Budget Numbers from Scratch

To enter the numbers from scratch, click in the Budget window or press the TAB key or SHIFT-TAB key combination to move from column to column, and start typing.

Don't forget to click the Save button periodically as you work on the budget. This way, you won't lose your work, and if you botch things up you can click the Restore button to get the last saved copy of your budget back. When you are done preparing your budget, click the Close button (the *X*).

| 2-Week | Click this button to budget for bimonthly paychecks. In the Set Up Two-Week budget dialog box, enter the amount you receive and the date that you will receive your next two-week paycheck. |
| --- | --- |
| Clear Row | Removes the budget amounts in the row the cursor is in so you can enter all zeros or start from scratch. |
| Clear All | Removes all amounts from the Budget window so you can start all over. |
| Autocreate | Enters data automatically from your account registers (see "Entering the Budget Numbers Automatically," the next heading in this chapter). |
| Fill Row Right | Copies the amount at the location of the cursor across the entire row to the right of the cursor. |
| Fill Columns | Copies the amounts in the column that the cursor is in to all the columns to the right of the one the cursor is in. For example, to copy the amounts from the top to the bottom of the third column to all the columns to its right, click anywhere in the third column and choose Fill Columns from the Edit menu. |
| Supercategories | Opens the Manage Supercategory dialog box so you can rearrange your supercategories (see "Putting Categories in a Supercategory" in Chapter 4). |

**habits & strategies**

*Entering the budget numbers automatically is the best way to formulate a budget. Not only are the numbers entered for you, but you can start with real data about your income and spending habits.*

Meanwhile the Edit button in the Budget window offers some handy options for entering numbers quickly:

# Entering the Budget Numbers Automatically

The fastest and maybe the best way to enter numbers in the Budget window is to have Quicken enter last year's numbers (or numbers from a previous time period) from the account registers. This way, the columns in the Budget window are filled with genuine, hard data about your income and spending. Instead of having to refer to reports to find

## habits & strategies

*To keep categories with nothing but zeros in them from crowding the Budget window, click the View button and choose the Zero Budget Categories option.*

out how much you spent or took in, the numbers are right there. All you have to do is tinker with them to formulate your budget. To go this route, however, you must have been using Quicken for a while.

To have Quicken enter data automatically from account registers in the Budget window:

1. Click the Edit button in the Budget window and choose Autocreate from the drop-down menu. You see the Automatically Create Budget dialog box shown in Figure 9.4.

2. In the From and To boxes, enter the date range for Quicken to draw data from.

3. In the Round Values to Nearest box, choose $1, $10, or $100 to tell Quicken how to round out the numbers it puts in the budget.

4. Click the Use Monthly Detail option button if you want Quicken to use real amounts from the time period you chose, or click Use Average for Period if you want Quicken to average out your spending or income and enter the same figure across all columns in the Budget window.

5. Click the Categories button to tell Quicken which categories to include in the budget. In the Select Categories to Include dialog box, yellow check marks appear beside the categories that will be included in the budget. Click the Clear All button to remove the check marks and then go down the list and click on each category that you want to

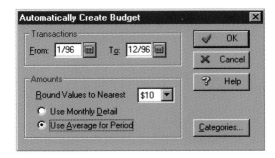

**Figure 9.4** Creating a budget automatically. Under Transactions, enter a time period to get sample data from, decide how to round the numbers, and click OK.

include in the budget to put a check mark beside it. When you are done, click OK.

Now a whole bunch of numbers appear in the Budget window. Play with them until you've formulated a budget or until the cows come home. Very likely, you have to decrease the amounts in the outflow (expense) categories. Click the Save button periodically as you work on the budget. By clicking Save, you save the budget data on-disk and you avail yourself of the opportunity to click the Restore button and get the last saved copy of your budget back if you botch things up. Click the Close button when you are done creating the budget.

## Creating a Second or Third Budget

You can create an army of different budgets, if you wish. To create another budget, get to the Budget window by choosing Features | Planning | Budget, and then click the View button and choose Other Budgets from the drop-down menu. You see the Manage Budgets dialog box. From there, click the Create button to see the Create Budget dialog box.

The name and description you enter here will appear in the Manage Budget dialog box. Under Create Budget Options, choose one of these options:

- **Autocreate Budget:** Creates the new budget with data found in the Quicken registers. When you choose this option, you see the Automatically Create Budget dialog box (see "Entering the Budget Numbers Automatically" earlier in this chapter).

- **Zero-Filled Budget:** Creates a *tabula rasa* budget.

- **Copy Current Budget:** Copies the budget that was onscreen when you chose Other Budgets on the Edit drop-down menu. Click this option to create a different version of a budget you've already created.

Click OK when you have made your choices in the Create Budget dialog box.

## OPENING A BUDGET step by step

1. To open a budget when you have created more than one, start by choosing Features | Planning | Budget.
2. In the Budget window, click the View button and choose Other Budgets from the drop-down menu.
3. In the Manage Budgets dialog box, click the budget you want to open.
4. Click the Open button.

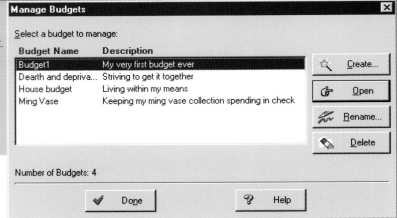

**Manage Budgets**

Select a budget to manage:

| Budget Name | Description |
| --- | --- |
| Budget1 | My very first budget ever |
| Dearth and depriva... | Striving to get it together |
| House budget | Living within my means |
| Ming Vase | Keeping my ming vase collection spending in check |

Create...
Open
Rename...
Delete

Number of Budgets: 4

Done    Help

## habits & strategies

*You can customize charts and graphs so they report only on specific categories or supercategories. See Chapter 7.*

# Seeing Whether You Met Your Budget

Now comes the moment of truth. You created a budget and have been doing your best to live with it for several months. Now it is time to find out how much self-discipline you have by creating a budget report and budget graph.

To create a budget report, start by opening the budget you want to see a report on, if you've created more than one budget. Then choose Reports | Easy Answer Reports. In the Easy Answer Reports & Graphs dialog box, click the seventh question on the list, "Did I meet my budget?" In the Details part of the dialog box, choose a time period from the list, and then click the Show Report button. You see a report similar to the one in Figure 9.5.

Where red numbers appear in the Diff column, you failed to meet your budget in a category or supercategory. Look down the Diff column, and when you see a red number, ask yourself, "How can I keep from spending more in that category?" Or, if you are staring at an income category, ask yourself, "Why didn't I earn enough money there?"

TEST2-All Accounts                                              8/23/96

# Budget Report
### 1/1/95 Through 12/31/95

| Category Description | 1/1/95 - 12/31/95 Actual | Budget | Diff |
|---|---|---|---|
| Dues | 23.40 | 24.00 | 0.60 |
| Entertainment | 500.04 | 504.00 | 3.96 |
| Fees | 196.55 | 192.00 | - 4.55 |
| Finance Charges | 24.70 | 24.00 | - 0.70 |
| Groceries | 5,051.55 | 5,112.00 | 60.45 |
| Hair | 105.50 | 36.00 | - 69.50 |
| Home Repair | 965.53 | 960.00 | - 5.53 |
| Housecleaning | 50.00 | 48.00 | - 2.00 |
| Insurance: | | | |
| Health | 1,872.00 | 1,872.00 | 0.00 |
| | | | |
| TOTAL Insurance | 1,872.00 | 1,872.00 | 0.00 |

**Figure 9.5** A budget report. Red numbers in the Diff column show where you failed to meet your budget.

Maybe the best way to see if you stuck to your budget is to create a graph. To do that, choose Reports | Easy Answer Reports and click the "Did I meet my budget?" question. In the Details part of the dialog box, choose a time period from the list, but this time click the Show Graph button.

Quicken creates a Budget Variance graph similar to the one in Figure 9.6. The bar chart at the top tells you how your actual and budgeted income compare. The one at the bottom tells you how your actual spending and budgeted spending compare. In the top chart, you

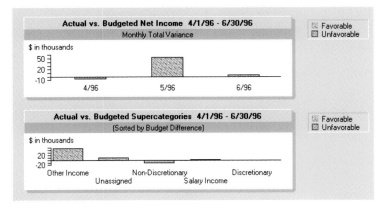

**Figure 9.6** A budget variance graph. A "variance" is the difference between budgeted amounts and real-life amounts.

*You can see the budget window*

*from which the data on the*

*progress bar was drawn. To do*

*so, move the pointer over the*

*progress bar. When the pointer*

*changes into a magnifying glass,*

*double-click to open the budget*

*window.*

know you received less income than you calculated if you see red bars dipping below the zero line. On the bottom chart, red bars tell where you went over budget and by what amount.

# Monitoring Budgets with the Progress Bar

Yet another way to find out how good a budgeter you are is to put the progress bar on the bottom of the Quicken screen and tell it to show how you are faring in one or two categories or supercategories. The progress bar appears along the bottom of the window, right above the Windows 95 taskbar.

The one here shows spending in two categories, Clothing and Leisure. The amount inside the gauge is how much was actually spent and the amount to the right of the gauge is how much the budget allowed for. This clotheshorse is about to overspend in the Clothing category and has gone way into the red in the Leisure category, where the budget called for $22 in expenses and this hedonist has spent $110. How could such a thing happen?

To see the progress bar, choose Features | Planning | Progress Bars. Then, to tell Quicken which categories to monitor, click the Cust button on the right side of the progress bar. You see the Customize Progress Bar dialog box shown in Figure 9.7. Under Left Gauge Type,

**Figure 9.7** The Customize Progress Bar dialog box, where you tell Quicken which categories or supercategories to put on the progress bar.

click the down-arrow and choose either Budget Goal or Supercategory Budget, depending on whether you want to monitor a budget category or budget supercategory. Next, click either the Choose Category or Choose Supercategory button.

In the Choose Category or Supercategory dialog box, click on the category or supercategory whose budgeting data you want to see. Then click OK to get back to the Customize Progress Bar dialog box, where, under Right Gauge Type, you can choose another category or super-category to monitor on the progress bar. Click OK when you are done.

The progress bar stays onscreen until you click the Close button on its left side to get rid of it. To see it again, choose Features | Planning | Progress Bars.

# SAVING TOWARD A FINANCIAL GOAL

To help you squirrel away money for trips, presents, and other enticing objectives, Quicken offers a feature called a "savings goal account." A savings goal account is a sort of ghost bank account. You transfer money into it, but not really. When you transfer money from a checking account to a savings goal account, the checking account balance shows a decrease even though no money has really left the checking account. Meanwhile, the savings goal account shows an increase, even though no real money has been passed between the real account and the ghostly savings goal account.

The idea is to keep you from getting your hands on the money you want to save. It is hidden in the savings goal account. In the checking account, you think you have less money than you really do, so you learn to live with less money.

However, if not knowing how much money is really in a bank account scares you, you don't have to handle the savings goal account

by artificially lowering the balance in the bank account. You can also
monitor a savings goal account with the progress bar along the bottom
of the screen or with the Savings Goal screen.

# Starting a Savings Goal Account

To start a savings goal account, choose Features | Planning |
Savings Goals or click the Planning button and choose Save for an
Upcoming Expense on the menu. You soon see the Savings Goals
window. From there, click the New button to get to the Create New
Savings Goal dialog box.

In the Goal Name box, enter a descriptive name for the goal. Enter
the amount you want to save with the help of the savings goal account
in the Goal Amount box. In the Finish Date box, Quicken has entered
the day a year hence. Change that date to the one by which you want
to have saved the money.

Click OK. Back in the Savings Goals window, you see the name
of your goal and the other information you entered, as in Figure 9.8.
Notice the "projected monthly contribution" that Quicken says you
need to set aside each month. If yours is a new savings goal, you don't
see a graph like the one in the figure.

# Setting the Money Aside

To set the money aside, you make a "contribution" to the savings
goal account. To do that, open the Savings Goals window by choosing
Features | Planning | Savings Goals. Then select the goal to which you

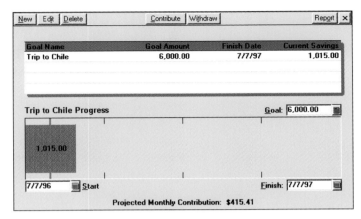

**Figure 9.8** The Savings Goals window. The bright green graph in the middle of the window shows how close or how far away you are from achieving your goal.

want to make the contribution, if necessary, and click the Contribute button. You see the Contribute to Goal dialog box:

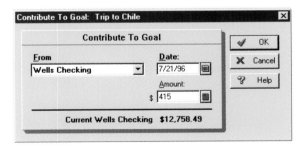

Click the From down-arrow and choose the account from which you want to make the pseudo-contribution. Then change the date if you want to and enter the amount of the contribution in the Amount box. When you are done filling out the dialog box, click OK.

# Seeing How Close You Are to Attaining Your Goal

In the Savings Goals window, a bright green graph in the middle tells you how close you are to realizing your savings goal.

Contribution towards goal
[Trip to Chile]

To see how the "shadow transfer" of money affects the account from which you made the transfer, try opening the account. Under Payee, it says "Contribution towards goal." In brackets in the Category box, you see the name of the savings goal account in brackets.

Meanwhile, the balance in the account that "contributed" to the savings goal is decreased by the amount of the contribution. However, to see how much money is really in the account, open its register, click the View button, and choose Hide Savings Goal. The balance in the accounts increases. Glance at the ending balance figure in the lower-right corner if you don't believe me.

If you get especially nervous about how much money is really in your account, you can always click the Withdraw button in the Savings Goals window and transfer the money back where it came from.

# The Progress Bar for Monitoring Savings Goals

Besides looking in the Savings Goals window, you can also see how close you are to attaining a goal by opening the savings goal account or looking on the progress bar. Savings goal deposits and withdrawals are recorded like those in normal accounts. Click an account tab or open the savings goal account from the Account List to see how close you are to achieving your goal.

Earlier in this chapter, I explained how to use the progress bar to monitor budgets (see "Monitoring Budgets with the Progress Bar"). To put a gauge that shows how close or far you are from reaching a savings goal on the progress bar, choose Features | Planning | Progress Bars to see the progress bar, if necessary, and then click the Cust button. In the Customize Progress Bar dialog box (see Figure 9.7), click the down-arrow beside Left Gauge Type or Right Gauge Type and choose Savings Goal, the first item on the drop-down menu. Then click OK. You see a savings goal on the progress bar similar to this one:

Click the Close button when you tire of looking at the progress bar.

## FULL SPEED AHEAD!

So ends the exciting chapter about budgeting and saving money. In the next installment, which starts very shortly, you will find out how to track loans, liabilities, and assets with Quicken.

# CHAPTER 10

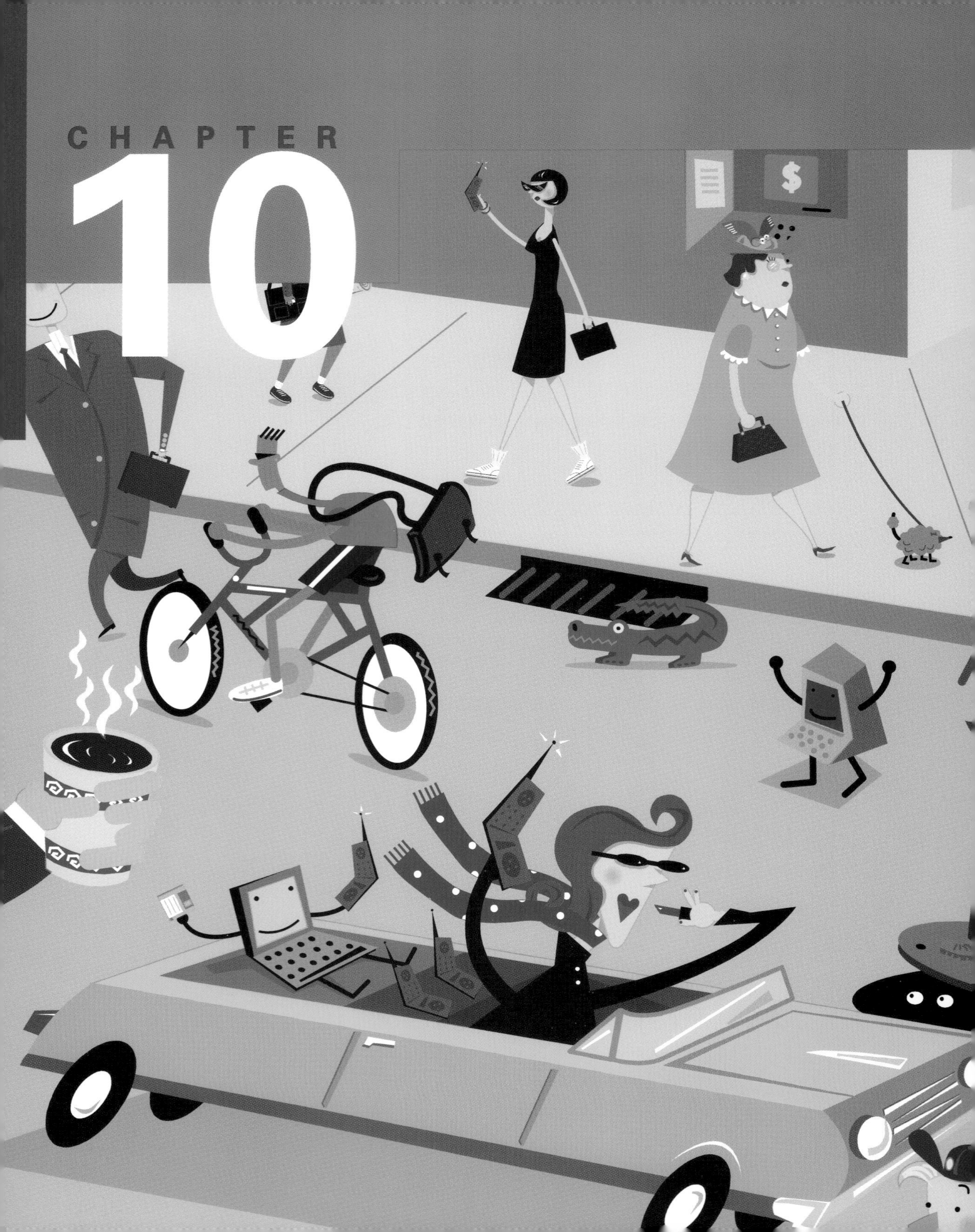

# Keeping Track of Loans, Liabilities, and Assets

# FAST FORWARD

## SET UP A LIABILITY ACCOUNT FOR TRACKING AN AMORTIZED LOAN ➤ *pp. 185-189*

1. Choose Features | Paying Bills | Loans (or press CTRL-H) to see the View Loans dialog box.
2. Click the New button to get to the EasyStep tab.
3. Answer the questions in the dialog box, clicking Next as you go. You are asked to name the account, for loan information, when payments are due,and what the loan's interest rate is.
4. When you get to the Summary tab, review your entries and click Next on each tab.
5. Click Done. You see the Set Up Loan Payment dialog box.
6. Choose Payment or Print Check in the Type box.
7. Click the Pmt Method button and fill out the Select Payment Method dialog box if you want to schedule loan payments.
8. Enter the lender's name in the Payee box.
9. Click the down-arrow in the Category for Interest box and choose an expense category for recording the interest portion of the loan payments.
10. Click OK to get back to the View Loans window, where all information about your amortized loan is recorded.
11. Click the Payment Schedule tab to get a look at when payments are due and what portion of each payment goes toward the interest and the principal.
12. Click the Payment Graph tab to see how the balance of the loan is affected when you make future payments.
13. Click the Close button.

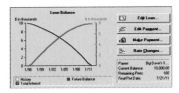

## RECORD A LOAN PAYMENT ➤ *pp. 189-191*

1. Choose Features | Paying Bills | Loans (or press CTRL-H) to get to the View Loans window.
2. Click the Choose Loan button and choose the loan to make a payment on, if necessary.
3. Click the Make Payment button to see the Loan Payment dialog box.
4. Click the Regular button to see the Make Regular Payment dialog box.

5. Enter the date the payment will be made.
6. From the Account to use drop-down menu, choose the account that the payment will be made against.
7. Click OK.

## RECORD AN EXTRA, UNEXPECTED PAYMENT ON A LOAN ➤ p. 191

1. Choose Features | Paying Bills | Loans (or press CTRL-H).
2. In the View Loans window, click the Make Payment button, and then click the Extra button in the Loan Payment dialog box.
3. In the Make Extra Payment dialog box, enter the amount of the extra payment in the Amount box. The amount you enter is applied directly to the principal.
4. Click OK.

## SET UP A LIABILITY ACCOUNT TO TRACK YOUR DEBT ➤ pp. 195-196

Liability accounts are similar to the other Quicken accounts, except payments made toward reducing the debt are recorded in the Decrease column, and increases in debt are recorded in the Increase column.

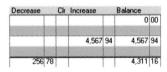

## TRACK THE THINGS OF VALUE THAT YOU OWN IN AN ASSET ACCOUNT ➤ pp. 196-197

Assets include IRAs, real estate, and even personal items like jewelry. Set up an asset account and categorize asset transactions as you would if you were working in another kind of Quicken account register. Record increases in the asset's value in the Increase column, and decreases in the Decrease column of the register.

This chapter delves into a subject that most people know more about than they care to know: paying off loans. It tells how to track how much of a loan payment goes toward paying the interest and how much goes toward reducing the principal. This chapter also explains how to keep track of liabilities and assets with Quicken.

## WHAT ARE LIABILITIES AND ASSETS?

A *liability* is simply a debt that you owe. Liabilities count against net worth. When Quicken lists net worth in the Account List window, for example, it subtracts liabilities from the money in savings and checking accounts. Credit card debt is an example of a liability. So is tax owed to the IRS. So is a mortgage, a car loan, and a student loan.

An *asset* is something of value that you own—stock, a house, jewelry, an IRA, a baseball card autographed by the great Willie Mays. Money that is owed you is an asset. The money in checking and savings accounts is considered an asset as well. Assets add to net worth. Create asset accounts in Quicken to get a better picture of what you are worth, not as a human being of course, but as a financial entity.

## THE BIG PICTURE: LOANS AND LIABILITIES

Although all loans are liabilities, since they count against net worth, Quicken makes a distinction between amortized loans and no-interest debt when it comes to setting up a liability account. If you are tracking an amortized loan, choose the Features | Paying Bills command, but if you are tracking no-interest debt or if you don't care to keep track of how much of your debt payment goes toward interest and how much goes toward reducing the principal, set up a liability account.

Either way, you end up with a liability account register for tracking how much you owe and how much you have paid on the debt.

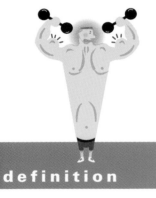

**definition**

*Amortized loan: A loan for which you make regular payments of equal size. With each payment, some money goes toward paying interest on the loan and some goes toward reducing the principal (the amount you borrowed).*

# TRACKING AN AMORTIZED LOAN

Setting up a liability account for tracking an amortized loan takes a while and can get pretty complicated, so before reading how to do it you ought to consider whether doing it is even necessary. It probably isn't necessary. As long as the lender tells you how much you owe after each payment and how much you are paying in interest, you really don't need to track the loan. You can simply get the numbers from the lender.

In the case of mortgages, business loans, and investment loans, the lender should send you a 1098 tax form at the end of the year that explains how much of your payments went toward interest. That is the amount you need to know, because the amount you paid to service interest on the loan is tax-deductible. As long as the lender tells you how much you can deduct from your income taxes in interest payments, you don't need to track the amortized loan yourself. Instead, create a liability account, and as the principal decreases, record it in the liability account's register.

If you do decide to track amortized loans, the loan payments are "split" in the Categories box:

*"Calculating the Price of a Loan or Mortgage" in Chapter 12 tells how to determine how much you can borrow and what the payments on a loan will be.*

- The portion of the payment that goes toward interest is recorded as an interest expense.

- The portion of the payment that goes toward reducing the principal of the loan is recorded as a money transfer to the liability account. That seems weird, but look at it this way: a liability account is just a normal account with a negative balance (negative because it represents money you owe). When you transfer money to the liability account, the money (a positive number) is added to the balance of the liability account, thereby reducing the amount of money that you owe. After a number of positive money transfers to your negative liability account, you finally reach 0 and pay off the debt.

## Setting Up the Loan Account

The first step in tracking an amortized loan is to set up the loan liability account. When you are done setting up the account, Quicken will have created a schedule for paying off the loan. The program will also have created a memorized transaction for the loan payment.

To set up a liability account for an amortized loan, press CTRL-H, choose Features | Paying Bills | Loans, or click the Home & Car button and choose Set Up or Track an Existing Loan. You see the View Loans dialog box shown in Figure 10.1. When you see it first, the dialog box is grayed out, but when you are done setting up the account, the View Loans window will look like the one Figure 10.1.

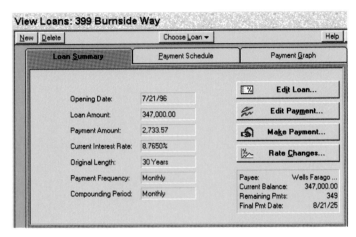

**Figure 10.1** When you finish setting up the loan account, the View Loans window looks like this.

For now, click the New button to get to the Loan Setup dialog box. This dialog box probably looks familiar because it is similar to all account setup dialog boxes. (Notice the car entering the driveway. If you look closely, you will see Homer Simpson running for his life to get away from the car.) Click the Next button to get to the EasyStep tab. From here out, you fill in the screens and click Next as you complete each one. The following list describes the questions you have to answer to set up the account. You might look at this list now and gather the necessary paperwork before filling in the Loan Setup dialog box and clicking Next as you go along.

- **What type of loan is this?** Make sure the Borrow Money option button is selected.

## CAUTION

*If you've made payments on the loan already, be sure to enter the original balance and not how much you owe. Quicken needs the original balance to make the payment schedule of the loan.*

*See "What to Do about Escrow Accounts" later in this chapter to learn how to handle payments that are kept in escrow.*

- **Choose a Quicken account.** Enter a descriptive name for the account you will use to track this loan.
- **Have any payments been made?** Click Yes or No.
- **Enter the initial loan information.** Enter the date the loan was created and the original balance of the loan. In other words, enter the amount of the loan.
- **Does this loan include a balloon payment?** Click Yes or No.
- **Enter the original length of the loan.** Enter a number and the length of the loan in years, months, or weeks. For a 30-year mortgage, you would type **30** and choose Years from the menu, for example.
- **Enter the payment period.** Tell Quicken how often you will make payments. Either click the down arrow and choose a time period or click the Other Period option button and enter the number of payment periods per year in the Payments per Year box.
- **Enter the compounding period.** Interest is compounded monthly or semi-annually. Check the paperwork that came with your loan and choose an option.
- **Do you know the current balance?** Click Yes or No.
- **Enter the current balance information.** If you answered "Yes" to the previous question, enter the most recent date for which you know the balance. If this is a new loan, the current balance is the same as the loan amount, but if you've made payments, the balance is something less than the original loan. Enter an amount here if you know what the balance is, but if you don't know it, Quicken can calculate the balance for you.
- **Enter the date of the next payment.** Enter the date when the next payment is due.
- **Do you know the amount of the next payment?** Click Yes or No.
- **Enter the amount of principal and interest in the next payment.** This confusing request simply means to enter the amount of the next payment.

- **Enter the interest rate for this loan.** Enter the interest rate that you are being charged for taking out this loan. If the loan you are setting up is an adjustable-rate loan, enter the current rate of interest.
- **Summary tab.** Take a look at the information you entered to make sure everything was entered correctly.

When you click the Done button, you see the Set Up Loan Payment dialog box shown in Figure 10.2. In this dialog box, you get one last chance to change the specifics of your loan. You also tell Quicken how to make payments and who is to be paid. Everything under Transaction in this dialog box gets "memorized."

After you've perused the Payment area to make sure it is correct, choose Payment or Print Check in the Type box to say how you intend to pay the loan installments. Then, if you want to schedule loan payments or online repeating payments, click the Pmt Method button and fill out the Select Payment Method dialog box.

In the Payee box, enter the lender's name. If you want, enter a few words that describe the loan in the Memo box. Finally, click the down-arrow in the Category for Interest box and choose an expense category for recording the interest portion of the loan payments you will make (probably Int Exp or Mort Int). Last but not least, click OK.

Back in the View Loans window (see Figure 10.1), you can see everything you need to know about your loan in its naked glory. The

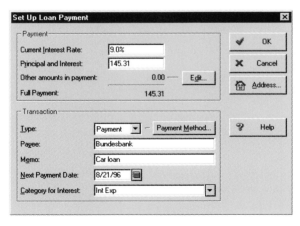

**Figure 10.2** The Set Up Loan Payment dialog box. Quicken "memorizes" the information in the Transaction part of this dialog box.

lower-right corner of the dialog box sums up what is owed, how many payments remain, and when the last payment is to be made.

Click the Payment Schedule tab to get a look at when payments are due and what portion of each payment goes toward interest and what portion goes toward reducing the principal of the loan.

Click the Payment Graph tab to see how the balance of the loan will decrease as you make future payments. That green line on the graph, by the way, shows what your total interest payments are on the loan. If you had saved and bought the thing without having to take out a loan, you would have been able to devote all the money on the green, right side of the graph to your pleasure or your principles instead of to a lender. As shown in Figure 10.3, it costs a little over $600,000 in interest payments to service a $350,000 loan. Over 30 years, the total payments will be about $950,000.

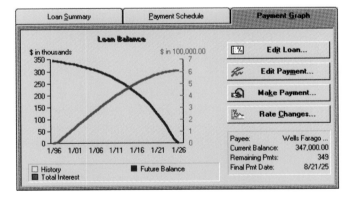

**Figure 10.3** The Payment Graph shows how the principal is reduced with each payment and how much is spent in interest payments over the life of the loan.

## Making a Loan Payment

When you are ready to make a payment on an amortized loan, press CTRL-H, choose Features | Paying Bills | Loans, or click the Home & Car button and choose Set Up or Track an Existing Loan. In the View Loans window (see Figure 10.1), click the Choose Loan button at the top of the window and choose the loan for which you want to make a payment, if necessary. Then click the Make Payment button. In the Loan

Payment dialog box, click the Regular button. You see the Make Regular Payment dialog box:

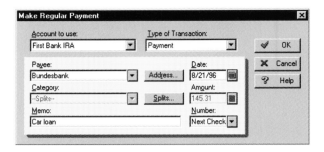

Enter a date. From the Account drop-down menu, choose the account that the payment will be made against. In the Number box, tell Quicken how the payment will be made. The rest of the boxes should be filled in correctly, since this is information you gave Quicken when you set up the loan account, but go ahead and make new choices if you wish.

When you click the OK button (wait a second before you do it), the amount that goes toward paying the principal of the loan will be recorded as a money transfer to the loan liability account you set up. The amount that goes toward the interest will be recorded as an interest expense. To see how this works, click the Splits button in the Make Regular Payment dialog box. You see a Splits window similar to this one:

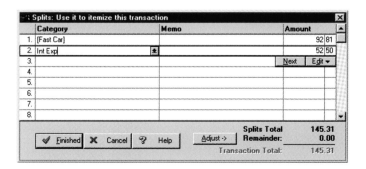

When the $92.81 shown here is transferred to the liability account, it will reduce the amount of the debt by $92.81. Meanwhile, the

$52.50 will be recorded in the Int Exp (Interest Expense) category. If you wanted to adjust the principal and interest amounts of this payment, you could do so from the Splits window.

Click Finished in the Splits window to get back to the Make Regular Payment dialog box, and then click OK.

To see how loan payments are recorded, open the liability account register for the loan you are tracking. You will see that the total amount you owe has been reduced by the portion of your payment that went toward reducing the principal:

| Date | Ref | Payee / Memo / Category | | Increase | | Clr | Decrease | | Balance | |
|------|-----|-------------------------|---|----------|---|-----|----------|---|---------|---|
| 7/21/96 | | Opening Balance | | 7,000 | 00 | | | | 7,000 | 00 |
| | | | [Fast Car] | | | | | | | |
| 8/21/96 | | Bundesbank | | | | | 92 | 81 | 6,907 | 19 |
| | | Car loan | [Wells Checking] | | | | | | | |

# Changing the Particulars of a Loan

When you need to change the particulars of a loan—the lender's name, the compounding period, or whatnot—press CTRL-H or choose Features | Paying Bills | Loans to get to the View Loans window (see Figure 10.1), and then click the Edit Loan button. That takes you to the Edit Loan dialog box, where you can make changes to your heart's content. When you're finished doing that, click Done.

# Paying Early and Often

It goes without saying, but the faster you pay off an amortized loan, the less you have to pay altogether, because much of the cost of an amortized loan goes toward interest payments.

To record a payment you've made above and beyond what the lender expects of you, press CTRL-H or choose Features | Paying Bills | Loans to get to the View Loans window (see Figure 10.1). From there, click the Make Payment button, and then click the Extra button in the Loan Payment dialog box. You see the Make Extra Payment dialog box.

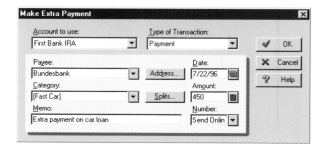

Fill in this box as you normally would, and enter the amount of the extra payment in the Amount box. Notice that the Category box doesn't say "Splits" as it usually does. It lists the name of the liability account, because the entire amount of the extra payment counts toward reducing the principal of the loan. When you pay extra, you help pay back the loan; you don't pay the lender for being generous. Click OK when you've filled in the dialog box.

# What to Do about Mortgage Escrow Accounts

An escrow account is a big drag to begin with, and tracking one with Quicken only adds to the misery. You can track an escrow account either by categorizing the portion of your loan payment that goes into the escrow account in a different way, or by setting up an asset account and transferring the escrow portion of the loan payment to the asset account.

With the categorizing method, you create subcategories for the escrow account that the mortgage company keeps for you. For example, if the mortgage company sets aside $100 of your monthly payment for homeowner's insurance and $100 for property taxes, create subcategories called Escrow:Home Ins and Escrow:Prop Tax. When you record a payment, apportion $100 to each subcategory. This way, you can track how much the mortgage company has set aside for you in escrow accounts.

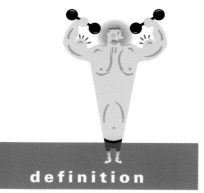

**definition**

***Escrow account:*** *An account that a mortgage company takes out on behalf of a borrower to make sure that property taxes and property insurance get paid.*

With the asset account method, you create an asset account to track the escrow account that the mortgage company keeps for you. ("Keeping Track of Assets" at the end of this chapter explains how.) Under this approach, the asset account mirrors the escrow account. Each time you make a loan payment, you transfer the portion of the payment that goes toward the escrow account to the asset account. This way, the asset account always tells you how much the mortgage company has set aside. When the mortgage company informs you that it has paid your property taxes, for example, you record a decrease in the asset account and categorize it as Tax: Property. When your homeowner's insurance is paid, you record it as a decrease and categorize it as Insurance: Home (or some such category).

Whichever method you choose to track an escrow account, you need to tell Quicken how to split the loan payment so that the escrow portion is recorded. After you have created the asset account or subcategories, go to the Edit Loan Payment dialog box. To get there, press CTRL-H or choose Features | Paying Bills | Loans, click the Choose Loan button at the top of the dialog box, choose the loan whose payments you need to split, and then click the Edit Payment button.

The Edit Loan Payment dialog box is where you change the details of a loan. It looks and works just like the Set Up Loan Payment dialog box (see Figure 10.2). To split a loan differently, click the Edit button. You see a Splits window. Enter the amount of the payment to be transferred to the asset account, or if you are using the category approach, enter the amounts to be categorized in different ways. In the Category column, choose expense subcategories from the list or go to the bottom of the list and choose the asset account the money will be transferred to. Then click Finished in the Splits dialog box and click OK in the Edit Loan Payment dialog box.

As you know if you read the past several pages, a loan payment is split between the portion that goes toward interest and the portion that goes toward reducing the principal. If you are tracking escrow accounts, the payment is split even further, with a portion going to an asset account or to subcategories as well as to interest and principal payments.

# Handling Adjustable-Rate Loans

If you have taken out a variable-interest loan and the interest rate has changed, you need to tell Quicken what the new interest rate is and have the program adjust your payments accordingly. To do that, press CTRL-H or choose Features | Paying Bills | Loans and click the Rate Changes button in the View Loans window. You see the Loan Rate Changes dialog box. Select the loan whose rate of interest needs changing and click the New or Edit button. The Insert an Interest Rate Change or the Edit Interest Rate Change dialog box appears:

These dialog boxes are for changing the interest rate and for having Quicken calculate what the new payment will be. The numbers you enter here mean nothing to the amounts already recorded in your registers—those numbers will not change. You do not need to enter anything in the Regular Payment box, because Quicken calculates what your new regular payment will be based on the new interest rate you enter. However, if you enter a regular payment amount, Quicken changes the length of the loan to accommodate the new payment schedule.

In the Effective Date box, enter the date when the rate change takes effect. In the Interest Rate box, enter the new interest rate. Enter an amount in the Regular Payment box if the payment amount has changed. Then click OK.

Back in the Loan Rate Changes dialog box, double-check the figures you entered, and then click the Close button. The View Loans window shows you the whole shebang once again, and you can click Close there as well.

## Paying Off a Loan

Once you've paid off a loan, and the amount in the Balance column of the liability account diminishes and changes from a red number to a black 0, congratulate yourself. Then choose Features | Paying Bills | Loans or press CTRL-H, click the Choose Loan button, choose the loan you have paid off, and click the Delete button.

Quicken asks if you want to hang onto the account records even though you are deleting the amortized loan. Click Yes if you want the loan data to appear on Quicken's reports and graphs. Click No if you would like to expunge all knowledge about the loan you've paid off. If the loan was a mortgage or student loan whose interest payments are tax-deductible, you most certainly want to click Yes. You will need the data at tax time.

## TRACKING A LIABILITY

A liability account tracks money you owe. A credit card account, for example, is a liability account, because it tracks the negative balance of what you owe the credit card issuer. Open a liability account in Quicken to track loans for which you pay no interest (or loans you do pay interest on but for which you don't care to track the interest and principal), income taxes, or anything else that counts against your net worth.

Figure 10.4 shows a liability account register. One glance at this figure tells you that a liability account is exactly like the other accounts in Quicken. It has places for entering dates, categories, and amounts. The only difference is that Increase and Decrease columns appear where Payment and Deposit columns might usually be. When something adds to your debt, enter it in the Increase column. When you pay off part of your debt, record the payment in the Decrease column. The Balance column (always negative, always red) tells your total debt.

To set up a liability account, click the Accts button on the iconbar, click the New button in the Account List, and click the Liability

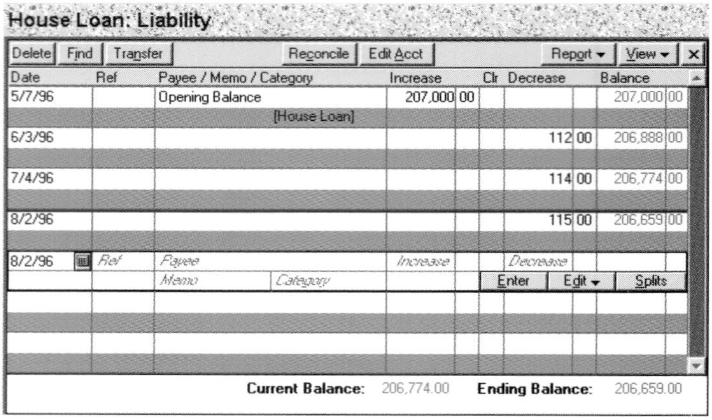

**Figure 10.4** A liability account for tracking a debt. By tracking liabilities, you know your net worth and can plan your spending better.

button. Then click Next and follow the steps in the Liability Account Setup dialog box.

# KEEPING TRACK OF ASSETS

Set up an asset account in Quicken to track things of value that contribute to your net worth: jewelry, an IRA account, a collection of nineteenth-century Shaker furniture, a Ming vase, an apartment building. In Figure 10.5, an author has set up an asset account to keep track of future royalty payments. The author is owed this money, so by tracking it in an asset account, the author can figure it into spending and budgeting plans.

To set up an asset account, click the Accts button on the iconbar, click the New button in the Account List, and click the Assets button. In the Asset Account Setup dialog box, answer the questions and click Finish or Done when you are done.

When the asset increases in value, enter the amount it has increased by in the Increase column. When it decreases in value, enter a number in the Decrease column.

When you pay for an item and record it in the checking register, rather than categorize it, you might record the expense as a transfer to

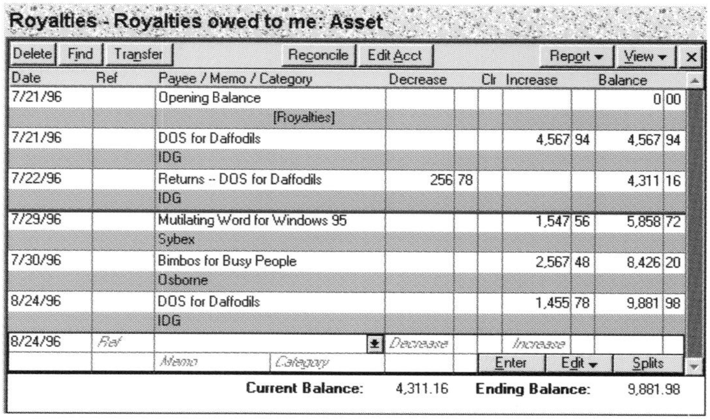

| Date | Ref | Payee / Memo / Category | Decrease | Clr | Increase | Balance | |
|------|-----|-------------------------|----------|-----|----------|---------|---|
| 7/21/96 | | Opening Balance | | | | 0 | 00 |
| | | [Royalties] | | | | | |
| 7/21/96 | | DOS for Daffodils | | | 4,567 94 | 4,567 | 94 |
| | | IDG | | | | | |
| 7/22/96 | | Returns -- DOS for Daffodils | 256 78 | | | 4,311 | 16 |
| | | IDG | | | | | |
| 7/29/96 | | Mutilating Word for Windows 95 | | | 1,547 56 | 5,858 | 72 |
| | | Sybex | | | | | |
| 7/30/96 | | Bimbos for Busy People | | | 2,567 48 | 8,426 | 20 |
| | | Osborne | | | | | |
| 8/24/96 | | DOS for Daffodils | | | 1,455 78 | 9,881 | 98 |
| | | IDG | | | | | |
| 8/24/96 | Ref | | Decrease | | Increase | | |
| | | Memo | Category | | Enter | Edit ▾ | Splits |

Royalties - Royalties owed to me: Asset

Delete | Find | Transfer | Reconcile | Edit Acct | Report ▾ | View ▾ | ×

**Current Balance:** 4,311.16    **Ending Balance:** 9,881.98

**Figure 10.5** An asset account register. Set up asset accounts to track things of value that contribute to your net worth.

an asset account. To see how this works, suppose you have an asset account to track the value of a house and you pay $2000 for a new deck for the house. Rather than categorize the expense, you could record it as a transfer to the asset account. In theory, anyway, the house is worth $2000 more with a new deck.

# ROCK ON!

Thus, and not a moment too soon, we bid adieu to the subject of loans, liabilities, and assets. I hope you have more assets than you have liabilities, but if that isn't the case, turn to the next chapter, which discusses how to plan ahead for a rosy, comfortable future.

# Planning Ahead
# with Quicken

# FAST FORWARD

## FIND OUT HOW MUCH YOU NEED TO SAVE ANNUALLY TO REACH A RETIREMENT INCOME ➤ *pp. 202-207*

1. Choose Features | Planning | Financial Planners | Retirement.
2. In the Retirement Planner dialog box, click the Annual Contribution option button under Calculate For.
3. Fill in the boxes under Retirement Information. These boxes ask for your current savings and how much income by percentage you expect them to generate, how old you are now and when you expect to retire, how long you expect to live on your retirement savings, and what you want your income in the retirement years to be.
4. In the Tax Information part of the dialog box, say whether your investments for retirement are tax-deferred or not.
5. In the Inflation area, tell Quicken what you expect the inflation rate to be in the future, and whether you want the calculations Quicken makes to appear in today's dollars, and whether you want to increase your contributions to account for inflation.
6. Click the Calculate button.
7. Look next to Annual Contribution in the dialog box—it tells how much you need to set aside each year. You can click the Schedule button to get a schedule of when and how much you need to contribute each year toward retirement.

## FIND OUT HOW MUCH TO SAVE FOR A CHILD'S COLLEGE EDUCATION ➤ *pp. 207-209*

1. Choose Features | Planning | Financial Planners | College.
2. In the College Planner dialog box, click one of the Calculate For buttons: Annual College Costs to figure out how expensive a college education you can afford, Current College Savings to see how much you need to have saved to reach a savings goal, or Annual Contribution to see how much you need to contribute each year.

3. Under College Information, tell Quicken what you expect college to cost, information about your child's age, how much you've saved, and how much you can save annually for college.
4. Under Inflation, say what you expect the inflation rate will be and whether you want to make larger contributions as the years go by.
5. Click the Calculate button.

## ESTIMATE HOW MUCH IN TAXES YOU WILL OWE ➤ *pp. 209-211*

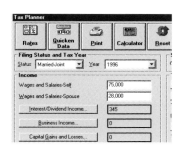

1. Choose Features I Taxes I Tax Planner to see the Tax Planner screen.
2. Click the down-arrow in the Status box and choose a filing status option.
3. Click the down-arrow in the Year box and choose the year for which you want a tax estimate. (If the year is not 1996, you may also have to click the Rates button, fill in the correct rates in the Tax Rates for Filing Status dialog box, and click OK.)
4. Fill in the boxes in the Tax Planner dialog box. To do that, either enter the numbers yourself or click the buttons to get to dialog boxes that help you calculate the numbers. You can also import the data from Quicken registers by clicking the Quicken Data button.
5. Look at the Remaining Tax Due box in the lower-right corner. It says what your estimated tax bill is.

## FIND HIDDEN TAX DEDUCTIONS ➤ *pp. 213-215*

1. Choose Features I Taxes I Tax Deductions to see the Deduction Finder window.
2. Choose a deduction type by clicking the down-arrow in box 1 and choosing an option.
3. In box 2, click a deduction you might be eligible for.
4. Click Y (Yes) or N (No) to answer the questions in box 3.
5. Click another deduction option in part 2 and answer its questions.
6. When you are done answering questions, Click the Action Plan tab. Quicken shows you different spending areas where you can take tax deductions.

This short chapter takes on something that is either dreadful or wonderful, depending on your point of view. It takes on the future. If you are a pessimist, this chapter shows how to avoid financial ruin in old age. It shows how to give your children the overpriced college education that everyone thinks is a necessity these days. It shows how to forecast what your taxes will be so you don't get hit hard in April.

If you are an optimist, on the other hand, this chapter shows how to plan for a glorious old age and how to give your children the college education that the little darlings so richly deserve. It shows how to make your tax bill smaller so you can enjoy the bright promise of springtime.

# PLANNING FOR YOUR RETIREMENT

Everyone has heard dire warnings about the imminent demise of the social security system. That being the case, setting aside money now for retirement is wise indeed. Moreover, with IRA and Keogh plans, the federal government has made saving for retirement very enticing, since money placed in IRAs and Keoghs is not subject to taxes. You can save *a lot* in income taxes by saving for retirement.

Quicken offers two ways to devise a savings plan for retirement. You can target how much income you need in your retirement years and calculate how much you need to save annually to reach the retirement income you want. Or you can punch in the numbers you are saving at present for retirement and see what kind of income your present savings will produce in old age.

## Aiming for a Retirement Income

To figure out how much you should save to reach a certain retirement income, you tell Quicken what you want your retirement income to be. Then Quicken asks a few personal questions about your age and how long you expect to live. When all the numbers are in, you find out how much to save each year.

Start by choosing Features | Planning | Financial Planners | Retirement. You see the Retirement Planner dialog box shown in Figure 11.1. This is where you give Quicken the information it needs to help you plan for retirement. When you are done filling in this dialog box, you will click the Calculate button, and Quicken will show you how much you need to contribute each year.

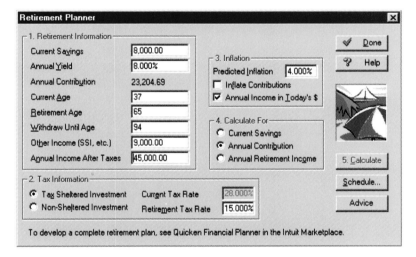

**Figure 11.1** The Retirement Planner dialog box, where Quicken figures out how much you need to save and how much income your present savings produce for retirement

Since you want to calculate how much to put away each year for retirement, click the Annual Contribution option button under Calculate For.

Next, fill in the boxes under Retirement Information:

- **Current Savings:** How much you have saved so far.

- **Annual Yield:** How much income, by percentage, you expect your investments to produce. As a yardstick, the stock market's average return in the past seventy years has been 10 percent, long-term corporate bonds have yielded 5 percent over the same time, and U.S. Treasury Bills have yielded 3.5 percent.

- **Annual Contribution:** You are trying to find out how much to contribute, so this box says CALCULATED. But if you had chosen Current Savings or Annual Retirement Income in the Calculate For part of the dialog box because you wanted to know what your current savings would produce in retirement income or how much a certain annual contribution would produce, this box would look like the others and you would enter the amount of money you expect to contribute each year toward retirement.

- **Current Age:** How old you are. No lying.

- **Retirement Age:** What age you would like or expect to retire.

- **Withdraw Until Age:** A dicey box, as this is where you say how long you expect to live. After you retire, you start withdrawing from your retirement income. By looking in my crystal ball, I see that you will withdraw until ... but now things grow hazy and now I cannot see...

- **Other Income (SSI, etc.):** Your social security or pension income. You can find out what your social security benefits will be by submitting form SS-4 to the Social Security Administration.

- **Annual Income After Taxes:** How much you want your annual income to be in your retirement years. You will withdraw this amount each year from your retirement savings after you retire. Be modest. As an old woman or man, your income probably doesn't need to be what it is now. The duplex might be paid off. The kids might be living on communes in Oregon. The dog might be dead.

With the Retirement Information part of the dialog box filled in, move on to Tax Information:

- **Tax-Sheltered Investment:** Click this option button if you are saving for retirement with IRAs, 401(k) plans, or other tax-deferred savings options.

- **Non-Sheltered Investment:** Click this option button if the investments you are squirreling away for retirement can be taxed before you reach retirement. Enter the marginal tax rate you expect to pay on these investments in the Retirement Tax Rate box.

Next you test your prognostication skills in the Inflation area of the dialog box:

- **Predicted Inflation:** What you expect the inflation rate to be between now and the time you retire. If it's any help, inflation in the past six decades has averaged 3.3 percent annually.

- **Inflate Contributions:** If you intend to make larger and larger contributions over the years to account for inflation, click this check box. If you choose this option, Quicken will make a schedule in which your annual contributions get larger as the years go by.

- **Annual Income in Today's $:** Click this box if you want to see what the money you are saving will be worth when you retire. If you want to see the figures in today's dollars, which are worth considerably more than tomorrow's dollars will be worth, remove the check mark. With the check mark removed, the figures are higher.

Now that you are finished filling in the dialog box, click the Calculate button and glance at the Annual Contribution box. It tells you how much you need to contribute annually to reach your savings goal. Next, click the Schedule button. You see the Deposit Schedule window shown in Figure 11.2. The Deposit column shows how much you must set aside each year to reach your retirement savings goal. If you scroll down the list to retirement age, you see in the Income column where you start withdrawing the money you are supposed to have saved.

At this point, most people get discouraged at how much they have to put aside each year, so they click the Close button, go back to the Retirement Planner, and tinker with the numbers. By way of consolation, most people fail to consider that their incomes, not just their retirement income needs, will rise over the coming decades. You will have many more opportunities than you do now to save money.

| Deposit Schedule | | | ☒ |
|---|---|---|---|
| Print | | | Close |

| Age | Deposit | Income | Balance |
|---|---|---|---|
| 0 | 0.00 | 0.00 | 8,000.00 |
| 38 | 23,568.36 | 0.00 | 32,208.36 |
| 39 | 23,568.36 | 0.00 | 58,353.39 |
| 40 | 23,568.36 | 0.00 | 86,590.02 |
| 41 | 23,568.36 | 0.00 | 117,085.58 |
| 42 | 23,568.36 | 0.00 | 150,020.79 |
| 43 | 23,568.36 | 0.00 | 185,590.81 |
| 44 | 23,568.36 | 0.00 | 224,006.44 |
| 45 | 23,568.36 | 0.00 | 265,495.31 |
| 46 | 23,568.36 | 0.00 | 310,303.30 |
| 47 | 23,568.36 | 0.00 | 358,695.92 |
| 48 | 23,568.36 | 0.00 | 410,959.95 |

**Figure 11.2** The Deposit Schedule window. The Deposit column shows how much you need to save annually to reach your retirement income goal.

# Seeing How Much Your Savings Will Produce

Besides aiming for a retirement income and working backwards to see how much you need to save each year, you can ask yourself what

## tricks of the trade

*Good health is wonderful. So is a nice place to live. But what you really need when you retire is money—money to pay your bills, with enough left over to do the things you want. The general rule of thumb is this: you'll need 70 to 80 percent of what you're spending before you retire, more if you have expensive hobbies or plan to travel extensively. For example, if your gross income while you're working is $6,000 a month—that's $72,000 a year— you'll probably need $4,800 a month, or about $57,600 a year, after you retire.*

*Kenneth M. Morris, Alan M. Siegel, and Virginia Morris,* The Wall Street Journal Guide to Planning Your Financial Future

you realistically can contribute and find out what those contributions will produce in retirement income. Or you can find out how much you need to start with to reach a savings goal.

To do that, choose Features I Planning I Financial Planners I Retirement and fill in the Retirement Planner as I explained to do in the preceding pages. Only this time choose either the Current Savings or Annual Retirement Income option button under Calculate For:

- **Current Savings:** Click to find out what you need to start with to reach the goal you are trying to achieve. After you have filled in the Retirement Planner, it tells you how much you need to start with.

- **Annual Retirement Income:** Click to find out what the yearly contributions you can realistically make will produce in retirement income. After you fill out the dialog box, look at the box next to Annual Income After Taxes to see what kind of annual income your yearly contributions will produce.

# SAVING FOR A CHILD'S COLLEGE EDUCATION

When the subject of higher education comes up at my kids' school, the parents go into a tizzy. They believe it is absolutely necessary for children to go to good (that means expensive) colleges and universities lest the children grow up to be economic eunuchs. Personally, I think that parents should pass along to their kids a love of learning and a curiosity about life instead of a swarm of anxieties about the future and the Scholastic Aptitude Test. People who love to learn and are curious go very, very far, no matter how close to the Charles River they went to college.

With Quicken, you can calculate how much you need to save each year toward a child's college education. Or you can calculate how much the savings that you can realistically set aside will produce in the years ahead to pay for junior's college expenses. Either way, choose Features I Planning I Financial Planners I College. You see the College Planner shown in Figure 11.3.

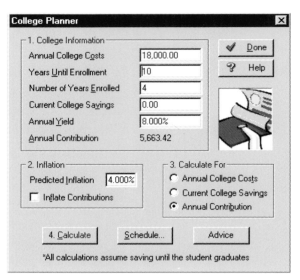

**Figure 11.3** The College Planner, where you calculate how much it costs to forge your child's ticket to the middle class

Choose how you want to conduct your investigation with the option buttons under Calculate For:

- **Annual College Costs:** Click to figure out how much in college expenses you will be able to pay annually with the money you've already saved plus the amount you intend to set aside each year till your child goes to college. In other words, click here to find out how swanky a university you can afford to send your daughter or son to.

- **Current College Savings:** Click to figure out how much you need to have saved already in order to send your child to college, not counting the amounts you intend to set aside annually till your child goes.

- **Annual Contribution:** Click to figure out how much you need to contribute each year in order to cover the annual costs of sending your child to college.

After you've clicked an option button, fill in the top of the dialog box. Except for Annual College Costs, in which you list the yearly cost (expenses plus tuition) of sending the child to college, most of this stuff is self-explanatory. To find out college costs, you can always call a university's administrative offices (call 617/495-1551 to find out how much it costs to send an undergraduate to Harvard University for a year).

Under Inflation, put what you think the inflation rate will be in the Predicted Inflation box, and click the Inflate Contributions check box if you intend to make your contributions larger over the years to account for inflation.

Click the Calculate button. You find out how much you are able to pay, how much you need to have saved, or how much you need to contribute annually. If you wish, click the Schedule button to see how much you need to set aside each month. Click Done when you've finished marveling at how much college costs.

# ESTIMATING HOW MUCH IN TAXES YOU WILL OWE

Yet another way to plan for the future is to use Quicken's Tax Planner. It never hurts to know how much in taxes you will owe, especially if you are the kind who doesn't like surprises. And the Tax Planner is a great way to see how purchasing a house or changing jobs will affect your taxes.

To see the Tax Planner screen shown in Figure 11.4, choose Features | Taxes | Tax Planner. On this screen, you start by telling Quicken what the tax rates are. Then you enter data about your income and expenses, or, if you have the time and the wherewithal, you tag Quicken's income and expense categories so that the data they track can be imported to the Tax Planner. As you enter the data, Quicken calculates what your total tax, marginal tax, and average tax rates are, and how much in taxes you owe. Finally, you can fool with tax rates by creating one, two, or three different tax scenarios.

## Telling Quicken What the Tax Rates Are

Before you can start estimating taxes, you have to tell the Tax Planner what your filing status is (Single or Married-Joint, for example) and what the tax rates are. The Tax Planner on your computer has the correct federal tax rates for 1996 and what the fortunetellers at Intuit

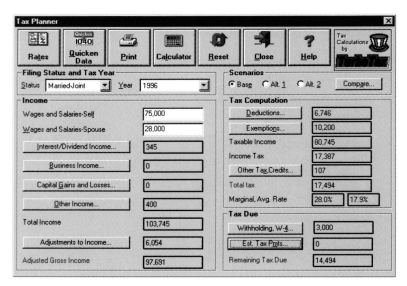

**Figure 11.4** Look in the Remaining Tax Due box in the lower-right corner of the Tax Planner screen to see what Quicken thinks your tax bill will be.

think the tax rates will be for 1997, so if you are reading this in 1997 or 1998 and you want to estimate taxes for those years, you will likely have to adjust the rates.

To tell Quicken what the tax rates are, choose Features I Taxes I Tax Planner (if you haven't done so already). Under Filing Status and Tax Year at the top of the dialog box, click the down-arrow in the Status box and choose a filing status option. Click the Year down-arrow and choose 1997, if that is the year you want tax estimates for. If you're prognosticating for 1998, choose 1997 anyway.

Next, click the Rates button in the upper-left corner of the screen. You see the Tax Rates for Filing Status dialog box shown in Figure 11.5. Not a pretty dialog box, is it? To fill it out, you probably need to know more about the tax codes than you ever wanted to. Fill in the correct rates as best you can. If you get tied up, click the Defaults button to start all over. Click OK when you are done.

## Entering the Tax Data

Now it's time to tell Quicken what your income and expenses were so it can calculate how much you will owe in taxes. To do that,

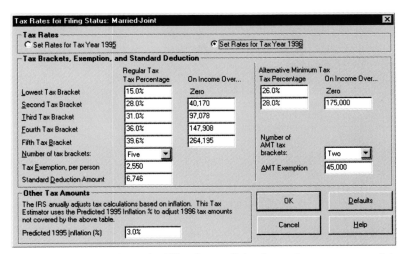

**Figure 11.5** The Tax Rates for Filing Status dialog box, where you can update the rates Quicken uses to estimate income taxes

either enter the numbers yourself or get as many numbers as you can from the Quicken category list and enter the rest of the numbers yourself.

*"Calculating the Price of a Loan or Mortgage" in the next chapter explains how to find out how big a mortgage you can afford and what your monthly payments will be.*

## Entering the Data Yourself

To use the go-it-alone method, start by getting the paperwork together. You need to know what your income is, what your mortgage interest payments are, if you are making mortgage payments, and everything else that you need to fill out tax forms. Of course, you can wing it if you want and make estimates, or you can use last year's tax forms.

In the Tax Planner screen, enter what you expect your total wages and salary to be in the first Income box, Wages and Salaries-Self. Then work your way down the Income column on the left side of the screen. Quicken offers buttons to help you fill in some of the boxes. For example, if you have or expect to have income from interest and dividends, click the Interest/Dividend Income button, fill in the dialog box, and click OK. After you finish the Income column, work your way down the Tax Computation column, too. As you go along, Quicken calculates your tax bill in the Remaining Tax Due box.

## Getting Tax Data
## from Quicken Categories

To have Quicken bring data from categories into the Tax Planner, you have to know which category gets plugged into which tax form. In other words, you have to know that dividend income, for example, is reported on Schedule B, and who knows that off the top of their head? If you know the tax forms well and you are especially keen on using the Tax Planner to stay on top of taxes, you can link different income and expense categories to the Tax Planner and have the Planner spit out tax data in an instant.

To do that, you have to leave the Tax Planner for an afternoon or so and choose Lists I Category/Transfer to get to the Category & Transfer List. From there, click the Tax Link button to get to the Tax Link Assistant dialog box. The three columns in the middle show categories, line items to which they've been assigned (if any), and tax form line items:

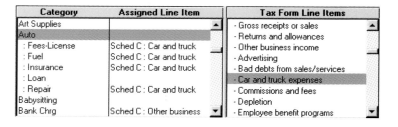

If you've been using ready-made Quicken categories, some categories already have line item assignments. To link a category to part of a tax form, click a category or subcategory, click its corresponding line item in the Tax Form Line Items box, and then click the Assign Line Item to Category button. When you're done assigning the categories that pertain to taxes to line items in tax forms, click OK. Now you can import the tax data you so laboriously assembled to the Tax Planner.

In the Tax Planner (choose Features I Taxes I Tax Planner to get there), click the Quicken Data button. You see the Preview Quicken Tax Data dialog box with its five mighty columns of data. This data comes from the transactions you entered so far this year in Quicken registers. Glance at it and click the OK button.

Back on the Tax Planner screen, most of the boxes are filled in. Go down the columns and make sure the data is accurate. If it isn't, enter the tax data yourself. Then have a look at the Remaining Tax Due box to see an estimate of what you owe.

# Playing with What-If Tax Scenarios

Should you sell the stock, even if it means taking the capital gains hit? Should you renounce all worldly goods to save on taxes? You can answer these and other questions by creating a second or third scenario with the Tax Planner. To do that, click the Alt 1 or Alt 2 button after you estimate your income taxes the first time. These buttons are in the upper-right corner of the Tax Planner screen. A dialog box asks if you want to copy the current scenario. Click Yes if you want to make the first scenario the starting point for the next one, or click No to start from scratch.

Now either tinker with the numbers in the Tax Planner dialog box or generate a new set of numbers. When you are done, you can click the Compare button to see how the different scenarios you created stack up:

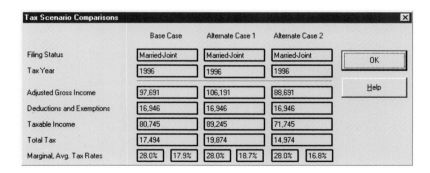

# Finding Ways to Reduce Taxes

On the subject of taxes, Quicken offers an electronic survey called the Deduction Finder to help you find out where you can take deductions and thereby lower your tax bill. The Deduction Finder asks questions and, on the basis of the answers it gets, draws up an "action plan" (actually it's a list of suggestions) for taking more deductions. To track where you can take deductions, the Deduction Finder offers to create special expense categories for the Category & Transfer List.

To try out the Deduction Finder, choose Features I Taxes I Tax Deductions. You see the Deduction Finder window shown in Figure 11.6. In box 1, click the down-arrow and choose a description that applies to you. Then, in box 2, click a deduction you might be eligible for and answer the questions in box 3. Answer by clicking Y (Yes) or N (No). You usually have to scroll down the list to answer all the questions. When you're done answering them, Quicken puts a green check mark next to deductions you might be eligible for or a red *X* next to deductions you can't take.

If you appear to be eligible to take a deduction, click the More Information button. You see a screen that lists the steps to take in Quicken to take advantage of the deduction. If you care to create a new category for tracking income or spending that pertains to the deduction, click the Create a Category button. You see a description of the category you are about to create, after which you can click OK to create it.

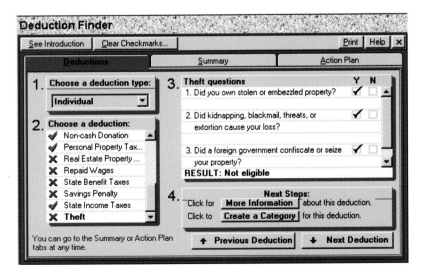

**Figure 11.6** The Deduction Finder window. Answer the questions and Quicken helps you find tax deductions.

Go back to part 1, click another option that applies to you, and answer the next round of questions. When you are done answering questions, click the Action Plan tab. It offers details about the deductions you can take, exactly what you must do to qualify, what kind of a paper trail to leave behind, and where on the tax forms you report the deduction.

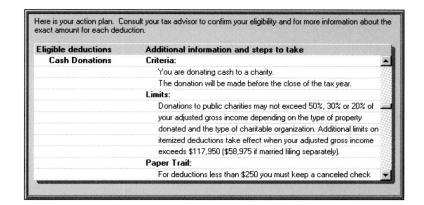

# AU REVOIR

So ends Chapter 11, the chapter that usually has to do with bankruptcy. However, if you follow the advice laid out here, if you save for retirement and for your kids' education, and if you plan for taxes better, you will never go into Chapter 11. You can go right to Chapter 12, which explains how to use Quicken as a financial analysis tool.

# Quicken as a Financial Analysis Tool

- Calculating the payments on a loan or mortgage

- Finding out how big a loan or mortgage you can afford

- Seeing whether refinancing a house is worthwhile

- Letting Quicken forecast your future income and expenses

- Determining the future value of an investment

- Calculating how to reach an investment goal

- Generating investment reports

- Creating an investment graph

# FAST FORWARD

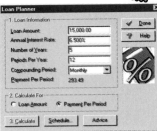

## FIND OUT HOW BIG A LOAN OR MORTGAGE PAYMENT YOU CAN HANDLE ➤ *pp. 221-222*

1. Choose Features I Planning I Financial Planners I Loan.
2. Under Calculate For in the Loan Planner dialog box, click the Payment Per Period option to find out how large your payments will be on a loan, or click the Loan Amount button to find out how large a loan you can realistically take out.
3. In the Loan Amount box, enter the amount of the loan you would like to take out. (If you clicked the Loan Amount button under Calculate For, it says CALCULATED next to the Loan Amount box, so enter nothing. The amount of the loan you can take out is what you want to calculate.)
4. In the Annual Interest Rate box, enter the interest rate you will be charged for the loan.
5. Enter the length of the loan in the Number of Years box.
6. Enter the number of payments you will make each year in the Periods Per Year box. If payments are due each month, for example, enter **12**.
7. Click the down-arrow in the Compounding Period box and choose Semi-Annually, if necessary.
8. In the Payment Per Period box, enter the amount you can realistically pay each month. (If you clicked the Payment Per Period option because you want to find out how large your payments will be, it says CALCULATED here, because the amount of each payment is what you are trying to calculate, so enter nothing.)
9. Click the Calculate button and look beside Loan Amount or Payment Per Period to find out either how big a loan you can take out or what your monthly payments will be.

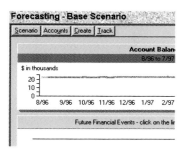

# FORECAST WHAT YOUR FUTURE ACCOUNT BALANCES WILL BE ➤ *pp. 225-227*

1. Choose Features I Planning I Forecasting.
2. If you have been using Quicken for a short while, you see the Automatically Create Forecast dialog box. Enter a time period in this box so that Quicken knows where to get forecast data from, and then click OK.
3. The Forecasting window appears. The yellow line in this window represents account totals from the past, and the blue line represents what they will be in the future. Click the down-arrow in the time period menu in the lower-left corner to view a different time period on the graph, if you want.
4. Click the Prev or Next button below the time period menu to "page through" your future or past account balances.

# CALCULATE THE RATE BY WHICH AN INVESTMENT GROWS AND HOW TO REACH AN INVESTMENT OUTCOME ➤ *pp. 227-230*

1. Choose Features I Planning I Financial Planners I Savings. You see the Investment Savings Planner dialog box.
2. Under Calculate For, click Opening Savings Balance to find out how much money you need to start with to reach an investment goal, click Regular Contribution to see how much you need to contribute periodically to reach the goal, or click Ending Savings Balance to find out what your present investment will be worth over time.
3. In the Opening Savings Balance, enter how much the investment is worth today. (This box says CALCULATED if you are trying to calculate how much money you need to start with to reach an investment goal.)
4. In the Annual Yield box, enter the percentage amount you think the investment will grow each year.

5. If necessary, click the down-arrow in the Number of box and choose a time period other than years to describe the length of the investment, and then enter a number in the box to the right.
6. Enter the amount of money you will contribute periodically to the investment in the Contribution Each Year box. (This box says CALCULATED if you are trying to see how much you should contribute.)
7. In the Ending Savings Balance box, enter the amount you would like the investment to be worth when the time period is over. (This box says CALCULATED if you are trying to find out what the investment will be worth over time.)
8. Click the Calculate button.

This short chapter explains how Quicken can help you make wise financial decisions. It explains how to calculate what the monthly payments on a loan or mortgage will be, and how to find out how much you can borrow. For people who already make mortgage payments, this chapter shows how Quicken can help you decide whether refinancing is worthwhile. This chapter also tells how to peek into the years ahead and see what your net worth will be in the future, how to calculate the future value of an investment, and how to use Quicken's investment reports to figure out whether your present-day investments are making you richer or poorer.

# CALCULATING THE PRICE OF A LOAN OR MORTGAGE

When you are contemplating a mortgage, car loan, student loan, or other kind of loan, the two most important questions to ask are "What will the monthly payments be?" and "How much can I afford to borrow?" Quicken's Loan Planner can answer these questions very, very quickly.

## Finding Out What Your Payments Will Be

To find out what the monthly payments on a loan or mortgage will be, choose Features I Planning I Financial Planners I Loan. You see the Loan Planner dialog box shown in Figure 12.1. Make sure the Payment Per Period option button under Calculate For is selected, and then enter the amount of the loan in the Loan Amount box. In the

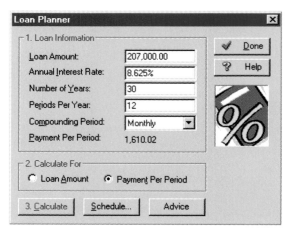

**Figure 12.1** Click the Payment Per Period option button and fill in this dialog box to see what your monthly payments will be; click Loan Amount to see how much you can borrow.

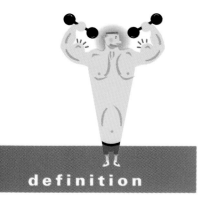

**definition**

*Principal: The actual amount of money borrowed on a loan. The principal is different from the interest, which is the price—expressed as a percentage of the loan amount—that you pay for borrowing the money.*

Annual Interest Rate box, enter the interest rate you will be charged for taking out the loan.

Enter the length of the loan in the Number of Years box and the number of payments you will make each year in the Periods Per Year box. For example, if payments are due each month, make sure 12 appears in the Periods Per Year box. Click the down-arrow in the Compounding Period box and choose Semi-Annually in the unlikely event that the lender compounds interest on a semi-annual rather than a monthly basis.

Finally, click the blue Calculate button. How much you have to pay each week, month, year, or whatever appears beside Payment Per Period in the Loan Planner dialog box.

Click the Schedule button to see the Approximate Future Payment dialog box. It shows how much of each payment is devoted to paying off interest on the loan and how much is devoted to actually reducing the principal. By scrolling down the dialog box, you can see how the principal of the loan is reduced over time. This illustration shows the figures for a monthly mortgage payment of $1,610.02. For the first payment, $1,487.81 is made in interest payments and $122.21 goes toward reducing the principal. After the first payment, the original debt of $207,000 is reduced to a mere $206,877.79.

| Approximate Future Payment Schedule | | | ☒ |
|---|---|---|---|
| Print | | | Close |
| Pmt | Principal | Interest | Balance |
| | | 8.6250% | 207,000.00 |
| 1 | 122.21 | 1,487.81 | 206,877.79 |
| 2 | 123.09 | 1,486.93 | 206,754.70 |
| 3 | 123.97 | 1,486.05 | 206,630.73 |
| 4 | 124.86 | 1,485.16 | 206,505.87 |

# Finding Out How Much You Can Afford to Borrow

Besides using the Loan Planner to see what the payments on a loan will be, you can also use it to find out how much money you can afford to borrow. To do that, choose Features | Planning | Financial Planners | Loan and click the Loan Amount option button under Calculate For in the Loan Planner dialog box (see Figure 12.1). In the Payment Per Period box, enter the amount of money that your budget, lifestyle, and personal inclination allow you to devote each month to paying off a loan or mortgage. Next, fill out the rest of the dialog box (read the previous few pages if you need help with that). When you click the Calculate button, Quicken tells you how much money you can afford to borrow.

## tricks of the trade

*What monthly mortgage payment can you afford? Calculate your monthly gross income by dividing your annual gross income by 12. Multiply that number by .36 to arrive at 36 percent of gross monthly income. That is the amount you can spend on your monthly mortgage payments, property taxes, homeowner's insurance, and repayment of outstanding credit debts or installment loans. Subtract your estimated monthly property taxes and homeowner's insurance and your monthly debt payments. What remains is the maximum monthly mortgage payment you can afford.*

*Janet Bamford, Jeff Blyskal, Emily Card, and Aileen Jacobson,* The Consumer Reports Money Book

## CAUTION

*The Refinance Planner doesn't take into account total interest payments on new mortgages. When you refinance, the amount of each monthly payment goes down, but the total number of payments, reset to 360, goes up, so you pay more in interest.*

# To Refinance or Not to Refinance

When interest rates start to fall, homeowners get itchy. They ask themselves whether now is a good time to refinance and lower their monthly mortgage payments. When it comes to refinancing, the question is whether the money saved by making lower monthly payments covers the cost of getting the new mortgage. With Quicken's Refinance Planner, you can find out how much you save each month by refinancing and how many months of lower monthly payments it takes to recoup the cost of getting the new mortgage. For example, if the present mortgage payment is $1,500, the new mortgage payment is $1,000, and the cost to refinance is $3,000, it takes six months to recoup the cost of refinancing ($3,000 = 6 months × $500, with $500 being the difference between the old $1,500 payment and the refinanced $1,000 payment).

To use the Refinance Planner, choose Features I Planning I Financial Planners I Refinance. You see the Refinance Planner dialog box shown in Figure 12.2. Under Existing Mortgage, enter how much your current monthly payment is in the Current payment box. If part of the payment is impounded or is tucked away in escrow accounts for insurance or property taxes, enter the amount in the Impound/escrow amount box.

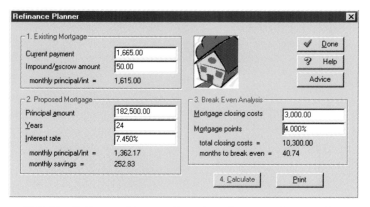

**Figure 12.2** The Refinance Planner dialog box shows you how much you save monthly by refinancing and how long it takes to recoup refinancing costs.

Under Proposed Mortgage, tell Quicken how much the new mortgage is, how many years it takes to pay it off, and its interest rate. Be sure to use the interest rate that the lender gives you, not the annual percentage rate, which is the *total* cost of borrowing, including loan fees and discount points.

Under Break Even Analysis, enter the closing costs in the Mortgage closing costs box. Closing costs include processing fees and appraisal fees. In the Mortgage points box, enter the loan fee and discount points. Points are expressed as a percentage of the loan. If 4 is the number of points the lender wants to charge you, enter **4**.

Last but not least, click the Calculate button. Then, under Proposed Mortgage, look at the monthly savings figure. It shows how much you save monthly by refinancing. Look under Break Even Analysis at the months to break even figure. It shows how many months of lower mortgage payments it takes to recoup the cost of refinancing.

# FORECASTING YOUR FUTURE INCOME AND EXPENSES

Quicken offers a means of forecasting what your future account balances will be, although I'm not sure how useful this device is. In the first place, no one can say what the future will bring, and in the second place, all Quicken does to make a forecast is total the amount in all the accounts, average out how much the total increases or decreases are each month, take into account scheduled transactions in the future, and extrapolate like a madman.

Figure 12.3 shows the Forecasting window. To see one of your own, choose Features | Planning | Forecasting. If you haven't been using Quicken very long, you see the Automatically Create Forecast dialog box, where Quicken asks for a time period from which to get the data for the forecast. Enter a time period and click OK to get to the Forecasting window.

The yellow line represents the sum of accounts in the past, and the blue line represents what they will be in the future. Funny how the yellow line is crooked and the blue line isn't. Personally, I think it's kind of interesting to click the Prev button in the lower-left corner of the

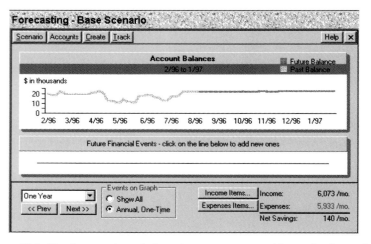

**Figure 12.3** The Forecasting window shows you past and future (estimated) account totals.

dialog box to get a graph of past account totals. I clicked that arrow once to get the graph shown in Figure 12.3.

Check out the lower-right corner of the Forecasting window. It compares the income forecast with the expense forecast and tells you what your per-month net savings are theoretically going to be.

For what it's worth (and it's not worth much if you are a busy person), you can create more scenarios and dabble in the Forecasting window. Here's how:

- **Scenario:** Click this button to get to the Manage Scenarios dialog box, where you can click New to create another scenario, click Edit or Delete to change the name of or remove a scenario, decide how forecast graphs should look in the window, and tell Quicken to compare one scenario to another.

- **Accounts:** Click this button to get to the Select Accounts to Include dialog box, where you can click next to account names to include or exclude them in forecast calculations.

- **Create:** Click this button to change the date range that Quicken uses to make forecasts. To begin with, Quicken uses data from the previous calendar year, but you can change that by changing the dates in the Automatically Create Forecast dialog box.

- **Track:** Click this button to create a budget with the data from a forecast.
- **(Time Period Menu):** Click the down-arrow and choose the time period for which you want to see forecast data onscreen. You can also click the Prev and Next buttons below this menu to make the graph move backward and forward in time.
- **Events on Graph:** Click the Show All option button to include scheduled transactions in the graph; click Annual, One Time to include only actions that have been recorded in registers.
- **Income Items:** Click this button to get to the Forecast Income Items dialog box, where you can include, exclude, or alter the income categories used in forecasting. Click in an amount category and then either change the amount by typing in a new amount, click the Delete button to exclude it from a forecast, or click New to create a new income category for forecasts.
- **Expenses Items:** Click this button to get to the Forecast Expense dialog box. You can do everything here that you can do in the Forecast Income Items dialog box, but from here you do it to expense categories, not income categories.

# CALCULATING THE FUTURE VALUE OF AN INVESTMENT

If, starting in 1996, you squirrel away $3,000 in a mutual fund account each year for the next 30 years, the fund grows by 9 percent annually, and the inflation rate is a steady 4 percent, how much will your shares in the fund be worth 30 years from now in 1996 dollars?

A. $448,725.65
B. $138,350.30
C. Some of the above
D. None of the above

Questions like these, which have stumped Econ 101 students for years, can be answered in about ten seconds with Quicken (the correct answer is B). You can find out how an investment grows over time, how much you need to invest annually to meet an investment goal, and how much you need to contribute and save to reach a certain amount of money.

## Seeing How an Investment May Grow

To find out how an investment may grow in the years ahead, choose Features I Planning I Financial Planners I Savings. You see the Investment Savings Planner dialog box shown in Figure 12.4. Make sure the Ending Savings Balance option button under Calculate For is selected, and then enter the amount of the investment in the Opening Savings Balance box.

In the Annual Yield box, enter the percentage amount you think the investment will grow each year. Your guess is as good as mine. On average since 1926, stocks have yielded 10 percent annually, long-term corporate bonds have yielded 5 percent, and U.S. T Bills have yielded

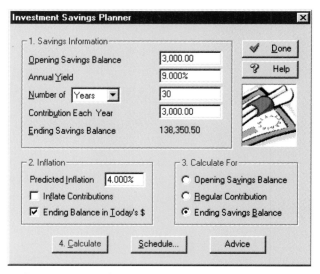

**Figure 12.4** The Investment Savings Planner shows how investments grow over time.

3.5 percent. If you are calculating the return on a mutual fund investment, you can find out what last year's return was. For a savings account, you can get the annual yield from the bank. For real estate, you are on your own.

Click the down-arrow in the Number of box and choose a time period if the length of the investment is not to be calculated in years. In the Number of box, enter the number of years, weeks, months, or quarters you will hang onto the investment.

The Contribution Each Year box is for entering the amount of money you intend to add to the investment each year, if you intend to do that. For example, if you are calculating what the value of a 401(k) or Keogh account will be and you intend to contribute each year, enter the amount of the annual contribution in this box.

In the Predicted Inflation box, enter what you think the inflation rate will be during the life of your investment. If it helps, the average inflation rate in the United States since 1945 has been 3.3 percent. Click the Inflate Contributions check box if you made an entry in the Contribution Each Year box and you intend to make larger contributions each year to account for inflation. Leave the Ending Balance in Today's $ box checked if you want to see the results of your contribution in today's dollars, not the inflated dollars of tomorrow. If you uncheck this box, the value of your future investment will seem quite large, but you will have to temper your initial pleasure at seeing how much your money grows by remembering that a dollar won't be worth as much tomorrow as it is today.

## tricks of the trade

*Buying stocks when the market picks up, and avoiding the market when it turns downward, is like buying underwear at Marshall Field's when you can get the same brand at Wal-Mart. There's a good chance that you'll be paying more than you need to.*

The Beardstown Ladies Investment Club and Leslie Whitaker, The Beardstown Ladies' Common-Sense Investment Guide

Finally, click the Calculate button and look beside Ending Savings Balance to see what your investment will be worth in the future. You can play around with the numbers, change inflation rates, and change contribution rates as you wish. You can also click the Schedule button to see how the investment will grow over time.

# Determining How to Reach an Investment Goal

Yet another way to use the Investment Savings Planner is to aim high and tell Quicken how much you want an investment to be worth in the years ahead, and then figure out how much you need to invest each year or how much you need to have invested to reach your goal.

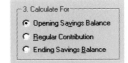

To use the Investment Savings Planner this way, choose Features I Planning I Financial Planners I Savings to get to the Investment Savings Planner dialog box (see Figure 12.4). Then, under Calculate For, either click the Opening Savings Balance option button to see how much you need to start with to reach an investment goal, or click the Regular Contribution option button to see how much you need to contribute each year to reach an investment goal.

Next, fill out the Investment Savings Planner dialog box and click the Calculate button when you are done (read the previous few pages if you need help). If you opted to see how much you need to start with to reach an investment goal, look at the figure beside Opening Savings Balance.

In the illustrations shown here, I used the Investment Savings Planner to find out what I need to do to reach an investment goal of $100,000 in 15 years, provided my investment grows at 9 percent annually. For the illustration on the left, I clicked Opening Savings Balance in the Calculate For part of the dialog box. Quicken tells me I need to start with $49,442.75 to reach $100,000 in 15 years. For the illustration on the right, I clicked Regular Contribution. Quicken tells me I need to contribute $6,133.81 annually to reach my $100,000 goal in 15 years.

 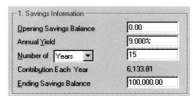

# REPORTS AND GRAPHS FOR ANALYZING INVESTMENTS

If you've already dabbled in investments, you can get Quicken to tell you how well your investments are performing. Do that by creating an investment report or by generating an Investment Performance graph.

*Chapter 7 explains how to tweak, customize, and memorize reports so you can use them again.*

To create an investment report, click the Reports button, click the Investment tab in the Create Report dialog box, and then click on the icon beside one of these reports:

- **Portfolio Value:** Lists the market value of the securities you own, how many shares of each you own, and how much they have increased or decreased in value.

- **Investment Performance:** Shows the return, by percentage and amount, of the securities in your portfolio.

- **Capital Gains:** Lists the capital gain or loss of securities you have sold.

- **Investment Income:** Totals investment transactions by income category and expense category.

- **Investment Transactions:** Lists all transactions from your investment account registers.

You can also gauge the performance of your investments by seeing an Investment Performance graph like the one shown in Figure 12.5. To see this graph, choose Reports I Graphs I Investments Performance, and click the Create button in the Create Graph dialog box. The first bar graph in the Investment Performance Graph window shows how the portfolio's value has changed over time. The second bar graph shows how the different parts of the portfolio have performed in comparison to the portfolio's average return.

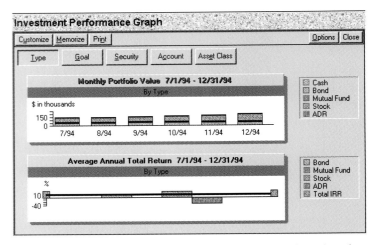

**Figure 12.5** An Investment Performance graph shows how the value of the portfolio has changed (top) and how its different parts have fared in comparison to the average return (bottom).

Click the buttons on the top of the graph to display investments by type, goal, security, account, or asset class.

You can also choose Reports I Graphs I Investments Asset Allocation to see a graph that shows your securities by asset class, if you have categorized them by asset class.

# THAT'S ALL SHE WROTE!

As Jane Austen used to say when she finished writing a chapter, "That's all she wrote." The next chapter leaves financial analysis behind and delves into the exciting and sometimes intimidating world of tracking investments with Quicken.

# CHAPTER 13

# Quicken for Investors

# FAST FORWARD

## SET UP AN ACCOUNT FOR
## TRACKING YOUR INVESTMENTS ➤ *pp. 240-241*

1. From the Account List window, click the New button.
2. Click the Investment option button and then click Next.
3. Click the Summary tab in the Investment Account Setup dialog box.
4. Name the account and describe it.
5. Click the Account Contains a Single Mutual Fund check box if you are tracking a single mutual fund; otherwise leave this check box blank.
6. If you are setting up an account to track the securities you buy and sell through a brokerage firm, fill in the CMA Information part of the dialog box. Click the Use a Linked Checking Account for my Cash Balance check box. Then click the New Account option button and either enter a balance and date to create a brand-new checking account, or click the Existing Account option button and choose an account you have already set up.
7. Click the Done button.

## LIST THE SECURITIES YOU OWN
## IN AN INVESTMENT ACCOUNT ➤ *pp. 242-244*

1. Click the EasyActions button in an investment register and choose Buy/Add Shares.
2. In the Buy/Add Shares dialog box, click the Summary tab.
3. Enter the date of the purchase.
4. Enter the name of the security in the Security box.
5. Choose the investment account you will add the security to.
6. Under Money from Quicken account?, choose the No button if you purchased this security in the past. If you purchased it with money from an account you have been tracking with Quicken, choose one of the Yes buttons.
7. Under Transaction, enter the price per share, the number of shares you purchased, and the commission, and then click Done.

8. In the Set Up Security dialog box, enter the security's name and its ticker symbol if you intend to download information about this security from Intuit.
9. Choose Stock, Bond, CD, or Mutual Fund from the Type drop-down list.
10. Click OK.

## RECORD THE PURCHASE OF SHARES ➤ *p. 245*

1. Click the EasyActions button and choose Buy/Add Shares.
2. Click the down-arrow in the Which Security? drop-down menu and choose the security whose shares you have purchased. Then click Next.
3. When Quicken asks if you used money from a Quicken account to buy the shares, click one of the Yes buttons and tell Quicken which account you got the money from. Then click Next.
4. In the next dialog box, say how many shares you bought, their per-share price, and the commission you paid, and then click Next.
5. Review the Summary tab to make sure you entered the data correctly, and click Done.

## RECORD INCOME
## FROM AN INVESTMENT ➤ *pp. 247-248*

1. Click the EasyActions button and choose Record an Income Event.
2. In the Record Income dialog box, enter the date of the income disbursement, not today's date.
3. Click the down-arrow in the security menu and choose which investment produced the income.
4. Under Distribution, enter the amount your investment earned in the box that describes how it was earned.
5. Click the Transfer Account down-arrow, choose the account you deposited the money in, and click OK.

This chapter explains how to use Quicken to track the value of investments, including mutual funds, stocks, bonds, and other securities. Investment accounts are similar to checking and savings accounts. Transactions are recorded by date, and Quicken tracks the value of the securities in a register.

What makes investment accounts different, however, is that Quicken tracks the price per share, the number of shares you have (as you buy and sell them), and the shares' market value, not just the account balance. Also, instead of the seven choices in the Num column that you know so well for describing checking and savings account transactions, there are no less than 30 different ways to describe a transaction in an investment account. Better read on...

# WHO SHOULD TRACK INVESTMENTS

For tax purposes and to understand how well investments are performing, everybody should track investments, except if they are tax-deferred. When it comes to investments like IRAs, SEPs, 401(k) accounts, or tax-deferred mutual funds, have the managers do the work for you. If the managers are worth anything, they send statements saying what your profits or losses are. Rather than go to the trouble of recording those profits or losses in an investment account (and the trouble can be significant), set up an asset account and record profits and losses as increases or decreases. Then, when you cash in part of a tax-deferred IRA, SEP, or whatever, record the transaction as income in a savings or checking account. You are a busy person. Take my advice about investment accounts and you won't be quite as busy.

# THE BIG PICTURE: TRACKING INVESTMENTS WITH QUICKEN

To track investments with Quicken, you start by setting up an investment account. If you want, you can track all your investments in

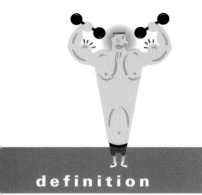

*Security: Bonds, stock certificates, and other financial instruments that can be traded and whose value fluctuates.*

a single account, but if you are tracking the securities you trade with a brokerage house, create one account for each brokerage house you do business with. That way, you simplify your record keeping, because you can enter data in the investment account straight from the broker's statement and even reconcile your account from the statements the broker sends you.

After you set up the account, you tell Quicken the names of the securities—the stocks, bonds, mutual funds, CDs, and so on—that go in the account. As you do that, you tell the program how many shares you own and what their values are. You can even record past sales and purchases of stock for analysis purposes, as long as you have the paperwork on hand and can record the transactions accurately.

Once the account has been set up and the securities entered, you record purchases, sales, share reinvestments, capital gains, dividends, stock splits, and what-all from the register. Or you can work from the Portfolio window, which lists all the securities you own and offers most of the commands found in an investment register. Figure 13.1 shows the Portfolio window. You can see all your securities in this window, if you so choose.

**Portfolio**

| Update Prices ▼ | | | Detail View | Register | | | Options | Report | × |

Prices as of: 7/31/96 ▣Account: All Accounts: ▼ View: Price Update ▼

| Security | Symbol | Mkt Price | | Chg | Shares | Last Price | Mkt Value | MktVal Chg |
|---|---|---|---|---|---|---|---|---|
| First Franklin CD | | 5,000 | e | | 1 | 5,000 | 5,000.00 | N/A |
| Intuit | Intu | 41 | e | ↑ | 65 | 41 | 2,665.00 | N/A |
| Microsoft | Microsoft | 48 | e | ↓ | 90 | 48 | 4,320.00 | N/A |
| Tristar | | 1 | e | | 30 | 1 | 30.00 | N/A |
| TycoTy | | 70 | e | | 8 | 70 | 560.00 | N/A |

| | | | | | N/A | 12,575 | 0 |
|---|---|---|---|---|---|---|---|

| Total Market Value: | 12,575 | e-Estimated |
| Total % Gain: | 2 | |

**Figure 13.1** You can record investment transactions starting from the Portfolio window or from an investment register.

# SETTING UP AN INVESTMENT ACCOUNT

Since you've come this far, I'll bet my eyeteeth you know how to set up an account in Quicken. Setting up an investment account is like setting up a savings or checking account, only you have to answer questions about tax-deferments and linked checking accounts. To set up an investment account:

1. Click the Accts icon on the iconbar to get to the Account List window, and then click the New button.
2. In the Account Setup dialog box, click the Investment option button and then click Next.
3. When you see the EasyStep tab, bypass it and click the Summary tab to go straight to the screen shown in Figure 13.2. Why not? You've created many accounts by now and you don't need all that hand-holding.
4. Under Account Information, name the account and describe it. If you are setting up an account to track the securities you buy and sell through a brokerage house, you could enter the house's name here.
5. If you are tracking a single mutual fund with this account, click the Account Contains a Single Mutual Fund check box.
6. Fill in the CMA Information part of the dialog box if you are setting up an account to track the securities you buy and sell through a brokerage firm. If you use a brokerage firm, you need an account—other than the one you are setting up—to handle the money you have banked with the brokerage firm. If that is the case, click the Use a Linked Checking Account check box. Then click the New Account option button and either enter a balance and date to create a brand-new checking account, or click the Existing Account option button and tell Quicken by way of the drop-down menu which account your new investment account is to be linked to.

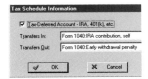

7. Click the Tax Info button if financial activity in the investment account needs to be reported on your income tax form. From the Tax Schedule Information dialog box, click the Tax-Deferred Account check box, if necessary, and then choose the tax form line item where transfers in and out of the account should be reported. If you fill in this dialog box, the data from your account is computed in tax reports. Click OK when you're done.

8. Back on the Summary tab, click the Done button. The Investment Setup dialog box appears so you can tell Quicken the names of the securities in the account you just created.

9. Click Cancel and then click Yes when Quicken asks if you really want to cancel. Instead of all this hand-holding, there is a faster way to enter the name of securities.

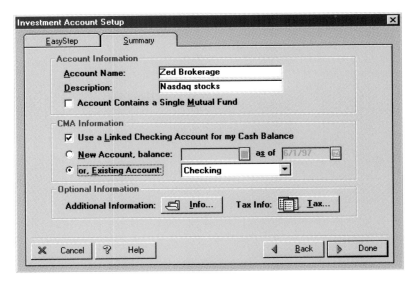

**Figure 13.2** The Summary tab of the Investment Account Setup dialog box, where you tell Quicken the name and particulars of the investment account you are creating

# THE BASICS: TRACKING MUTUAL FUNDS, STOCKS, AND BONDS

No matter what the security you are tracking, you start by recording when you purchased it, how much you paid for it, and how its market value has changed. If you sell all or part of it, you have to inform Quicken of that, too. This part of the chapter explains the basics of tracking a security. The techniques described here apply to mutual funds, stocks, and bonds, as well as IRAs, Keoghs, CDs, treasury bills, annuities, precious metals, collectibles, REITs, unit trusts, and baseball cards.

## Entering Your Securities in the Investment Account

After you set up an investment account, the next step is to tell Quicken which securities go in it and how much the securities are worth. To do that, open the investment account register, put the cursor in the first empty row, click the EasyActions button in the upper-left corner, and choose Buy/Add Shares from the drop-down menu.

You see the Buy/Add Shares dialog box. Enter the name of the stock, bond, security, or whatever it is you are trying to track in the Which Security? box. If you were buying more shares of a security you already own, you would choose it from the Which Security? drop-down menu. Click Next.

You see the Set Up Security dialog box shown in Figure 13.3. The name you enter here will appear in the Security List. Meanwhile, enter a ticker symbol in the Symbol box if you intend to download information about this security from Intuit. The ticker symbol is the abbreviated name of the company. You see them in the cryptic pages of the *Wall Street Journal* and other newspapers. (If you have a modem, you can click the Lookup button and find out what the ticker symbol is.)

From the Type drop-down menu, choose Stock, Bond, CD, or Mutual Fund. Making a choice in the last two drop-down menus is up to you. Choose an option from the Goal menu to see securities grouped by goal on reports and graphs. The options on the Asset Class menu are also for grouping securities on reports and graphs.

*How to download stock quotes from Intuit is described in Chapter 14.*

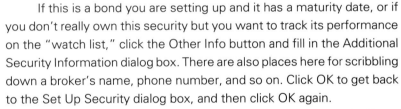

**Figure 13.3** In the Set Up Security dialog box, enter the security's name, its ticker symbol, its type, and (if you want) an investment goal and asset classification.

## CAUTION

*In the date box, enter the date you purchased the shares, not today's date. Quicken uses the dates you enter to calculate capital gains taxes.*

If this is a bond you are setting up and it has a maturity date, or if you don't really own this security but you want to track its performance on the "watch list," click the Other Info button and fill in the Additional Security Information dialog box. There are also places here for scribbling down a broker's name, phone number, and so on. Click OK to get back to the Set Up Security dialog box, and then click OK again.

After you click Next, the Buy/Add Shares dialog box asks if you used money from accounts you track with Quicken to buy the shares. Since you are telling Quicken about securities that you had in the past, let the No option stand. If you were buying securities, you would click one of the Yes buttons and tell Quicken which account you got the money from, if necessary. Click Next.

Now you see the Start tab of the Buy/Add Shares dialog box shown in Figure 13.4. I hope you have the paperwork in front of you, because you need to enter the number of shares you own in the Add box, the dollar value of each share in the $ box, the date you purchased the shares or first acquired them, and the commission, if any.

If the security you are setting up is a bond, enter the number of bonds you bought times ten in the Add box, and enter the dollar value of the bond divided by ten in the $ box. In other words, if you are buying

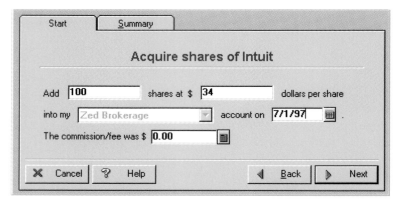

**Figure 13.4** List how many shares of the security you own and how much they are worth in this dialog box.

a $1000 bond, enter **10** in the Add box and **100** in the $ box. Do this because bonds are quoted at a percentage of their face, or par, value.

For a CD, put **1** in the shares box and the total value of the CD in the $ box.

**tricks of the trade**

*One way to measure the relationship of risk versus reward is to balance how much you think a stock is likely to rise against how far it could fall from its current price. If a stock selling for $20 could go up to $50 or fall to $10, its ratio is 3:1 (or 30 up/10 down). If the price goes up to $45 but could still fall to $10, the ratio is 1:7 (or 5 up/35 down) which may make it too risky.*

Kevin M. Morris and Alan M. Siegel, The *Wall Street Journal* Guide to Understanding Personal Finance

Click the Next button, take a gander at the Summary tab to make sure all is well, and click Done. Your entry appears in the investment register:

| Date | Action | Security | Price | Shares | Amount | | Clr | Cash Bal |
|------|--------|----------|-------|--------|--------|---|-----|----------|
| | Memo | | | | Comm/Fee | | | |
| 4/1/96 | ShrsIn | Intuit | 34 | 100 | 3,400 00 | | | 0 00 |
| | | | | | 3,400 00 | | | |

# Buying Shares

Buying shares is very similar to entering them in the investment account, only now you tell Quicken where the money to buy the shares came from. To record a purchase of shares, go to the last line of the investment register, click the EasyActions button, and choose Buy/Add Shares. Click the down-arrow in the Which Security? drop-down menu and choose the security whose shares you have purchased. Then click Next.

Fill out the Start tab of the Buy/Add Shares dialog box (see Figure 13.4 and the accompanying text, if you need to). First, Quicken asks if you used money from a Quicken account to buy the shares. Click one of the Yes buttons, tell Quicken which account you got the money from, and click Next. On the next screen, make sure to enter the date of the sale, not today's date. Enter the number of shares you purchased, how much each share cost, and the commission, if any. Click Next again. Review the Summary tab to make sure you entered the data correctly, and click Done. The account you took the money from shows a transfer to your investment account.

# Selling Shares

If you just read the last few pages, my apologies for being repetitive. The dialog boxes that you get when you choose options from the EasyActions menu in investment registers start to look alike after a while, but I guess that's good, because, at least where computers are concerned, familiarity doesn't breed contempt; it breeds confidence.

To record a sale of shares, click the EasyActions button and choose Sell/Remove Shares. In the Start tab you see next, click the down-arrow in the Which Security? box and choose the security whose shares you sold. Then click Next. On the next screen, tell Quicken in

**SHORTCUT**

*Besides using the dialog boxes, you can describe investment transactions by choosing options straight from the Action drop-down menu inside an investment register. You have to know the options well, however, to do it that way.*

which account you want to stash the proceeds from the sale, and then click Next again. You see a dialog box that looks very similar to the Buy/Add Shares dialog box (see Figure 13.4), only it has a Sell box where the other had a Buy box. Fill in this dialog box and click Next. You see the Summary tab of the Sell/Remove Shares dialog box shown in Figure 13.5.

**Figure 13.5** From the Summary tab, you can choose which of your stocks to sell by clicking the Lots button.

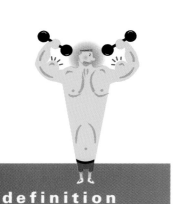

**definition**

**Lot:** *A group of securities purchased at the same time at the same price. Also a nephew of Abraham whose wife was turned into a saltshaker.*

If you are selling all your securities, or if you purchased the securities all at once, you can click Done and be done with it. If you bought the securities in lots, however, you need to click the Lots button and tinker with the Specify Lots dialog box shown in Figure 13.6.

Select the lot you will be selling the shares from and then click either Use All or Use Part. If you click the Use Part button, Quicken asks you by way of a dialog box how many shares from the lot you want to sell. You can also click the Maximum Gain button to have Quicken choose which lots you can sell and gain the highest profit by; click Minimum Gain to get the lowest profit and save on capital gains taxes. First Shares In sells the earliest shares you bought and Last Shares In

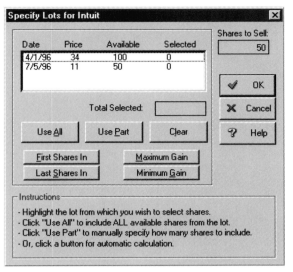

**Figure 13.6** Click a lot at the top of this dialog box and then click the buttons to tell Quicken which lots or which parts of lots you sold.

sells the most recent. Click the Clear button to start all over if you have to, but in any case click OK and then click Done to record the sale.

*See "The Portfolio View for Managing Investments" later in this chapter to learn how to update the price per share of a security.*

# Recording Dividend, Interest, Capital Gain, or Other Income

You became an investor with the hope that your investments would turn a profit, and when they do, you have to record the income you made in the investment register. These instructions tell how to record income you receive by check. If the income from your investment has been reinvested in the security that produced it, see the next part of this chapter.

To record income from an investment, go to the last row in the register, click the EasyActions button, and choose Record an Income Event. You see the Record Income dialog box in Figure 13.7.

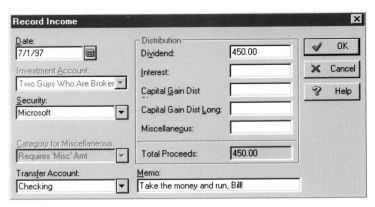

**Figure 13.7** To record investment income, enter a date, enter the amount in a Distribution box, choose the account the money will be deposited in, and click OK.

Enter the date of the income disbursement, not today's date. Next, click the down-arrow in the Security menu and choose the lucky investment that produced the income. Under Distribution, enter the amount your investment earned in one of the boxes:

- **Dividend:** A quarterly (or one-time) stock or mutual fund dividend.
- **Interest:** Interest income from a security.
- **Capital Gain Dist.:** A mutual fund capital gains distribution.
- **Capital Gain Dist. Long:** A mutual fund long-term capital gains distribution.
- **Miscellaneous:** A "none of the above" means of acquiring income from an investment.

Finally, click the Transfer Account down-arrow, click the account you will deposit the money in, write a memo in the Memo box if you want, and click OK. In the investment register, the transaction is recorded as a transfer to another account.

## Reinvesting Shares

Sometimes income from a mutual fund or stock is reinvested in the security. To record profits that have been reinvested, go to the last row in the register, click the EasyActions button, and choose Reinvest Income. You see a dialog box by the same name. One is shown in Figure 13.8.

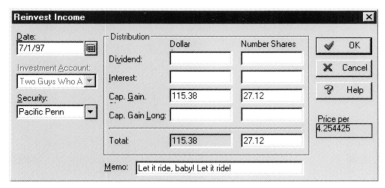

**Figure 13.8** When profits from a security are reinvested, fill in this dialog box and enter how many new shares were purchased with the reinvestment.

If you read the last two pages or so, this dialog box looks painfully familiar. Fill this out as you would the Record Income dialog box (see Figure 13.7), only enter the number of shares the reinvestment purchased as well. Notice the Price Per box on the right. The price per share shown here should match the price per share on the statement you were sent that notified you of the reinvestment.

## tricks of the trade

*It's a mistake to dismiss load mutual funds out of hand. If your investment is for your retirement nest egg or your toddler's college education, a load should not stand between you and the best possible fund. After all, even an 8.5 percent load—and there are very few of them left—over a 10-year period works out to less than 1 percent per year. That kind of burden can be easily overcome in the performance of an exceptional load fund versus a mediocre no-load.*

*Jeffrey M. Laderman, Business Week Guide to Mutual Funds*

# Transferring Cash In and Out of Investment Accounts

If the investment account you set up with Quicken tracks a brokerage account, you have to record when you put money in or take money out of the account. Doing that is pretty simple: click the Easy Actions button in the account register and choose either Transfer Cash Into Account or Transfer Cash From account.

Filling in the Transfer Cash In or Transfer Cash Out dialog box is pretty simple, and as you are a Quicken aficionado, I'm sure you know what to do with it. Just remember to choose the right account from the Transfer menu.

# Recording Annual Fees, Exit Fees, and Other Miscellaneous Fees

Sometimes you get charged an out-of-the-blue fee from a fund manager or broker. When that happens, and a checking account is linked to the investment account you are using to track the security, simply record the fee in the checking account. But if an account is not linked to the investment account, you have to choose another means of recording the fee.

To do that, click the Easy Actions button in the register and choose Miscellaneous Expense to get to the dialog box by that name. Enter the date and, in the Security box, choose a security if the expense is associated with a single security. Then fill in the amount, categorize the expense, choose an account to transfer it to, and click OK.

# When Stocks or Mutual Fund Shares Are Split

Occasionally, stocks and mutual fund shares are split to lower the price of individual stocks or shares and make them seem more attractive to investors. In a 2 to 1 split, for example, investors are given twice as much stock, but the value of individual stocks is half what it was before, so the owner of 100 shares worth $1000 now owns 200 shares worth the same amount, $1000.

To record a mutual fund share split or stock split, click the Easy-Actions button and choose Stock Split. In the Stock Split dialog box, enter the date, choose the security whose stock has been split, enter how many shares of the split stock you own, and how many shares of the old, unsplit stock you owned. If you want, you can update the price of the stock by making an entry in the Price after box. Click OK when you have finished.

# THE PORTFOLIO VIEW FOR MANAGING INVESTMENTS

After you set up an investment account, Quicken sticks a new icon on the iconbar called Port. Click this button to get to the Portfolio window shown in Figure 13.9. It shows the securities in one investment account at first, but you can choose another account from the Account menu or choose All Accounts to see all your securities. The bottom of the window shows the total market value of your securities, how much they have grown by percentage, how much income they have generated, and the return on your investments (ROI). The arrows in the Chg column tell you whether the value of the security is going up or down.

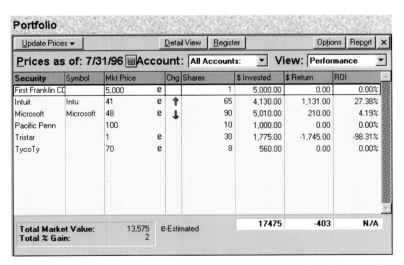

**Figure 13.9** In the Portfolio window, you can get a good look at how your investments are performing.

**habits & strategies**

*To make all your securities appear whenever you open the Portfolio window, click the Options button, click the Miscellaneous tab, click the Show All Securities check box, and click OK.*

To find out more about an individual security, double-click it in the Portfolio window or select it and click the Detail View button. You see a Security Detail View window similar to the one in Figure 13.10. Everything you can do from a register can also be done from this window. The options on the EasyActions menu are the same as the options on the EasyActions menu in registers. You can click the tabs at the bottom of the window to get to different securities. The price history, a graph, and the most recent transactions in the register are all there for your viewing pleasure. As the next few pages explain, this window is where it's at as far as managing investments is concerned.

# Recording the Current Market Value of Securities

The market price of securities changes quite often, and each change affects the value of the securities you own. To stay up to date with the market, click the Prices button and click either Get Online Quotes or Edit Price History from the menu (the Update Prices menu in the Portfolio window offers these same two options). How to get online quotes is explained in the next chapter. If you choose Edit Price History, you get a chance to update the price of the security yourself.

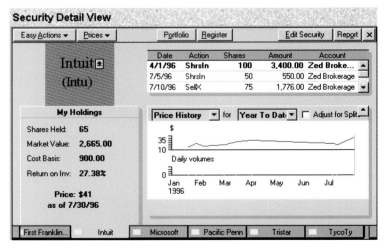

**Figure 13.10** From the Security Detail View window, you can make investment transactions, update market prices, and even graph the history of an investment.

From the Price History For dialog box, click the New button to see the New Price For dialog box, shown in Figure 13.11, where you can enter the price of the security as of a certain day (you can enter the volume of sales and other information as well). Click OK when you've finished. The Edit button in the Price History For dialog box is for correcting market quotes that were entered inaccurately, and the Delete button is for deleting quotes. The market prices entered here are used to plot the graph that appears in the Security Detail View window.

# Graphing a Security's Performance

The graph in the lower-right corner of the Security Detail View window shows the price history of the security in the past year, but you can tinker with the graph and squeeze other juicy information out of it. Click the menu on the left side of the graph and choose Market Value to see how the monetary value of the stock you own, not its per-share price, has changed. Click a time period from the middle menu to plot the graph across different periods of time. If the shares or stock in the security have been split, be sure to click the Adjust for Splits check box to get a realistic picture of the value or per-share price of the security.

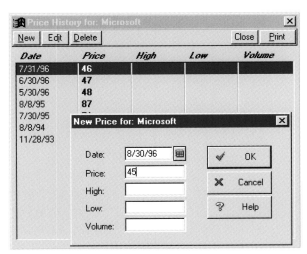

**Figure 13.11**  To keep your portfolio up-to-date, enter the current price of securities in the Price box.

And, when you've finished journeying in the Security Detail View window, click the Close button or the Portfolio button to get back to the Portfolio window. Remember, you can do everything from the Security Detail View window that you can do in a register (click the EasyActions button if you don't believe me). If you're an investor, camp out in the Security Detail View window.

# SPECIAL STOCK TRANSACTIONS

If you click the EasyActions button in an investment register or in the Security Detail View window, then click the Advanced option at the bottom of the menu, you see a submenu with a number of esoteric options for handling esoteric stock transactions. Here is a rundown of those options and why you would choose them:

Margin Interest Expense
Transfer Shares Between Accounts
Corporate Name Change
Corporate Securities Spin-Off
Corporate Acquisition (stock for stock)
Stock Dividend (non-cash dividend)
Reminder Transaction

- **Margin Interest Expense:** Choose this option when you borrow money from a broker to pay for a security. In the Amount box, enter the amount in interest on the loan that you have to pay.

- **Transfer Shares Between Accounts:** Choose this option to transfer a security from one investment account to another.

- **Corporate Name Change:** Choose this option to change a security's name without changing the financial records you have diligently kept.

- **Corporate Securities Spin-Off:** When a corporation spins off, drops off, or lops off part of itself and you own shares in the corporation, choose this command to record how many new shares the corporation is issuing for each old share.

- **Corporate Acquisition (stock for stock):** When one corporation merges with another and the two swap stocks, choose this command to record how many shares are being issued for each share of the parent company, and the share price that the parent company has to pay for each share of the company it has swallowed.

- **Stock Dividend (non-cash dividend):** Choose this
  command when dividends are paid in stock, not cash.

# RECONCILING AND UPDATING INVESTMENT ACCOUNTS AND SHARE PRICES

*Chapter 5 explains the particulars of reconciling an account.*

Reconciling an investment account is done the same way as reconciling a savings or checking account. When the statement comes from the brokerage house, open the investment account and click the Recon button. You will see a dialog box for entering the starting cash balance, the ending cash balance, and the statement date. Click OK in that dialog box and you get to a familiar Reconcile Account window, where you can reconcile the broker's records with your own.

A simpler, easier way to reconcile an investment account is to open the account in question and choose either Features | Investments | Update Cash Balance to update the cash value of a brokerage account, or Features | Investments | Update Share Balance to record the correct number of shares you own. To make sure your records are correct, fill in these dialog boxes and click OK:

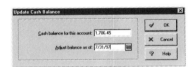 

# GOING THE WHOLE HOG!

So ends Chapter 13, which explains how to record investment transactions in Quicken. I was told that it is bad luck to put investment instructions in unlucky Chapter 13. I was told to put the investment stuff in lucky Chapter 7, but I ignored that advice. You can't be superstitious when it comes to investing. You have to be cool-headed and rational. You have to keep your nose clean and look straight toward the future. Speaking of which, the next chapter explains how to turn your cold hard cash into data bits and hurl it across cyberspace. The next chapter explains how to make financial transactions online with Quicken.

# Going Online with Quicken

257

# FAST FORWARD

## SEND PAYMENTS, BANK STATEMENT REQUESTS, AND MONEY TRANSFERS ONLINE ➤ *pp. 266-267*

1. Click the Online button on the iconbar.
2. On the Transactions, Payments, Transfers, and E-mail tabs of the Online Banking/Investments Center window, tell Quicken what you want to do online.
3. Click the Go Online button.
4. In the Instructions to Send dialog box, click next to each instruction you *do not* want to send to remove the check mark, or leave the check marks to send all the instructions.
5. Enter your PIN number in the Instructions to Send dialog box.
6. Click the Send button.
7. Enter a password, if necessary.

## GET AN UP-TO-DATE BANK STATEMENT ONLINE ➤ *pp. 268-270*

1. In the Instructions to Send dialog box, make sure a check mark appears beside the Download transactions instruction.
2. Click the Go Online button. After the transactions have been downloaded, look at the online statement to see what the balance is and which transactions have cleared.
3. Click the Compare to Register button.
4. Click the Accept All button in the window that shows the account register and the online statement. Transactions that "match" in your register and the bank's records are given a *c* (for Cleared) in the Clr column. "New" transactions that appear in your register but not in the bank's records are entered in the register.
5. For transactions that don't match, Quicken displays the Duplicate Check Number Found dialog box. Click the Skip button in this dialog box to continue accepting the downloaded transactions without entering the online version of the transaction in your register. When all the approvals have been made, go back into the register and change the transaction so it jibes with the bank's records.

6. In your register, enter names in the payee boxes and categorize the transactions that Quicken entered in the register because they are "new."

## TRANSFER MONEY BETWEEN ACCOUNTS AT THE SAME BANK ➤ *pp. 270-271*

1. Click the Online button on the iconbar.
2. In the Online Banking/Investments Center window, click the Transfers tab.
3. In the Transfer Money From box, choose the account from which you will transfer the money.
4. In the To box, choose the account that gets the money.
5. Enter the amount of money that is being transferred in the Amount box and click the Go Online button.

## PAY BILLS ONLINE ➤ *pp. 272-273*

1. Click the Online button on the iconbar and click the Payments tab.
2. From the Payee drop-down list, choose a payee name. (The names on this list come from the Online Payees list, which you construct by choosing Lists | Online Payees.)
3. Enter the amount of the payment and categorize the payment as you would if you were filling in the Write Checks window.
4. Click the Enter button and enter another online payee and amount, if you wish.
5. Click the Go Online button to make the payment.

## GET STOCK QUOTES ONLINE FROM QUICKEN ➤ *p. 274*

1. Click the Port button on the iconbar.
2. Click the Update Prices button and choose Get Online Quotes from the drop-down menu.
3. In the Online Quotes dialog box, click Continue.
4. In the Update Quicken Live Features dialog box, click the Update Now button.
5. Enter your password and click the Connect button.

**T**his chapter delves into the futuristic and sometimes unnerving world of Quicken's online services. It explains how to keep tabs on a bank account with the Online Banking service and how to pay bills electronically with another service called Online Payment. It also shows how to update the stocks in your portfolio by downloading stock quotes from a Quicken Web site.

This chapter describes the most useful online services that Quicken offers. You have to do a little setup work before you can reach out to Quicken's corner of cyberspace, and you'll find out how to do that in the pages that follow, too.

# A SURVEY OF QUICKEN'S ONLINE SERVICES

 Quicken offers the following online services. Prices listed here were current as of September 1996. An asterisk in the list means that the service is only available to users of Quicken Deluxe.

| Service | Description |
| --- | --- |
| Online Banking | Gives you an electronic bank statement with up-to-date information about a bank account. After you have downloaded the statement, you can find out the account's balance and see which transactions have cleared. You can also transfer the downloaded data into an account register (which saves you the trouble of entering it yourself) and send e-mail to a bank. Some banks allow money to be transferred between accounts within the same bank. To use this service, you must sign up with a bank. *Cost:* Varies from bank to bank; some banks charge nothing for the service. |
| Online Payment | Lets you pay bills electronically. The order to give the online payment is sent from your computer to Intuit. Intuit "withdraws" the amount of the payment from your bank account and either issues a paper check to the payee or sends the money electronically (if the payee accepts electronic money transfers). To use this service, you must sign up with a bank. *Cost:* Varies from bank to bank. My bank charges $5 per month for the first 25 payments (that's 20 cents apiece), after which the payments cost 40 cents apiece. |
| Online Quotes | Lets you download stock quotes into the Portfolio View window. *Cost:* Free as long as you are using Quicken 6, the most up-to-date version of Quicken. |

| Service | Description |
|---|---|
| Quicken Financial Network* | A Web site where you can get banking and investment information. Click the QFNet button on the iconbar. |
| Credit Report* | Lets you run a credit check on yourself. Choose Features \| Planning \| Check My Credit Online. *Cost:* Free if you print out the application and mail it in. If you get the results of the credit check online, the cost is $6. |
| Mutual Fund Finder* | Lets you shop for and compare mutual funds. Choose Features \| Investments \| Mutual Fund Finder. |

# ARE THE ONLINE SERVICES FOR YOU?

| Online |
|---|
| Go to the Online Banking & Investments Center |
| Get Started with Online Banking... |
| Download Quotes and Update my Quicken 6 |
| Check out the Best Financial Web Sites |
| View Current Quicken Tips and Important News |
| Go Online to Quicken Financial Network |

By now you must have noticed how eager the Intuit Corporation is for you to sign up with its online services. Every time you set up a new account, Quicken bids you to use it together with the Online Banking and Online Payment services.

Intuit and others are betting that, in the same way that people rely on ATM machines to do most of their banking today, they will soon rely on home computers to pay bills and get bank statements. However, sending hard-earned money across cyberspace is a bit disconcerting, especially if you are not comfortable with computers. And when you make an online payment, you don't have a paper record to show for it. To dispute a bill, you can't wave a check in front of the merchant and say, "See, I paid for this and here's the check to prove it."

On the other hand, paying bills online is a bit cheaper than paying them by check. And if you are a stock market maven, the Online Quotes service is a must, because the service makes it very, very easy to update a stock portfolio.

# GETTING READY TO USE THE ONLINE SERVICES

Before you can begin using the online services, you have to tell Quicken how your modem works and how you want to connect to the Internet. How to do that is the subject of this part of the chapter.

*If you use an online service
such as CompuServe, you can
quickly find out what your
modem settings are by opening
the dialog box in the online
service where modem settings
are listed. These modem
settings will work with
Quicken as well.*

# Introducing Quicken to Your Modem

Before you can use Quicken's online services, you have to make
sure Quicken and your modem are on speaking terms and understand
each other. To do that, choose Features | Online | Modem Setup. You
see the dialog box in Figure 14.1.

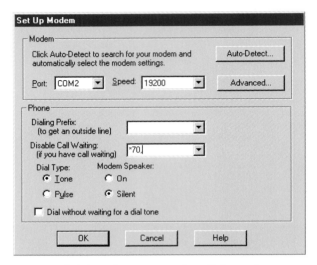

**Figure 14.1** Telling Quicken about your modem. If the settings are wrong
here, change them and click OK.

If you are lucky, Quicken "auto-detects" the right modem settings
and you don't have to tinker with this dialog box. If these modem
settings are wrong, consult the dreary manual that came with your
modem, change the settings in the dialog box, and click OK.

Subscribers to call-waiting services must be absolutely certain to
choose an option in the Disable Call Waiting box. Unless call waiting is
disabled, incoming calls can interrupt the phone connection and ruin
your data transmissions.

# Telling Quicken How to Connect to the Internet

To access Quicken's online services, you can do it either through
an Internet provider you subscribe to already or through Intuit. Begin by

choosing Features | Online | Internet Connection Setup. As shown in Figure 14.2, you see the Internet Connection Setup dialog box with its three check boxes for establishing the connection:

- **Existing dialup Internet connection:** Choose this option, click Next, and answer a series of questions about the Internet connection you have. Quicken asks the name of the service you use, what type of Web browser you have, and whether you want to "test drive" the connection to see if it really works with Quicken.

- **Direct Internet connection:** Choose this option if you are running Quicken on a network. You are asked for the Web browser that you use, the proxy server, and whether you want to do a "test drive."

- **Free, limited access account:** Choose this option for free access to the Quicken Web page only. You answer a handful of questions about yourself, after which you are given an account. Don't forget the password to the account, because you will need it when you access the

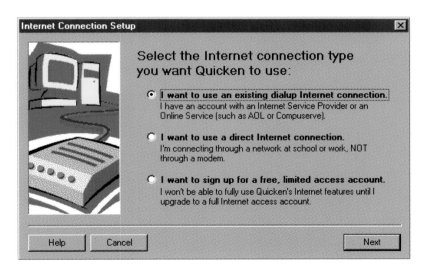

**Figure 14.2** Establishing a connection with the Internet

account. Be sure to write down your password and user ID when Intuit gives you the account, because you will need the password to access the account later.

# THE ONLINE BANKING AND ONLINE PAYMENT SERVICES

After your modem is set up and you have established a connection to the Internet, you can begin using the online services. This part of the chapter explores two of the most useful services, Online Banking and Online Payment. With these services, you can download information about an account, pay bills, transfer money between accounts, or send e-mail messages to a bank.

## The Big Picture: Online Banking and Online Payment

Online Banking and Online Payment are separate services, but they work similarly. To use either service, you have to find out if your bank offers it. If your bank does, you apply for the service by calling the bank and making arrangements to bank online. A few days later, the bank sends you a confirmation notice that includes a PIN, identical to the PINs used at ATM machines. You have to supply a PIN whenever you make an online transaction.

When you make your first transaction online, you are asked as a security measure to change the PIN the bank gave you to a PIN you invent yourself. For security purposes, Intuit asks for your PIN whenever you submit an online transaction.

Intuit acts as the "middleman" in all online transactions. When you update a bank account with the Online Banking service, your computer calls Intuit, and Intuit calls your bank's computers, gets the data, and hands it back to your computer. When you pay a bill with the Online Payment service, your computer calls Intuit, and Intuit withdraws the amount of the payment from your account and relays it to the payee either in the form of a paper check or as an electronic funds transfer.

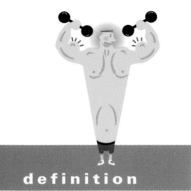

**definition**

***PIN:*** *A **p**ersonal **i**dentification **n**umber that safeguards financial transactions. You must submit the correct PIN in order to complete an online transaction with Quicken.*

# Applying for the Services

You can apply for the Online Banking and Online Payment services by going online and doing it through the Internet, but a better way is to call your bank. That way, you can ask questions of a bank representative. Find out how much the services cost, whether you can transfer money between bank accounts, whether the bank offers a trial period, and whether you will be charged on a per-account or a per-customer basis for the services.

To find out if your bank offers the services, choose Features | Online | Get Started. In the Get Started dialog box, click the Financial Institutions button. You see a scroll list of banks and their logos. Scroll to the bank that safeguards your money, click it, and click the More Info button. Among other enticements, you will see a number to call. Call that number to apply for the services.

If you decide to go through with it, hang on to the PIN number the bank sends you—you need it to use the services.

# Setting Up an Account for Use Online

The next step is to mark the account or accounts you will go online with as online accounts. To do that, go to the Account List, click an account, and click the Edit button to get to the Edit Bank Account dialog box. From there, click the Online Information check boxes, and then click Next and answer the many questions that Quicken asks you:

- **Financial Institution:** Click the down-arrow, scroll to the name of the bank you trust your money to, and click the name.

- **Routing Number:** The *routing number* is the first nine numbers in the lower-left corner of checks. On either side of the routing number is a colon. In the case of a savings or other type of account besides checking, get this number from the account information sheet or call your bank.

- **Account Number:** You can get this number from a check, too. It is the last nine or ten numbers in the lower-left corner. The routing number comes first, then the check number, then the account number.

- **Account Type:** Click the down-arrow, if necessary, and tell Quicken which kind of account this is.
- **Social Security Number:** Your social security number.

When you are done setting up the account, a yellow lightening bolt appears in the Account List next to your new, online bank account.

## MAKING AN ACCOUNT ONLINE step by step

1. Click the Accts button on the iconbar.
2. In the Accounts List window, click on the account that you want to turn into an online account.
3. Click the Edit button.
4. Under Online Information in the Edit Bank Account dialog box, click either or both the Enable Online Banking check box and the Enable Online Payment check box. Then click Next.
5. In the following Edit Account screen, choose the name of the financial institution that handles the account, enter the account's routing number (you can get it by reading the first nine digits in the lower-left corner of a check or from an account information sheet), enter the account number, choose an account type, and enter your social security number. Then click Done.

6. Read the service agreement and click OK.
7. On the screen that asks if you want to set up more accounts, click the No option button and then click Next.
8. On the "Congratulations" screen, click OK.

## Going Online

Whether you want to bank online or make an electronic payment, the procedure for getting online is the same. Start by clicking the Online button. You see the Online Banking/Investments Center window.

If you are signed up with more than one bank, click the Financial Institution down-arrow and choose the institution you need to deal with now. Then click one of the tabs—Transactions, Payments, Transfers,

or E-mail—and give instructions for downloading transactions from the bank, paying a bill, transferring money between accounts, or sending an e-mail message (the following pages explain how).

Next, click the Go Online button. You see the Instructions to Send dialog box. These are the instructions you entered on the tabs in the Online Banking/Investments Center window. Make sure that a yellow check mark appears beside the instructions you want to send. To keep from sending an instruction, click its yellow check mark to remove it. In the dialog box shown here, instructions are being sent to make an electronic payment, to transfer money, to send e-mail, and to download a statement from a bank.

Next, enter your PIN and click the Send button to send the instructions to Intuit.

## GOING ONLINE THE FIRST TIME step by step

1. Click the Online button to get to the Online Banking/Investments Center window.

2. Click the Go Online button.

3. In the Instructions to Send dialog box, click next to an instruction to remove the yellow check mark if you don't want to send the instruction. Otherwise, let the instructions stand.

4. Click the Send button. Since this is the first time you have tried to go online, you see the Change assigned PIN dialog box.

5. Enter the PIN that the bank sent you in the Assigned PIN box. Asterisks appear instead of letters or numbers as you type.

6. Under Change to, type a new PIN in the first box. Be sure to observe your bank's rules about passwords.

Some banks don't allow letters in passwords, for example.

7. In the Re-enter new PIN box, type the new PIN a second time. If you fail to enter it the same way twice, Quicken gets angry and doesn't let you proceed. Don't forget the new PIN. Getting a new PIN if you forget the one you have is a big, big hassle.

8. Click OK.

9. Fill in the Intuit Online Services User Profile dialog box. Some of this information should already be entered, since you gave it to Quicken when you registered the program. Click OK when you are done.

10. A series of online status boxes appears (this could take a minute or two). Finally you see a message box

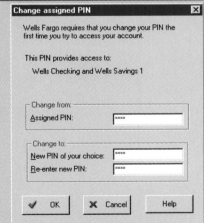

that tells you whether the transmission was successful and whether you changed PINs successfully. Click the Close button.

# Getting Accurate, Up-to-Date Account Information

With the Online Banking service, you find out how much money is in an account and which transactions have cleared the bank. After you get this information, you can compare it to what you have entered in the account register and update the register with the downloaded information, if you wish.

To update a bank account, make sure that the Download Transactions instruction appears in the Instructions to Send dialog box (see the previous step by step box to learn how to send instructions online). After the information has been downloaded, Quicken either informs you that no new transactions have been recorded since the last time you went online, or it displays a Transactions tab like the one shown here:

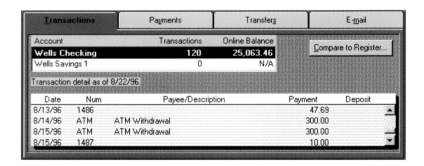

Peruse the statement to find out the account's balance, to find a transaction you're looking for, or do whatever it is you went online to do. The balance, date, and transactions listed here are up to date as of 4:00 P.M. on the last business day when the bank closed. Notice the account list. If you have funneled your money into more than one account at this bank, click another account to see its balance, transactions, and so on.

By clicking the Compare to Register button, you can clear the transactions that have been recorded by the bank, fix discrepancies between your records and the bank's, and even enter transactions that you haven't recorded yet in your register. After you click the Compare to Register button, you see a window like the one in Figure 14.3.

| Date | Num | Payee / Memo / Category | | Payment | | Clr | Deposit | | Balance | | ▲ |
|------|-----|------------------------|---|---------|---|-----|---------|---|---------|---|---|
| 8/20/96 | ATM | Withdrawal | | 300 | 00 | | | | 2,631 | 63 | |
| | | | Misc | | | | | | | | |
| 8/21/96 | DEP | tricom systems | | | | | 1,610 | 00 | 4,241 | 63 | |
| | | | Income:Trimcom | | | | | | | | |
| 8/21/96 | DEP | Credit Union | | | | | 20,000 | 00 | 24,241 | 63 | |
| | | Loan | Second mortgage | | | | | | | | |
| 8/2/96 | 1469 | *Payee* | | 100 | 00 | c | *Deposit* | | | | |
| | | *Memo* | *Category* | | | | Enter | Edit ▾ | Split | | ▼ |

**WELLS FARGO**  Online Balance as of 8/22/96: $25,063.46    0 of 119 items Accepted

| Status | Date | Num | Payee/Description | Payment | Deposit | |
|--------|------|-----|------------------|---------|---------|---|
| Match | 8/19/96 | ATM | Exp ATM Transfer | | 3,700.00 | **Accept** |
| Match | 8/20/96 | 1488 | | 211.57 | | **Accept All** |
| Match | 8/20/96 | ATM | Exp ATM Deposit | | 20,000.00 | |
| Match | 8/21/96 | ATM | Exp ATM Deposit | | 1,610.00 | **Delete** |
| New | 6/24/96 | 1308 | | 22.62 | | |
| New | 7/2/96 | | Cust Check Order | 1.16 | | **Help** |
| New | 7/2/96 | | Cust Check Order | 1.20 | | **Done** |
| New | 7/2/96 | | Cust Check Order | 5.16 | | |

| Addie IRA | Peter IRA | Peter's SEP-... | Savings-Cre... | Wells Check... | Wells Savir ▸ |

**Figure 14.3** Comparing your records with the bank's

The Status column on the left side of the transactions list says "Match" when your records and the bank's jibe, or "New" when a downloaded transaction hasn't been entered in the register yet (scroll to the bottom of the list to see new transactions). In the Payee/Description column, Quicken has tried its best to describe the transaction, but it can't list payee names except in the case of payments made with the Online Payment service.

To record this data in the register, either click on the transactions one at a time and click the Accept button, or click the Accept All button. The word "Accepted" appears in the Status column when you record a transaction. Meanwhile, in the register, Quicken puts a *c* (for Cleared) in the Clr column to show that a transaction has cleared the bank (next time you click the Recon button to reconcile this account, check marks will appear beside cleared transactions in the Reconcile Bank Statement dialog box).

When you accept a "new" transaction on the bottom of the list, Quicken enters it in the register. In the case of a check, you have to go into the register, enter the payee's name, and categorize the transaction, since Quicken can't do that for you.

To Quicken, a "new" transaction is simply a downloaded one that doesn't match a transaction that has been entered in the register.

## CAUTION

*When you "accept" a downloaded transaction, you are, in effect, reconciling that transaction with the bank. Don't "accept" transactions if you want to reconcile the account from the paper statements the bank sends you. You can reconcile on paper or online, but you can't do both.*

Therefore, sometimes what Quicken calls a "new" transaction is really just a transaction that you entered incorrectly. For example, my register showed check number 1466 for $46.56, but the bank's records said the check amounted to $56.46, so when I clicked on the Accept All button to record all the downloaded transactions, Quicken stopped on check number 1466 and showed me this dialog box:

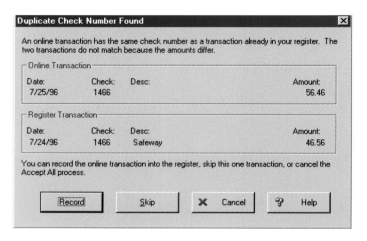

When you see this dialog box, take note of the date of the duplicate transaction and click the Skip button to let what Quicken calls "the Accept All process" continue. Later, find the transaction by date in the register and change it to what the bank's records say it should be. Banks rarely err when it comes to recording the amount of money transacted.

Click Done when you are finished with clearing downloaded transactions.

## Transferring Money Between Accounts

To transfer money from one account to another, ask yourself whether both accounts are signed up with the Online Banking service. If both are, click the Online button on the iconbar, and, in the Online Banking/Investments Center window, choose a bank from the Financial

**CAUTION**

*Not all banks allow money to be transferred electronically between accounts.*

Institutions drop-down list, if necessary. Next, click the Transfers tab, shown here:

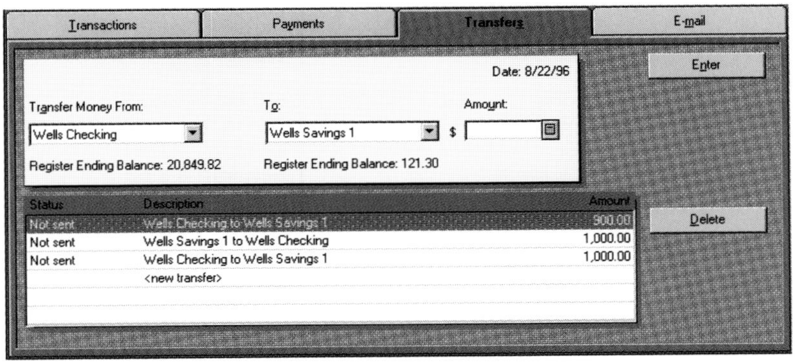

In the Transfer Money From box, choose the account you are transferring the money from, and in the To box, choose the account that will receive the money. Click the Enter button, then the Go Online button, and review the "Going Online" section earlier in this chapter for sending the transfer instruction. If you decide against transferring the money, highlight the transfer order on the Status list and click the Delete button.

After the transfer has been sent, EFT (electronic funds transfer) appears in the Num box of the register where the transfer was recorded. Meanwhile, a *c* (for Cleared) appears in the Clr column. All online transactions are cleared in the register after they are sent.

# Sending E-Mail to the Bank

As a fringe benefit of the Online Banking service, you can e-mail to a bank. To do that, click the Online button on the iconbar and then click the E-mail tab. From there, click the Create button. In the Select Message Type dialog box, click OK if you want to send a message to your bank, enter the message and all its particulars in the Message To dialog box, shown next, and click OK again.

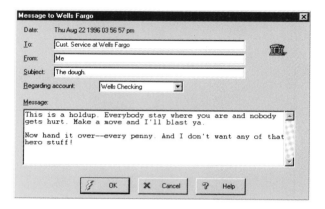

If you are inquiring after a bill, on the other hand, click Inquire about a Payment in the Select Message Type dialog box, enter your inquiry, and click OK.

Back on the E-mail tab, the date and the recipient's name appear on the Status list. Click on a message on the list and then click Read to read it, or click Delete to delete it. To send a message, click the Go Online button and see the instructions under "Going Online" earlier in this chapter.

# Paying the Bills Online

The first step to using the Online Payment service is to make a list of the people and parties you intend to pay. To do that, choose Lists | Online Payees. In the Online Payee window, click the New button to get to the Set Up Online Payee dialog box (shown here). In most cases, Intuit sends a paper check to the party you are paying, so it is important to enter information correctly in this dialog box. You can click the down-arrow in the name box and choose names from the Memorized Transactions list. If the payee doesn't have an account number, you will be asked to enter the payee's last name in the Account # box. Click OK (not shown here) when you have filled in the dialog box.

The payee's name appears in the Online Payee window. The lead time shown in this window is the number of days that the payment is expected to take to reach the payee. After you start sending payments online, Quicken may change lead times in the Online Payee window if it recognizes payees as parties to which it can send electronic payments. Keep clicking the New button and filling in the Set Up Online Payee dialog box until you put together a list of the parties to whom you will send payments online. You can click the Edit button to change payee information or the Delete button to remove a payee from the list.

When you are ready to send the payments, click the Online button on the iconbar, and then click the Payments tab in the Online Banking/Investments Center window. This tab is shown in Figure 14.4. Click the Payee down-arrow and choose a payee from the list. Then fill in this dialog box as you would the Write Checks window and click the Enter button. When you have entered all the payees, click the Go Online button and follow the directions in the "Going Online" section earlier in this chapter to send the payment across cyberspace.

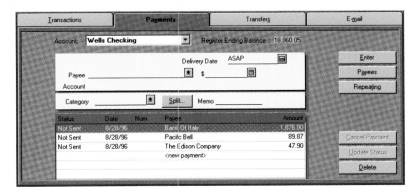

**Figure 14.4** Making an online payment

After you send payments, a message box tells you that they were sent and which check numbers they have been assigned. Meanwhile, the Status column on the Payments tab states "Sent" instead of "Not Sent." In the Num box of the register, a lightening bolt appears beside the check number.

To delete a payment that has been sent, select it on the Status list on the Payments tab and click the Cancel Payment button. You can also click the Update Status button to inquire about the status of a payment—whether or not the payee has received it—the next time you go online.

**SHORTCUT**

*You can send online payments straight from an account register. To do so, choose Send Online Payment in the Num box menu. What's more, by doing it this way, you also make sure that you don't use duplicate check numbers.*

## DOWNLOADING STOCK QUOTES step by step

**1.** Click the Port button on the iconbar.

**2.** In the Portfolio window, choose All Accounts from the Account drop-down menu.

**3.** Click the Update Prices button and choose Get Online Quotes from the menu.

**4.** Click Continue in the Online Quotes dialog box.

**5.** In the Update Quicken Live Features dialog box, click the check marks (to delete them) beside Best of the Web and What's New if you don't want that stuff, but make sure a check mark appears beside Online Quotes.

**6.** Click the Update Now button.

**7.** Enter your password, if necessary, and click Connect.

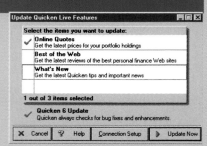

# GETTING STOCK MARKET QUOTES ONLINE

You can update the stocks in your portfolio by way of Quicken's Web site. The following step by step box explains how. Being able to download stock quotes this quickly is a very, very nice feature of Quicken. And to top it off, downloading stock quotes is free.

# A PLEASANT TRIP

This is your captain speaking. Please do not leave your seats until the plane has stopped moving. As you depart, check the area around your seat and the overhead luggage compartments to make sure you haven't forgotten anything. I hope you enjoyed flying with Quicken. Have a pleasant trip.

# Index

**S**

**T**